Kiss my genders

Kiss my genders

HAYWARD GALLERY
PUBLISHING

TEXTS AND POEMS

ARTIST PLATES

RALPH RUGOFF
Director, Hayward Gallery

Foreword

Spanning the past 50 years, *Kiss My Genders* looks at how artists have explored and evoked identities that do not conform to traditional gender categories. This thoughtfully adventurous exhibition brings together works made by different generations of artists and from different parts of the world. While they engage a range of approaches and draw on an expansive inventory of historical references, all of these artworks share an interest in articulating more fluid, non-binary positions of subjectivity, often implicitly addressing related social and political contexts. Placing a special emphasis on artists who revisit traditions of photographic portraiture, the exhibition also features works in a wide variety of media, including painting, installation, video and sculpture. In ingeniously resisting locked-down conceptions of social identity and gender, the works in *Kiss My Genders* exemplify the open-ended, category-defying character of the very best contemporary art.

I would like to thank former Hayward Senior Curator Vincent Honoré, currently Director of Exhibitions and Programmes at MoCo, Montpellier Contemporain, France, for his conscientious research and insightful approach to organising this exhibition. He has been ably supported by Hayward Assistant Curator Tarini Malik and Curatorial Assistant Thomas Sutton. Former Hayward Associate Curator Eimear Martin has also played a key role on this project. I am additionally grateful to Exhibition Organiser Eimear O'Raw, who made substantial contributions to the final stages of realising this exhibition. The innovative exhibition design by Diogo Passarinho Studio, meanwhile, has earned all of our admiration.

I would also like to thank the many lenders – including artists, estates, public institutions and private individuals – who have generously lent us key works from their collections. For their generous support of *Kiss My Genders*, I wish also to extend our gratitude to Thomas Dane Gallery and WHATIFTHEWORLD, Cape Town.

So much has been written in recent years on the subject of gender, but the authors in this book have all managed to contribute fresh and original new thinking on the subject. Our thanks go to Amrou Al-Kadhi, Paul Clinton, Charlie Fox, Jack Halberstam, Manuel Segade and Susan Stryker for their thoughtful essays. We are also grateful for the fascinating roundtable discussion featuring artists Ajamu, Travis Alabanza and Victoria Sin along with Vincent Honoré. In addition, reprints of an essay by artist Renate Lorenz and poetry by Travis Alabanza, Jay Bernard, Tarek Lakhrissi and Nat Raha have all added critical layers to the contents of this publication. Thanks also go to Lucy Biddle, Thomas Sutton and Wong Bing Hao for their informative texts on individual artworks. Studio Frith have earned our appreciative admiration for the elegant design of this book. I am also grateful to Diana Adell, who has served as Publishing Project Manager, and to former Hayward Publisher Rebecca Fortey, who initiated the early work on this publication.

Far more people have contributed to the realisation of this exhibition than can be mentioned here, but a special thank you goes to Hayward Installation Manager Juliane Heynert and Senior Installation Technician Chloe Brooks for their work in planning and executing the installation; Hayward Senior Registrar Imogen Winter for overseeing the transport of works; Exhibitions Interpretation Manager Lucy Biddle for her concise and illuminating interpretative texts; and Hayward General Manager Aoife Leach for skillfully guiding all the many moving parts and keeping the big picture in focus. As always I am grateful for the support and enthusiasm of Southbank Centre CEO Elaine Bedell, as well as Southbank Centre's Board of Governors, and Arts Council England.

Finally, our most profound gratitude and appreciation goes to all of the artists participating in *Kiss My Genders*, for making compelling and nuanced artworks that open up new ways of seeing and thinking around this very important subject.

Kiss My Genders: A Conversation

Vincent Honoré, chair, exhibition curator [VH]: *Kiss My Genders* is a group exhibition celebrating artists whose work explores and engages with gender identity. Working across painting, sculpture, poetry, photography and film, many of these artists treat the body as sculpture and, in doing so, open up new possibilities for gender, beauty and the representation of the human form. *Kiss My Genders* originated from discussions with artists, writers and activists. Conceived as a celebration of difference and of the rich spectrum of gender identity, it features a multitude of voices and approaches. Even the title of the exhibition – a lyric from Planningtorock's song 'Transome' – comes from an existing work. In keeping with this approach, I made the decision not to provide a curatorial introduction to this book but rather to stage a conversation with you – each of whom are featured in *Kiss My Genders* or the accompanying programme – about some of the issues raised by the exhibition. So I guess we should start by talking about how each of you position yourselves within *Kiss My Genders*.

Victoria Sin, artist [VS]: It's really important to have these views and stories, narratives and representations, coming from the queer artists themselves, rather than having other people speak about our identities.

Ajamu, artist [A]: I like the title – *Kiss My Genders*; it's about kissing my ass, basically! [Laughter] Straight away there is a certain energy, or an attitude. There is always a danger with talking about any kind of identity – even queer identity. I would maybe move 'queer' from an identity to a politics, as in, what is a queer 'doing'? Then it becomes more messy, more murky, harder to articulate, because, actually, we inhabit many internal worlds simultaneously. We too often try to bring [that reality] back down to 'identity' to hold it, to articulate it. The exhibition operates in a different register – as an attitude or an energy, or something else.

Travis Alabanza, artist [TA]: I'm so glad you started with the title, because that's why I didn't ignore the request to be involved in this. We just came out of a year of institutions doing stuff about gender – I was feeling fatigued! I was just so done with these stale conversations about gender; they would bring in these really exciting artists, but the institution would work its magic to make their work seem more mundane or serious about gender than I know those artists intended. And what I love about* Kiss My Genders *is what you were saying – that same playfulness in the title, for me, invites the artists, the audience and the visitors to have that same playfulness too. I think that's what's been left out over these last two years – the playfulness that I and so many other trans, queer, gender non-binary artists have. The reason this feels important is that it's an exciting way to say 'Look, this thing is real – this exists in nightclubs, this exists on our record players, this exists when we're dancing around.'

A: That playfulness or that mischievousness is no less political; although it is not seen as political, because people assume it's not doing that sociocultural work.

TA: It's the most political thing I think we can do sometimes. People always see us and our conversations – especially with trans folk – in direct relation to violence. So when me and my friends play, I'm, like, 'This is incredible, because you're having to learn about us through us being joyous, being playful, pretending.'

VS: One of my main things about drag is that it's inherently playful. There's always comedy, it's always going to be a bit silly. You're asking yourself to step outside of yourself and do something that you would not do in your day to day. It's like a tool that can be used to gain a better idea of, actually, how serious gender usually is, and that's where the power is: making fun of gender.

I also think about this in relation to science fiction and fantasy in queerness, because these are places that you can say, 'Actually, here's a completely new world that is separate to the societal context that we're in, and I'm gonna change these things, I'm gonna play with it.' The whole point is that queerness is playful and it can change, and probably will, because who's the same thing for the rest of their lives?

A: It makes me think about queer and punk. They're both doing something very specific. They are mischievous, they are deviant. But now the word 'queer' has been co-opted for all forms of difference, right? I'm not sure that all forms of difference can be queer. That's why I think I'm pushing back against 'queer' as an identity

position, but not necessarily 'queer' as an attitude or an energy. I would actually like to reclaim the deviant queer, the dirty queer.

TA: The 'doing word'.

VS: This is often said about ally-ship: [an ally is] not something that you are, it's something that you do. Maybe queerness is in that same vein.

VH: The exhibition focuses on recent works but also includes works from the late 1960s and early 1970s. The radical social changes initiated in the 1960s, with the rise of feminism, gay rights and unconventional notions of masculinity, as expressed in glam rock, disco or punk – and seen in the exhibition in the works by Luciano Castelli [pp. 114–17] and Jimmy DeSana [pp. 120–25] – paved the way for changes in how gender was socially perceived and is now considered. How do you connect with previous generations? Who are your 'transcestors'?

A: The one artist I keep coming back to, decade after decade, is Pierre Molinier [pp. 164–69]. There was an exhibition [of his work] at Cabinet Gallery in Brixton in 1993. I was totally bowled over by it, partly because it was confusing – I couldn't work out where Pierre was in the image, and there are times his body has morphed. It not only played around with gender, it explored fetishism, voyeurism and spectatorship.

VS: It's important to have intergenerational conversations, because if you don't, then you just start trying to reinvent the wheel every time – and why start all over again when you can learn from people before you?

A: What are the things that you steal from another generation, and what then do you invent? What are the tensions?

VS: I remember realising that I was an artist who was into gender, who was into science fiction, who was into sex and pornography. I found the work of Shu Lea Cheang, a Taiwanese artist. She made a queer, sci-fi porno called I.K.U. *[2000]. Finding her work for me was, like, 'Oh my god, I'm not alone in this – here is another person who's come before me that my work can be in dialogue with.'*

I remember also thinking, 'who are the drag queens that I can look to in the past?' Then I looked back at Cantonese opera. This was a space where men would play women, women would play men; I found out that these two iconic actors called Yam Kim-fai and Bak Sheut-Sin were actually two actresses who played romantic lead roles opposite one another in 1960s films, and who maintained a 'close' friendship for over 40 years. These narratives, they do exist, and, really weirdly, sometimes they exist in very heteronormative contexts.

TA: I love Jo Clifford – I think she's one of the best playwrights ever. I was looking for trans people that are grotesque; I hope she doesn't mind me saying this but, among many other things, her work is sometimes gross. I was looking for a way that trans people can make performance that doesn't feel like it needs to be pretty and attractive, and can be mean and horrible. Jo Clifford's work was a real invitation to make the audience angry and upset, but it would be about their pain rather than hers.

A: For me it wasn't just artists, but also people like Miss Gold walking around Brixton in the late 1980s – people who were never trans non-binary, but presented another kind of gender: Jamaican queens who were just walking around in Brixton, Chapeltown, Toxteth, just taking up space. Because I couldn't work them out, I found them frightening. They didn't apologise for presenting themselves in ways that would seem unacceptable in black culture, and gay culture too. It's that confidence to be different – that energy – that I kind of took with me as part of my own politics. So now I say to myself, 'I am now one of those queens that scares people' [laughter].

VS: A similar experience brought me to drag. Sneaking into gay bars when I was 17 in Toronto and seeing my first drag shows, seeing these queens who were using femininity – a queer femininity, a femininity that most people would say should not exist, or is existing in a way that's very improper – but using it to take up space and command a room; I was absolutely infatuated. I wanted to be like that, and use femininity in a way that is not intended to be consumable from the viewpoint of a heteronormative, cis[gender] gaze.

VH: This makes me think of [artist] Peter Hujar's comment: 'My work comes out of my life. The people I photograph are not freaks or curiosities to me. I like people who dare.'[1] It is about daring, as well as being part of a community. What is your relationship to your community, and how does it feed your art?

VS: I wouldn't be able to exist in any kind of healthy way without a community; I definitely would not be able to make the work that I'm making.

TA: I live with three other black, gender-nonconforming people, and my close circle of friends are all black, won't-be-defined fags, freaks, whatever you want to call us – or we call ourselves freaks. That, for me, powers my work. But sometimes it's hard to grasp what we mean by community in a physical form. Maybe four years ago, when I was first starting to make work in a 'community', I found it useful; then, recently, I've actually found it not so useful to see myself so directly linked to this thing that I can't quite grasp. At the moment, my work is coming out of quite a selfish need. If that work then helps someone else or is useful in a community, it's fine. Maybe that's the sense of community that I enjoy: just like really supportive aunties, cheering each other on.

A: I think for me, my relationship to the notion of a community has shifted, and it keeps changing. So I'd rather use the word 'networks', because I find the meaning of 'community' depends on who's using the word. Community always sounds like a fixed space – somehow it locks in something – and how do we break out of those notions?

VS: When I say community I mean my friends, basically. 'The LGBT community' is just everyone who's not cisgendered and straight, and we're not necessarily a community. Having come up in the drag scene, I would not be doing what I'm doing without an LGBT network. The reality is, though, that there is definitely a glass ceiling within the 'drag community' and after a while I was, like, 'Well, why should I keep on existing to serve a community that actually has not really any interest in recognising me? Because this community has deep issues with racism, misogyny and transphobia.'

A: For me, it's about how I *feel* community. I could feel community with some people irrespective of their race, sexuality and gender.

VH: [Artist] Catherine Opie [pp. 182–89] said: 'I take a very traditional way of looking at portraiture to photograph a non-traditional and misrepresented community in a loving and dignified way.'[2] Interestingly, she links the representation of her community to a traditional visual approach – a traditional approach that can be seen in the works by Peter Hujar [pp. 145–51], Zanele Muholi [pp. 176–81] and Del LaGrace

Volcano [pp. 224–27], as well as your own work [Ajamu, pp. 82–89; Sin, pp. 216–19], and in Travis's play, *Burgerz* [2018].

A: I don't think that they're mutually exclusive. I'm part of some tradition that I do love, and the work is in conversation with that tradition and contests it at the same time.

VH: Travis uses the word 'freaks'. [American academic] Susan Stryker notes that contemporary gender representation must still contend with the historical legacy of transgender lives being viewed primarily through the depersonalising lenses of criminality or pathology. A traditional approach is also a way to reclaim the dignity of representation.

TA: The reason I use the word 'freaks' – I use it a lot – is that what we've seen in a post-Caitlyn Jenner era of conversation around transness is an effort to sanitise gender and transness. The type of trans visibility that's accepted is 'if you look like a proper woman' or 'like a proper man' and, to me, that is the complete antithesis of queerness. The reason that I love saying 'I'm a freak'? I don't understand my gender, so I'm not trying to come up with words that make it sound me. Yeah, some days I feel like a fucking freak.

VS: It's so important when queer artists are making their own work to represent queer identities. I think, going back to what you were saying about traditional methods of representation. It's useful to adopt normative systems of looking and interrupt them with queer subjects and ideas, [in order] to infiltrate systems of representation. When I make films and when I make images, I use something that you've seen before – maybe the pose of a sitter in a painting, or the way a camera moves across a feminine figure's body – drawing you into typical ways of looking. You think you're consuming something you're familiar with, but then you realise you're actually looking at something completely constructed, something completely queer.

A: I have the word 'freak' on my arm. In the 1990s, a lot of the work by gay photographers concerned the typical type of male body. 'Freak' is the total antithesis of that, so, for me, 'freak' is actually a political position – the ultimate form of difference with the body. I would like a freakish body, or a different body. We talk about difference, but what does it mean to really embrace difference?

VH: This is a notion that deeply informs the exhibition. We are reprinting one of Renate Lorenz's texts [pp. 66–77], in which they argue we should go beyond queer theories to embrace a freak method, to freak the world. In the exhibition, to borrow from an essay by [gender theorist] Judith Butler, we will be showing 'bodies that matter', with portraits by Zanele Muholi, Del LaGrace Volcano and Catherine Opie, as well as portrayals of the artists, including Pierre Molinier, Martine Gutierrez [pp. 130–35] and Juliana Huxtable [pp. 152–55]. Most of the works go beyond queerness to create a different sense of bodily representation – of being a body in the world and being a represented body. Some artists embrace abstraction, treating the body as a concept or a form – like Sadie Benning [pp. 98–99] and Ad Minoliti [pp. 162–63] – while others frame them as structures or systems – like Jes Fan [pp. 126–27] and Flo Brooks [pp. 108–13].

VS: For me, it's just about shifting the paradigm a little bit, you know? I want to create the world that I want to live in. That's my fantasy – that's the reason why I make work.

A: My work is never necessarily about finding an answer; it's trying to pose other kinds of questions. But, yes, bodies matter – black bodies matter, all bodies matter.

VS: That issue of questions versus answers is so important, because I would always be suspicious of somebody who seems to have answers, or claims to. We should be thinking, how can we ask better questions?

TA: In my work, I want, not just me, but you and everyone, to be able to not be desired: for the other person to find you maybe gross, for the other person to be shocked, for the other person to find you repulsive, but you still be safe and still be seen as cared for. That's what my work is trying to do with gender. I actually don't need you to understand me – I actually don't need you to get what I'm saying. I just want your understanding of me not to be a correlate of my safety. I want a world where you can say, 'Be a freak, be whatever you want', and you can still get from A to B and not die. This is why the attitude of this exhibition seems different to that of so many other exhibitions; they've got it wrong with this idea of understanding being the goal.

VS: There's this thing about assimilating queer narratives into terms that can be understood by a mainstream, social-institutional context, and that's where a lot of things go wrong. We shouldn't be looking for acceptance, or to be assimilated within the institutional cog-work. We should be looking to be celebrated, and making space.

VH: This is what we are aiming to do – a celebration of multiple genders, a spectrum of identities. We are not trying to provide answers. Politics of course will be important in the exhibition, although possibly less frontal than expected. Some works are more directly political: *The Memorial Dress* by Hunter Reynolds [1993–2007; see p. 207], addressing the AIDS crisis; the 1992 presidential campaign by American drag queen Joan Jett Blakk [p. 157]; the installation by Hannah Quinlan and Rosie Hastings looking at the disappearance of safe spaces in the UK for the queer community [p. 199]; or the video installation by Pauline Boudry / Renate Lorenz looking at silence as both a gesture of oppression and an act of resistance [pp. 104–07].

A: Celebrating multiple experiences is political. Artists are always political – every piece of work is part of some political, doctrinal framework. I've stepped back from lots of LGBT work and black LGBT work because, actually, the artist is slightly sidelined if not seen as doing social justice work. [But] you cannot have social justice work that doesn't account for pleasure and joy, for celebration and aspiration. To celebrate – in this context, in this moment – is political.

VS: I remember having this conversation about drag, and there were a few drag queens in the community that were really criticising my work because it was too political. When you're playing with gender, it's always going to be political. I think it's important that people are representing their own voices or that artists themselves are representing their own bodies, or their own experiences at least. But I know from personal experience – and I'm sure that both of you can also attest to this – when you're a little bit visible, and your experiences are underrepresented, suddenly people come to you and they're like, 'Thank you for just being visible, because now I feel validated.'

A: I totally understand it, I support it, but representation will not save you from having your face kicked in. That's why I think that we mustn't get locked into representation and visibility only around our politics as artists. That's what happens with black and brown and queer artists' work – it's talked about in terms of representation; people then totally exclude form and process, push it to one side. You cannot have a conversation about an artist and their practice if you push formal process to one side.

TA: I definitely saw it with my recent work,* Burgerz. *I just watched all these people from my community not being able to talk about it without referencing back to identity. I saw that, sometimes, the trap isn't from this external gaze, it's actually from our internal ways, the only ways we know about talking about work. I think that's what oppression does, it flattens out people. A side-effect of queer- and transphobia is to flatten us out. So I hope that the politics of this show is one that goes against this – I can be angry and also sad and happy; and I can be visible and also hide.

VH: This is so crucial. That's the main principle of this show. And a good conclusion for our conversation.

TA: Absolutely, Kiss My Genders!

NOTES

1. Peter Hujar entry in an unidentified directory of photographers, late 1970s, Peter Hujar Collection, as cited in Joel Smith, 'A Gorgeous Mental Discretion,' in *Peter Hujar: Speed of Life* (New York: Aperture; Madrid, Spain: Fundación MAPFRE, 2017), p. 12

2. Catherine Opie, quoted in Colette Dartnall, 'Interview with Catherine Opie, July 11, 1997,' in Stephanie Emerson (ed.) *Catherine Opie* (Los Angeles: Museum of Contemporary Art, 1997), n.p.

The Sea

TRAVIS ALABANZA

I

Sometimes I stand by the edge of where the ocean meets
the beach, and look out into the sea, so I can see
something that does not have an end.

I often get asked what my gender feels like,
and I want to say: it is more like, what I wish it
could feel like?
I wish it could feel like this moment.
Like it does not have a beginning or an end.
That you cannot see where it starts or stops.
That it just continues to exist, or not exist.
That it is a vast space of nothingness in one wave, and
holds so much in the next.
That it is like the moment where the sea feels endless.

Sometimes I stand by the edge of where the ocean meets
the beach, and look out into the sea, so I can feel
like something that does not have an end.

II

Cis people ask me what my gender feels like and that
never allows me to say what my gender really is.
My gender feels like something stopped halfway through.
A badly formatted tape to CD conversion, missing full
potential.
The second character on a video game, without levels,
no up or down.
It feels like an unfinished
A body of water, potential to do so much, yet
eventually bottled.

Sometimes I stand by the edge of where the ocean meets
the beach, and look out into the sea, that looks out
over my gender, that pours over my body, and makes me
feel like nothing.

JACK HALBERSTAM

Making a Move – Object Lessons in Trans* Art

In his brilliant, humorous and whimsical parody of *The Smithsonian's History of America in 101 Objects* (first published 2013), artist Chris E. Vargas, in 2015, invited visitors into his imaginary Museum of Transgender *Hir*story and Art (MOTHA) to see a show titled *Transgender Hirstory in 99 Objects: Legends and Mythologies.*[1] Riffing on the self-importance of the original book title, the precision of its '101' objects and its investment in the notion of authentic history, Vargas called attention to the way that a history of gender variance will necessarily fall by the wayside in any canonical account of American history and will require its own object lessons. The objects that collectively tell the story of gender variance are counter-intuitive and suggestive, risqué and emblematic. For Vargas's show, the objects ranged from queer banners by Brooklyn-based artist Tuesday Smillie to sculptures of hybrid creatures and photographic records of transgender lives gone by.[2] What *Transgender Hirstory in 99 Objects* made clear, however, was that a trans* history is all at once a mobile set of materials and an archive of mobility.[3]

While the transgender *hir*story that Vargas imagined played out through the works of a specifically North American group of artists, the show was not supposed to be definitive, and another iteration of this history could easily stretch far beyond this regional context. As many of the works in *Kiss My Genders* prove, trans variant imagery is now part of many different art worlds, from Europe to South Africa, from China to India.

In recent years, breathless media coverage has hailed our era as a 'transgender tipping point' and as a new day for transgender visibility.[4] Articles in the *New York Times*, *Time* magazine and the *Atlantic* have both celebrated a tendency towards gender flexibility among young people and puzzled over what it all means. Our era, at any rate, is understood to be marked by the emergence of public discussions of transgender embodiment and by debates over trans children, transgender soldiers, non-binary bathrooms and so on. Of course, just as the public debate picked up steam in 2016, Donald Trump was elected president of the United States, and the boulder of transgender rights that had been patiently pushed up various legal hills, quickly fell back down to the bottom.

Which is not to say that nothing has been achieved, but only to note that state recognition and protection of transgender populations will shift and change as the wind blows and that, at a certain point, queer and trans* populations will have to say 'kiss my genders' to the state while walking towards different understandings of liberation, acknowledgement, life and love. Once we do kiss off normative conceptions of history, progress, visibility and existence, we are ready to enter the looking-glass world of art and transformation, and there we will find those 99 objects Vargas sought to curate, and 999 more. In the museums in our heads, kaleidoscopic panoramas of bodies and change swirl around, not seeking to settle into one or two clear images but always providing fantastically unstable footing, in the hopes that we will slip and slide into a world so much more inventive than our own.

Kiss My Genders, a survey of gender-dissident bodies in art, offers a collage of gender-variant forms that gesture towards this other world of invention. In one, startlingly timely, poster image, drag persona Joan Jett Blakk, in dark glasses and with an impressive Afro, sits in a wicker chair, an automatic rifle in hand, with the banner 'Joan Jett-Blakk for President' running above the image and 'By any means necessary' running below. This was an image used in Jett Blakk's 1992 campaign for US president, when she ran against Republican incumbent George H.W. Bush under the slogan 'Lick Bush in '92'. This presidential campaign, campy as it was – Jett Blakk had a lesbian militant running mate and wanted to rename The White House The Lavender House – offers a serious critique of a political system that claims, and fails, to represent massive swathes of the North American population. Indeed, in 1996, when Jett Blakk declared her intention to run for office again, she asked people to vote for her by *refusing* to vote and, in this way, counted 440,000 non-votes in her favor. This tactic – offering voters a way out of the enforced choice between candidate A and candidate B, both of whom inevitably represent white people, straight people, big business and the status quo – is a powerful articulation of a trans* politics of dis-appearance. The non-voters who did not go to the polls and did not show up for their candidates, represent another population of gender-variant queers – the unrepresented, unpresentable, unfit, dispossessed, unelectable don't-wanna-bes who do not seek recognition within a system built upon their exclusion but who want to tear the system down, by any means necessary.

The imaginative politics of Joan Jett Blakk exemplify what American academic C. Riley Snorton has called 'the mechanics of invention', or the modes by which black trans* life can be seen to emerge, in the form of fugitive figures, from archives that have been overlooked or discounted. Snorton begins his history of black trans* life and death, not with medical technologies of the twentieth century, but with slavery and the concept of fungibility as it was applied to slave bodies.[5] In *Black on Both Sides* (2017), Snorton writes: 'captive flesh figures a critical genealogy for modern transness, as chattel persons gave rise to an understanding of gender as mutable and as an amendable form of being.'[6] As we see in Snorton, the mutability of flesh is not necessarily a progressive idea; even as the flexible body becomes a representation of new forms of identity in the twenty-first century, it hearkens back to earlier models of fungibility that allowed for black bodies to function as interchangeable commodities. It is this trans* history from which Jett Blakk's campaign for president emerges, as an affront to and rejection of the political process that situates her as the problem to be solved and as a figure for a totally different conception of the political altogether.

New work in transgender studies by Snorton and others has pushed away from the, by now well-known, accounts of theatrical drag, medical breakthroughs and liberal activism. The new edge of trans* studies looks for leverage in dark corners of history, science and the art world. In *Kiss My Genders*, we see these shadow archives of trans* life sitting uneasily alongside images that have circulated widely. And so, while Catherine Opie's luscious images of genderqueer icons like Justin Vivian Bond (p. 183) and Del LaGrace Volcano's adoring stills of butches and kings continue to exert immense power some 20 years after their making, we also need to look again at new and old images that move beyond portraits of genderqueer bodies and locate transness and queerness in dream worlds, fantasies of fugitivity, abstract systems and modes of unbecoming.

Examples from the more surrealistic side of trans* visual history reside in this wide-ranging show. Pierre Molinier, for example, a French photographer born in 1900, used the fetishist's wardrobe of stockings, suspenders, corsets and stilettos to create fantastical non-human forms. In *Grande Mêlée*, a photomontage from 1968 (pp. 164–65), a scrum of bodies resembles a mythical beast, or a many-legged creature, with several butts and heads too. The octopus-like form that *Grande Mêlée* represents is reprised in the work of a more contemporary artist, Ajamu, a queer visual activist who, in one image, offers us a remarkable view of a foot entangled with an octopus (*Feet of Duane Cyrus, Dancer*, 2015; p. 89). In another work, *Marker Cones (No Head)* (1982, pp. 120–21), punk artist (or anti-artist, as he preferred) Jimmy DeSana captures a torso as it balances precariously upon four orange cones. With the head of the model bent out of view and the inverted cones serving both to prop up the body and cover its extremities, the torso loses all specificity and takes the form of an unreadable geometric shape. The cones mimic stilettos or claws, and the dominant orange colour gives the whole figure a crustaceous appearance. As in Molinier's image, DeSana's figure slips away from the human altogether and foregrounds the indecipherable quality of embodiment. DeSana, in this way, does not try to turn human into animal so much as he buries the recognisable features of the human in animal-like appendages.

Surprisingly (or maybe not), many of the images in *Kiss My Genders* obscure not simply the gender of the body, but its humanness. The work of Zanele Muholi presented here, for example, is taken not only from their now well-known images of queer, black, gender-dissident communities in South Africa; we also see a photograph from their ongoing series *Somnyama Ngonyama: Hail the Dark Lioness* (p. 177). In this series of self-portraits, Muholi documented their own travels through time and space and into art world spaces that have often been closed to black artists. Many of the images from *Somnyama Ngonyama* are remarkable for the way they include ready-made objects and found materials – black rubber gloves in one, headphones in another, clothes pegs in another – and for the exaggeration of stereotyped features of black and African femininity. In some of the images, the visual activist appears in massive wigs; in others they peer out from plastic material arranged to look like a shawl. In all of them, they attach the mutability of the racialised body – in relation to race, gender, sexuality, regionality – to a world of objects. Muholi has said of this series that it investigates 'how photographers can question and deal with the body as material or mix it with objects to further aestheticise black personhood.'[7] Dealing with the human body as material rather than as an exceptional form of being questions the meaning of the human altogether. Here Muholi reminds us that the human as a category has been theorised mostly by European discourse and used within colonialism to separate out the human from object worlds and animals. Their work makes the human part of a wider world of things.

These artists, and particularly Zanele Muholi, deploy images of bodily transformation to put pressure on the human. In an attempt to extend Jamaican writer Sylvia Wynter's racial critiques of the human to transgender archives, Snorton asks: 'How does one access a language outside of and in contradistinction to the governing codes that currently determine human definition such that it gives rise to new meanings, forms of life, and genres of being?'[8] Muholi's answer is to make transformation the foundation of their practice – not just in terms of their aesthetic but in every aspect of their work. Thus, Muholi sometimes travels with a large group of South African artists, singers and dancers, and they situate themself not as the singular and chosen black queer artist from South Africa, but as a visual activist and part of an evolving community of artists. Their work reimagines the role of the artist, the status of the art object and the meaning of the body altogether.

Other artists in *Kiss My Genders* also extend this new visual language for the body, the human and gendered being; some use collage, others graphic novels and performance. Juliana Huxtable uses her body to make original marks in the visual landscape. She poses against candy-coloured backdrops and uses her body to make a visual exclamation mark. In one image, *Untitled (Lil' Marvel)* (2015, p. 155) she is dressed in a black leotard and, as her black braids fly behind her and a black background with streaks of purple offers a sense of forward motion, she reaches towards the edge of the frame, grasping the space between herself and the viewer and pulling us into the void.

Trans* bodies here are bodies that twist and turn between meanings. They are bodies that emerge from lost archives and that visit from the future. Trans* bodies do not seek to be seen as real or true, as found or discovered, as recognisable or understandable. Instead, as gathered here under one sign, the kiss, they gesture hello and goodbye at the same time and intimate eroticisms that are yet to be imagined. The bodies relentlessly pose, reach out from the frame, retreat back into it, disappear and refuse to present themselves. They preen and pop, bleed and beckon. And, in one work, the body is gone altogether, or at least dispersed across a series of steel frames, none of which can be confidently called 'the body'. Jes Fan calls their work a 'material inquiry into otherness as it relates to identity politics' and works at the intersection of de-colonial imaginaries and transgender art.[9] Fan's work often investigates how social identity is projected onto the bodily materials of hormones, melanin and other chemicals. In describing some of Fan's work that focuses upon race, for example, Ari Larissa Heinrich writes: 'In *Obscure Functions: Experiments in Decolonizing Melanin*, Jes Fan approaches the molecularization of race through aesthetics by abstracting melanin from its usual associations with what they call the "social organizing principle… known as race."' Heinrich goes on to describe how Fan distils melanin, mixes it with rubber and places the mixture in bubbles of crystal custom glass, which are then displayed in an installation that frames the melanin sculptures.[10] Heinrich describes Fan's process as akin to 'destroying "nature"'.[11] In other work, Fan dismantles nature to isolate estrogen and testosterone and in *Testo-Candle* (2017) they contrast medical vials of injectable testosterone with a candle made of the same fluids. In this way, Fan both distills hormones from the body and extracts them from their medical context. By inviting gallery visitors to touch these materials and interact with them, Fan turns the body inside out and, using Heinrich's term, redistributes its chemical and biological materials across the room and in relation to the bodies present.

In some ways, Jes Fan's highly inventive environments force viewers to let go of all preconceptions about the meanings of bodies, mutability, representation and legibility. The dispersal of bodily materials across time and space in *Kiss My Genders*, and in the work of the artists gathered here and beyond, refuses the media-ready image of the body in drag – rouged up and ready to entertain. Instead, *Kiss My Genders* leads us into a moment that is neither tipping point nor aftermath, neither history nor prediction. This moment, like the intentionally blurred images by Lyle Ashton Harris (pp. 94–97), will come and go, break up upon contact, and insist always upon multiplicity and illegibility. The trans* objects in this museum of mobility force a new view on the history of gender variance; not a subject in drag tiptoeing through the archive, not an accumulation of evidence forcing a 'tipping point', not a newly neoliberal subject, trans* here is a magnetic field of energy that exceeds the frame of the human and opens towards the end of the body as such.

NOTES

1. The exhibition was staged at ONE National Gay & Lesbian Archives at the USC Libraries, Los Angeles, between 21 March and 1 August 2015.

2. The show featured the work of nine contemporary artists alongside objects from the ONE Archives collection, including a photo album with pictures of one of the archives' founders, Reed Erikson.

3. I use the term 'trans*' in order to recognise the variation that exists under the sign of transgender. For more explanation on the asterisk, see Jack Halberstam, *Trans*: A Quick and Quirky Account of Gender Variation* (Oakland, CA: University of California Press, 2018)

4. 'The Transgender Tipping Point' was the headline on the cover of *Time* magazine for a story by Katy Steinmetz, on 29 May 2014. The cover featured transgender actress Laverne Cox.

5. Fungibility refers to the status of slave bodies as commodities. Because slave bodies were bought and sold they were constituted by a logic of exchange and their identities were seen as unstable and mutable. For a full theory of fungibility and transness, see C. Riley Snorton, *Black on Both Sides: A Racial History of Trans Identity* (Minneapolis, MN: University of Minnesota Press, 2017)

6. Ibid, n.p.

7. Artist's statement, Stevenson Gallery [stevenson.info/exhibition/1440, accessed 5 February 2019]

8. Ibid.

9. See 'Jes Fan: Visual Arts Residency', in Pioneer Works [pioneerworks.org/residency/jes-fan/, accessed 5 February 2019]

10. Ari Larissa Heinrich, 'Applied Co-Enmeshment' (written in parallel with Jes Fan), in Recess, October 2018 [recessart.org/arilarissaheinrich/, accessed 5 February 2019]

11. Ibid.

SUSAN STRYKER

On the Transfeminine

Kiss My Genders offers a timely intervention into the lived and imagined complexities of embodied identity at this overwrought historical moment, as the global geopolitical order rearranges itself, Brexit and Trumpism roil nations on both sides of the Atlantic, racialised fears of immigrant hordes spark mass reactions, and hysteria reigns supreme regarding gender diversity.

If one were to believe everything one reads in the newspapers these days – particularly in the British press – it would appear that trans women[1] (i.e. 'men', for a disconcerting number of cisgender people across the political spectrum) represent a growing, well organised, well funded, tragically misguided (perhaps psychotically deranged) political lobby, hell-bent on endangering the future of the race through voluntary sterilisation, disruption of the family, harming 'real' women and girls, harassing lesbians by pestering them for sex, trespassing against such gender-segregated spaces as public toilets, having the gall to ask society to pay for their perverse and mutilative surgeries as well as their health-destroying hormones, demanding changes in routine bureaucratic identity documentation that works just fine for everybody else, and insisting that the basic rules of English grammar be altered to accommodate their 'preferred' or 'gender-neutral' pronouns.

Or, to say the same thing more economically, many people find it psychically impossible to accept trans women as women. Instead, in incomprehension or hostility, they fantasise the worst of us, in telling, self-revelatory fashion. We are thought to be both in thrall to, and the bearers of, a suspect set of beliefs increasingly encapsulated by the term 'gender ideology', often conflated with a vulgarisation of Judith Butler's theory of gender performativity that reduces it to and mischaracterises it as the false notion that one can become whatever one says one is, 'reality' be damned. Trans people – transsexual women in particular – are construed as the monstrous and preposterous prodigy of this fundamentally flawed proposition.

I dissent, to put it mildly, from the current moral panic surrounding transgender and gender ideology, and, to the contrary, would go so far as to suggest that contemporary notions of gender and trans gender, as well as prevailing versions of feminism and homosexual emancipation, often actually work to the detriment of trans women.

Following an argument made by literary critic Emma Heaney, the transfeminine – a broad descriptor referring to all that is encompassed within subjectivities emanating from bodies assigned male at birth, whose self-understanding and self-expression answers to the hailing of the pronoun 'she' – has been a problem for transatlantic modernities, particularly those that are white and anglophone, since at least the turn of the twentieth century, and, arguably, long before.[2] The rise of feminism, in this view, has been predicated on the desirability of the movement of women into an androcentric public sphere in which the liberated 'New Woman' refashions herself along masculinist lines in pursuit of expanded suffrage and citizenship – a history that runs from Hillary Clinton's trouser-suits all the way back to Mary Wollstonecraft's vindication of the rights of women to the extent that they imitated 'manly virtues' that would 'raise females in the scale of animal being'.[3]

Similarly, homosexual emancipation has been predicated on the disavowal or disparagement of effeminacy and a subordination of the feminine as the less-valued term of the masculine/feminine, male/female and man/woman binaries. As the lesbian feminist anthropologist Esther Newton put it in her classic work on gay male drag culture, *Mother Camp* (1972), 'the struggle to come to terms with the stigma of effeminacy' resulted in 'a shift from effeminate to masculine styles' in the wake of 'transformations wrought in the gay community by the gay-pride movement'. Or, as she said differently: 'Sissies are out.'[4]

Within this problematic, the transfeminine falls between the cracks. The dominant modes of social and psychical transformation – driven by the legitimate social justice struggles of those minoritised and oppressed by gender and sexuality – exclude the transfeminine, which remains a particular kind of problem to be solved, contained, absorbed, reframed or eliminated, quite distinct from the trajectory of masculine-trending transformation privileged within both feminism and gay liberation. It is the grit that goads modernity to encase it in pearl, smothering it and smoothing it over into something that no longer irritates, but which remains, at heart, a contradictory provocation.

The transfeminine, historically, has taken two forms. The first – well represented among the works featured in *Kiss My Genders* – is disjunctive. It is anchored, in Heaney's telling, in the 'riotous, resistant'[5] vernaculars associated with mollies, fairies, queens and other effeminate, sex-working street subcultures, which long predate the contemporary organisation of identities and the social movements associated with them. Not 'women' exactly, but 'femmes', who manifest a femininity detached from biological femaleness in ways that align that detachment with a cultural politics that imagines conven-tional womanhood as something to be overcome, refigured, reformulated, transmogrified or dismantled, rather than inhabited, mobilised or deployed.

This is where the action is, aesthetically speaking: the blurred superimpositions of Amrou Al-Kadhi in Holly Falconer's photographic portrait, which refuse to cohere into a single image (*Glamrou*, 2016, p. 91); the brawn of a back as backdrop to a pair of out-of-kilter bra-straps in Ajamu's *Body builder in bra* (1990, pp. 82–83); the fetishistically fragmented reductions and multiplications of sexualised feminine signifiers in Pierre Molinier's seductively kinky photo-montages; the hint of beard-shadow on Justin Vivian Bond's lovely face in Catherine Opie's formal portrait. Perhaps Joan Jett Blakk's campy subversion of Black Panther icon Huey Newton's macho posturing captures this sensibility best, to suggest that the visually discordant transfeminine carries a revolutionary potential. It is the blowing-up of the sex/gender relationship, not the putting of it back together with a difference, that matters, that counts as critically important. For Italian radical queer theorist Mario Mieli, it was the discovery and liberation of *transessualità*, the woman psychically present within the man (or vice versa), that was the cornerstone of, and foundation for, the project of anti-capitalist social transformation that he announced in his landmark work *Towards a Gay Communism* (1979).[6]

Distinct from Mieli's *transessualità*, a dissonant interior essence, is the English word 'transsexuality', a category of transfeminine personhood that, as Heaney sees it, descends directly from the generic heroine of the medico-scientific case study: the suffering and psychiatrised invert of nineteenth-century sexology. This is the other, less celebrated, and largely unrecuperated form of the trans-feminine. Relative to the 'genderqueer' strategy of staging the disjunction of sex and gender through a disruption of normative gender signification, the trans-sexual strategy of bringing feminine identification and modes of self-expression into visual alignment with conventional female morphology, through a working of flesh initially understood to be biologically male, is drastically undervalued. Understandably so, given that the better this strategy succeeds, the more it disappears into imperceptibility.

To the extent that transsexuality in this sense is understood as having a politico-aesthetic dimension at all, beyond its utilitarian function as a practice of caring for one's health, it is typically dismissed as the uninteresting act of producing, at best, an overpriced knock-off or a kitschy imitation of the real thing and, at worst, an unappealing visual failure. Almost entirely unrecognised as yet, however, is the extent to which the act of engaging in transsexual surgical practices can also have radical political implications.

Of all the artists represented in *Kiss My Genders*, it is Juliana Huxtable who has addressed these implications most directly. In conversation with scholar and activist Che Gossett at the New Museum, New York, in 2016, Huxtable discussed her recent shift towards writing and performance, and an even more recent hiatus from making visual work at all, as 'relevant ways to deal with a lot of the questions surrounding trans people' – by which she meant, particularly, black trans women such as herself – 'or how to represent them in this moment'[7] in history.

Huxtable's perception that she has been tokenised, fetishised and exoticised within the international art world as 'the black trans woman artist' is a minor matter relative to her deeper concern with the potentially lethal downside of greater visibility. Heightened cultural attention to trans issues has, perversely, fuelled a dramatic rise in often fatal violence towards black trans women, who are already vulnerable to racialised misogynistic (or misdirected homophobic) harm. In response to the fraught context of her art-making, Huxtable's artistic response was, in her words, to 'disappear into myself', focusing less on gallery work she wanted to make and 'more on how I want to be positioned as a person, and how I want to carve out the space necessary for me' simply to live.[8]

Part of that 'disappearing act' involved aesthetic practices entirely different to those that she learned in art school: self-conscious observation and emulation of the quotidian appearance-making practices of older generations of urban black transsexual women. Huxtable came to see her elders' sense of style and fashion – their clothing and accessorising, as well as how they fashioned their bodies – as literal survival strategies. Rather than dismissing them as mere 'passing',[9] she saw them as ways to navigate public and private social worlds that both expressed their sense of self and kept them safer by allowing them to disappear into the norms and ideals of feminine beauty.

This shift in the register of Huxtable's image-making – not externalised, but auto-directed – allowed her some breathing room before taking the next turn in her career. It can be understood as a profound instance of what ancient Greek philosophers called *epimeleia heautou*, or 'the care of the self' – an everyday art of living that takes 'art' off the gallery wall and puts it instead onto the skin and into the streets. It is a vernacular art that, in this instance, enables a black trans woman to lessen her chances of being killed as expendable gendertrash, and to thus become capable of making other art in the future.

In asserting that 'it's actually really radical to insist on [...] traditional ideas of what beauty is, but in a really intense way',[10] Huxtable reframes transfemininity in a transfeminist mode. Transfeminism is more than the mere inclusion of trans women within a feminism that remains centered on cisgender women and girls. Rather, it is a coalitional, anti-misogynistic praxis that doesn't pay attention to whether the myriad diminishments, subordinations and violences directed against the feminine take aim at bodies born with vaginas or those that acquire them later in life, those whose normative feminine appearance disappears into the fiction of a natural fact or those who disrupt the fictive naturalness of the sex/gender system. It is a perspective capable of countering the moral panic targeting trans women without in any way sacrificing the very real political concerns of those assigned female at birth.[11] To the extent that the works presented in *Kiss My Genders* foster greater appreciation for the radical potential of this transfeminist proposition, the exhibition will have succeeded as a social intervention as well as an aesthetic provocation.

1. I use the term 'trans woman' here, instead of 'transwoman', in order to emphasise the notion of a shared womanhood modified by a type of specifier – whether race, class, disability, etc – rather than naming a different kind of person than a woman.

2. Emma Heaney, *The New Woman: Literary Modernism, Queer Theory, and the Trans Feminine Allegory* (Evanston, IL: Northwestern University Press, 2017)

3. Mary Wollstonecraft, *A Vindication of the Rights of Woman and A Vindication of the Rights of Men* (Oxford: Oxford University Press, 2009 [1792]), p. 72

4. Esther Newton, *Mother Camp: Female Impersonators in America* (Chicago: University of Chicago Press, 1979), p. xiii

5. Ibid.

6. Mario Mieli, *Towards a Gay Communism: Elements of a Homosexual Critique*, trans. by David Fernbach and Evan Calder Williams (London: Pluto Press, 2018 [1977])

7. Che Gossett and Juliana Huxtable, 'Existing in the World: Blackness at the Edge of Trans Visibility', in Reina Gossett/Eric A. Stanley/Johanna Burton (eds.), *Trap Door: Trans Cultural Production and the Politics of Visibility* (Cambridge, MA: MIT Press, 2017), p. 49

8. Ibid, p. 53

9. Passing, in both transgender and racial contexts, is usually meant pejoratively as successfully presenting oneself as belonging to an identity group to which one does not properly belong.

10. Gossett/Stanley/Burton (2017), p. 54

11. For a broader exploration of the concept of transfeminism – that is, the articulation of a feminist politics which is informed by and inclusive of transgender perspectives – see Susan Stryker/Talia Bettcher (eds.), 'Trans/Feminisms', a special issue of *TSQ: Transgender Studies Quarterly*, Vol. 3, Nos. 1–2 (2016)

PAUL CLINTON

Useless Man

On What Occasions Do You Lie?
On What Occasions Do I Breathe?
Leigh Bowery, responding to a questionnaire[1]

In the mid 1990s – during the last few years of his life – club performer, costume designer and artist Leigh Bowery became notorious for an act in which he would give birth to his assistant (and, later, wife) Nicola, live on stage. Wearing some disturbing approximation of middle class respectability – a tweed twinset with a rubber fetish mask, for instance – he would sing before collapsing on the ground as his 'daughter' emerged from between his legs, covered in fake blood and viscera. Often the song would be 'Useless Man', a litany of unspeakable sex acts and bodily functions recited to the tune of a Pepsi commercial and attributed to some unnamed male.[2] The abject, vulgar and 'common' becomes a means to shame and debase conventional ideas of masculinity, childbirth and straight family values. Illicit desires, unsightly bodily functions and lurid acts are normally mentioned only on the fringes of society, not in polite, middle class company. But Bowery associates all that is decent and proper with all that isn't, showing how images of motherhood often repress the horrors of the body, and representations of masculine authority ignore their implication in sordid abuses of power. Bowery – in a way perhaps characteristic of UK gender-dissident performance – tested the norms of gender by disturbing conventions of class and propriety.

This focus on class or issues of social inclusion and hypocrisy might be surprising, as artists who engage with gender play through the manipulation or depiction of their own bodies are often misread as indulging in narcissism or solipsism. But, from Bowery's bawdy nightclub acts to artists Hannah Quinlan and Rosie Hastings – whose recent work concerns local and national identity – self image and physical transformation have acted as a means to talk about broader cultural and political issues. Far from navel-gazing, artists have used gender insubordination as a means to journey outwards into the world at large.

Any account of recent gender-nonconformist art in the UK, starting with Bowery, is bound to have more holes in it than a pair of fishnet stockings, but some themes and figures can be singled out nonetheless. Drag performance, and particularly female impersonation, were, at least in the twentieth century, associated with working class culture in the UK. In his book *Queer London* (2005), Matt Houlbrook explains that drag shows were a regular feature of pubs and working men's clubs.[3] He also finds that proletarian homosexuals were more likely to display overt effeminacy, and wear nail polish and make-up. Houlbrook argues that in this context, such displays were a way of conforming to the norms of gender, rather than disrupting them: working class homosexuals explained their desire for other men by imitating the attributes of women.

In other contexts, such gender- and class-crossing performances were a means of undoing distinctions between masculine and feminine. Lily Savage, comedian Paul O'Grady's drag alter ego, entertained television audiences in the 1990s with a parody of a working class woman from Liverpool. Part of the joke was that her vulgar, no-nonsense demeanour made her tougher than any man. It is worth noting that, while this kind of classed gender play had mainstream appeal in the UK, in North America it was largely the province of underground performers like Charles Ludlum, Jack Smith, The Cockettes and the queen of trash, actor and drag artist Divine. There are also significant differences in approach between US and UK gender performance. Where the impoverished black and Latinx transgender and drag performers of the film *Paris Is Burning* (1990), which documents New York's voguing ball culture, imitated and parodied luxurious lifestyles they could not afford, artists like Bowery rejected them outright.

Bowery's primary means of expression was through his visual appearance, and his often shocking bodily modifications were, like the work of his collaborator, choreographer Michael Clark, influenced by the antisocial aesthetic of the 1980s post-punk and New Romantic subcultures. His dirty songs and highly sexualised appearance – chest fat pushed upwards to form breasts, genitals artfully tucked to look like an exposed vagina – also contrasted with the asexuality of other well-known gender nonconformists of the time. If one underground, confrontational style of gender-nonconformist performance, such as Bowery's, took place in nightclubs and art galleries, a neutered version played out for the wider public on television and in newspapers. Lipstick-wearing raconteur Quentin Crisp and pop star Boy George found public acceptance for their ambiguous appearances by removing any sense of sexual threat from their public personae: George famously quipped 'Sex? I'd rather have a cup of tea.' Working in the 1980s, amid the ongoing AIDS crisis, Bowery's overt vulgarity was, by contrast, an unapologetic act of confrontation at a time when queerness was considered dangerous.

His bloody nightclub performances – giving birth, squirting enemas, swinging through plate glass – led critic Hilton Als to compare Bowery's work to dissident surrealist Antonin Artaud's visceral and ritualistic 'theatre of cruelty', although there is no evidence that the artist himself made the reference.[4] Bowery's looks would become increasingly surreal: body modifications such as creating the illusion of a vagina or taping his waist would give way to costumes that went beyond recognisable gender – his head becoming a pompom or his limbs padded and distended. As the quotation at the start of this essay signals, Bowery made no claim to be expressing some authentic, true or essential self, instead seeing the body and identity as illusory and ripe for change.

In this regard, his looks and performances resonate with ideas of gender performativity – most notably queer theorist Judith Butler's claim that all gender is an imitation of social conventions for which there is no original.[5] We are all gendered, willingly or not, by society at large. But the fact we have to reassert our gender repeatedly – through gesture, naming and behaving – signals that it is not so innate, natural or secure as we might assume. Drag, for Butler, acts as a subversive and parodic version of the kinds of gender imitation all subjects, heterosexual or not, engage in during daily life. Bowery's performances for mirror in Charles Atlas's video *Teach* (1992–98) or Cerith Wyn Evans's documentation of the performer's residency at Antony d'Offay Gallery in 1988, toy with this practice of learning and mimicking gendered gestures. In the former, an emotive song by Billie Holiday plays while Bowery mugs for the camera, wearing feminised plastic lips that cover his own. Authentic feeling and insight into the soul of the performer are promised by the music and his expressive eyes, but the alternately smiling and pouting false lips indicate that this is all for show, and that there is nothing beyond or behind the performance. In the latter, his changing looks and carefully constructed self-image emphasise identity as surface effect.

A performative view of gender, combined with unapologetic depictions of sexuality, can also be found in the work of photographer Ajamu. In common with a number of other black British artists who came to prominence in the 1980s and 1990s – artists like Sonia Boyce, Rotimi Fani-Kayode, Isaac Julien and Ingrid Pollard – his work is concerned with how perceptions of race identity shape those of gender and sexuality. Where Fani-Kayode used allusions to artists like Caravaggio as an aesthetic foil for depictions of black gay men, Ajamu's work is confrontationally sexy. Overt homoeroticism combines with femininity – a black male hand in a delicate lace glove holding an erect penis, for example (*Cock and glove*, 1993; p. 84). Both masculine and feminine, erotic and highly constructed, the image does not offer a key according to which one gender is the truth hiding behind another, nor any other details which might resolve the confusion. By presenting scenes of ambiguous sexual fantasy, Ajamu also avoids the urge to document and locate an essential black, gay male identity: his photographs, as art historian Kobena Mercer put it, are about difference, not identity.[6]

Stuart Hall, also speaking on this artist's work, has argued that for members of the black diaspora, identity – and, by inference, gender identity – is particularly important, as it gives a sense of belonging to those who do not otherwise feel at home.[7] Ajamu's ambiguous photographs are a challenge, both to white audiences who fantasise about black male virility and to black audiences looking for a fixed sense of self. Throughout his work, too, are found jarringly anachronistic accessories: pearls, evening gloves, a chaise longue. These luxurious but outmoded metonyms for feminine glamour show how norms of gender change over time, and that access to them depends upon race and class position. The signifiers Ajamu uses to convey femininity all carry associations of luxury and wealth, indicating that working women may be at a disadvantage in imitating standards of womanly beauty.

Queer theories of gender performativity, which came to the fore in the early 1990s, had a pervasive effect on art-making in Britain, including on work that came to be viewed as post-feminist. This is a misleading term, as certain strains of feminism, particularly from France, have long argued that gender is a set of norms rather than a biological fact. Nevertheless, post-feminism became the phrase attached to work by women who refused to be defined by their bodies, from Sarah Lucas's ironic takes on misogynistic working class jokes (*Two Fried Eggs and Kebab*, 1992) and her reproductions of tabloid sex scandals (*We Score Every Night*, 1992), to the feminine abjection explored by Helen Chadwick or Rachel Evans-Milne. The latter two both featured in the influential 'Bad Girls' season of exhibitions at London's Institute of Contemporary Art in 1994. This brought together queer, punk and feminist impulses to present female artists who rebelled against both feminist and patriarchal definitions of women. An altogether different strategy was taken up by artist Rose English, who, from the 1980s onwards, played upon the idea of femininity as performance, in highly theatrical works that made much of the difficulty of separating truth from illusion.

The same decade would also see a flourishing of drag king performance (impersonations of masculinity), in which a number of artists, such as Ashley Hans Schierl and Del LaGrace Volcano, participated. Schierl moved to London from Austria in the mid 1990s and set up a warehouse studio and living space that became a meeting place for artists who identified as queer, transgender and/or lesbian. The results of their collaborations became the film *Dandy Dust* (1998). This sci-fi romp not only depicts gender dissidence, but attempts to produce a cinematic structure that reflects this refusal to define identity: the film eschews narrative coherence, and characters often change gender, or form, from one scene to the next, with no sense of resolution. Also, among Schierl's collaborators at the time was the artist Oreet Ashery, whose early work exploring the effects of cultural identity upon gender included performances in which she dressed as a fictional orthodox Jewish man, Marcus Fisher.

For all that queer theories of performativity liberate the concept of gender from essentialism, they have been accused of ignoring the body altogether, including the bodies of transgender subjects such as those represented by Schierl. Those who surgically transition have been accused of reinforcing the idea that gender is a fixed state, tied to certain physical attributes. But it has often been the gender identity clinics, not trans people themselves, who have made patients conform to various behaviours in order to access treatment. Not everyone who opts for surgery sees their gender as defined by it, nor do they seek to identify with any one role, and not all trans people seek physical interventions. In not distinguishing between stages and styles of transitioning, be they surgical or otherwise, Schierl's film arguably comes closer to writer Paul B. Preciado's claim, in *Testo Junkie* (2008), that bodies do not exist in a natural or permanent state, but are constantly being manipulated by society, industry and pharmacology.[8] From the discovery of the reproductive function of wombs in the eighteenth century, through to the invention of the contraceptive pill or Viagra, the body itself is being continually reshaped, intellectually and physically. Biological sex, Preciado argues, is no less historically or culturally contingent than gender, and those who seek to transition are simply appropriating technologies of transformation already at work in us all.

Butler's use of drag as an example of subversive gender performance has also been criticised for being ahistorical, ignoring circumstances that render it at certain periods a far from dissident practice. Such a social and historical context is examined by Hannah Quinlan and Rosie Hastings in their 2018 film *Something for the Boys* (p. 199). The last two decades in Britain have seen increasing recognition of transgender and non-binary rights. At the same time, they have been years of marked economic austerity, in which the gap between rich and poor has vastly increased.[9] Quinlan and Hastings's film depicts the declining seaside resort of Blackpool, on the UK's west coast, as in the grip of a nostalgia for a pre-war time of prosperity – a nationalistic yearning that has driven its population to vote overwhelmingly in favour of Brexit. They find that this extends into the city's gay scene, where campy drag musical revues and go-go dancing bars also hark back to values of an earlier era. Just as Houlbrook argues that, in twentieth-century working class communities, drag was a means of conforming, so Quinlan and Hastings, through a mix of documentary and staged performance, suggest that, in the Blackpool scene, it may be unwittingly complicit in the conservative politics of nostalgia. Tension between community inclusion and the risk of non-heterosexual subcultures assimilating to normative social values also pervades the work of Jenkin van Zyl (pp. 220–23). Using ensemble casts and borrowing from the language of horror movies and sexual fetishes, Van Zyl invents fictional communities that are neither clean nor family friendly, in a way that recalls Bowery's defiant blood-and-guts performances.

Far from being restricted to self-portraiture or autobiography, the artists discussed here work across group and individual performance, sculpture, installation, photography, and even in disparate genres such as horror and science fiction. More than this, their work is not solely about gender or defined by their own identifications. In depicting the social construction of masculinity and femininity, they also dissect other forces in society that determine who you are, such as race, class or historical context. This approach, which has come to be called intersectional, argues that what it means to be male, female, trans or non-binary cannot be understood in isolation from a range of social and political issues. Perhaps the prominence of the class system in the UK has meant that this subject in particular has been unavoidable for the nation's queer, trans and drag artists. By drawing attention to the ways in which factors like class or race change how masculinity or femininity are performed, they show that norms affect everyone, even the straight, white, cis majority. The task of troubling gender is one that falls to us all.

NOTES

1. Leigh Bowery quoted in Hilton Als, 'Cruel Story of Youth', in *Leigh Bowery* (London: Violette Editions, 1998), p. 23

2. Minty, 'Useless Man', in *Open Wide* (London: Candy Records, 1997)

3. Matt Houlbrook, *Queer London: Perils and Pleasures in the Sexual Metropolis, 1918–1957* (Chicago: University of Chicago Press, 2005), pp. 140–41

4. Als (1998), p. 21

5. Judith Butler, 'Imitation and Gender Insubordination', in Diana Fuss (ed.), *Inside/Out: Lesbian Theories, Gay Theories* (Abingdon: Routledge, 1991), pp. 13–31

6. Kobena Mercer, speaking in the film *The Homecoming*, dir. Topher Campbell, 1995, 17 min

7. Stuart Hall, ibid.

8. Paul B. Preciado, *Testo Junkie: Sex, Drugs and Biopolitics in the Pharmacopornographic Era* (New York: The Feminist Press, 2013)

9. Statistics from the Institute for Public Policy Research in 2018 have ranked the UK the fifth most unequal country in Europe in terms of income, with inequality having significantly worsened since 2008; 'How Unequal Is Britain and Are the Poor Getting Poorer?', in the *Guardian*, 5 September 2018 [www.theguardian.com/inequality/2018/sep/05/qa-how-unequal-is-britain-and-are-the-poor-getting-poorer, accessed 12 February 2019]. The Equality Trust has also cited the UK as having 'a very unequal distribution of income' compared to other developed nations. 'The Scale of Economic Equality in the UK', in the Equality Trust [www.equalitytrust.org.uk/scale-economic-inequality-uk, accessed 12 February 2019]

Lingerie

JAY BERNARD

Lingerie was not on the shopping list.
Down the aisle
the bras were prawn cracker white, the lace cerulean
the frills soft as young pig
and each mushroom cup hung with
aloof authority.
But our basket was filled with
eggs and seven day bread.
It is why, at twelve, I had sagging breasts.

There was no silk
rampart, no delicate clip to
keep them in; polyester wakens the rage of
the most patient saint and it chafes
the petalled skin of tiny
new gods
who command
an imperious trot punishing
fun with excruciating pain.

I eyed them in the mirror.
          There seemed to be no solution –
they grew and grew until I had to accept them.
But what child, I thought, would want them?
                    If I could not reveal them now
from the silk case of a good bra
how would I ever learn?
          and how many lovers would
be crushed in that sickening
          fold where each breast hung
soft and fat and waxen?

          Mother, my galaxy might once have been
your breasts. I may have put a rounded mouth
on either tether, and spent the tiny,
silent night sucking; I may
have drained you every evening of your whiteness,
so that you staggered into banisters,
when putting me to bed –

          I'm sorry for my babyhood,
for the wet fisted selfishness, for that
day, by the knickers, when something stirred
between us, something like wind
against pendulous bells –
          vast and ineffable changes
that present themselves as soft, budding
aureoles, ones I sucked to be closer to you,
and mine, which I cage in tight,
black bras like prisons
sheared from panther –

CHARLIE FOX

Chimeras

I was 7 years old when I fell in love with the chimera.

Her picture was in a book on monsters in Greek mythology. 'The chimera', it told me, 'is a fire-snorting beast with a lioness' head and paws, a goat's midriff and a serpent's tail.' Homer records that the chimera was gruesomely slain in battle with this dude Bellerophon astride Pegasus the winged horse. My mind melted into goo thinking about this fantastic beast, sprung from a trippy synthesis of different creatures.

Who could kill a beautiful thing like that?

I wanted to climb on her back and run far away from home.

Growing up, there was only a scrambled galaxy of clues, which I'd need to witchily synthesise to figure out what it was I liked.

Mythology always tells you how strange creatures are born.

Maybe I saw Nan Goldin photographs when I got into my early teens. (Transgender slip: Bill Clinton called her 'Dan Goldin' in 1997, when condemning heroin chic.) There were no *Drag Race* gifs. I hadn't seen Leigh Bowery talking about how he liked to 'become a thing' with his discombobulating costumes. I hadn't seen the eerie creatures invented by Jesse Kanda for the covers of Arca's records, which exist in some angelic zone beyond boy and girl.

I saw Marilyn Manson on the cover of *Mechanical Animals* (1998), with his prosthetic alien breasts and vanished genitals staring at me like a strung-out angel.

And when I was 16, I had a VHS tape of this documentary where Nan Goldin was shooting a transwoman in what seemed like a swank Manhattan hotel suite. It was so classy.

'Marilyn never looked so good...' Nan purrs.

'Marilyn Manson?' the sly blonde answers, pretending to be dumb.

Hot joke.

Biological factoids about genitalia and who fucks what are more significant to a lot of people thinking about trans or queer bodies than their magical ramifications. But a werewolf knows plenty about being trans, craving escape from his sack of wretched human flesh to reveal the cute beast hidden inside. Awooool! Swirl 'trans' around your mouth like a potion until it turns into transmogrification and transhuman. Think about superhero Swamp Thing, 'A Real Doll' (1990) by A.M. Homes ('Have you ever been held captive in the dark cavern of someone's body?' Barbie asks a twisted little kid) or *The Cremaster Cycle* (1994–2002). The freaky bodies on @matieresfecales, an Instagram account run by two kids in Montreal who like to dress up as aliens, are wildly new and simultaneously ancient as Ovid's *Metamorphoses*. John Waters said Divine always wanted to be Godzilla.

Too skinny, too fat, too oddball? 'Don't dream it, be it!' Transform into a disorientating monster.

It's mainstream now, longing for creatureliness to escape the horror of being ~~human~~. Pass the OxyContin. Cosplay frolics and hallucinogenic Furriness are on TV – did you watch *Secret Life of the Human Pups* (2016)? Spend Halloween as the killer female cyborg from the anime *Ghost in the Shell* (1995); hang out with the kids who identify as mermaids. Those cute Instagram filters make you look like a fluffy-hearted cartoon hound or bunny. At last, with the ascent of unashamedly hateful right-wing politics, everybody got sick of being sold the same monochrome romance and only seeing gay kids in 'very special episodes' of TV shows. The internet allowed them to explore their kinky, multicoloured lusts in full. Prince sang as his female alter ego Camille, voice pitch-shifted to mimic a squeaky teen princess: 'Rebirth of the flesh! Let it in, y'all!'[1]

This desire to be *something else* never goes away in childhood. Maybe transhumanism came out of the dark because the first generation of kids to ingest Disney flicks on demand with their VCRs watched carefully and discovered being human is for suckers. Belle falls in love with the Beast when he's still a furry monster. Anthropomorphic lunacy reigns! Smooth-talking tigers, the tree that speaks in *Pocahontas* (1995), hyenas cracking jokes and the genie (not even flesh and blood!), shape-shifting all the time. You don't know where a body begins or ends. In another @matieresfecales post, the girl creature wears fleshy prosthetic devil horns with pink bruises blushing around her eyes. It's captioned, 'What I always wanted to look like as a child.'

'Why do you wear that stupid bunny suit?', Donnie Darko asks his evil pal Frank

And he answers, 'Why do you wear that stupid man suit?'

I freeze-framed a moment from 'Two Dozen and One Greyhounds' (1995), that episode of *The Simpsons* where Bart is trying to explain himself to his family at breakfast while dressed in candy-floss pink socks and culottes. I wonder what kind of confession he could be making...

BART: I've got a crush on a girl from ballet!

HOMER (*chomping pancakes*): Ballet? You mean the act with the bear in the little car? (*He giggles and hums a circus tune, suddenly lost in daydream...*)

MARGE: Like a romantic crush, honey?

BART: No, like I wanna *be* her! I wanna be that magical girl!

Shocked pause.

LISA: Go Bart!

HOMER: Marge, if Bart's a girl now, can we call him Batwoman?

And I like pretending Bart was mesmerised by a parade of transgender minxes he saw on an awful talk show – *Geraldo* (1987–96), maybe – where the audience shrieked and gasped at them like they were new creatures from the zoo. 'So hardcore', he thought. Or he listened to Kurt Cobain howling 'Daddy's little girl ain't a girl no more!' on 'Negative Creep' from *Bleach* (1989) and felt... *excited.*

'My mom and friend both believe that Kurt was trans', somebody writes into the Reddit vortex. 'I mean, it's not an unheard of theory.'

'You've felt it your entire life,' wizardly Morpheus tells Neo in *The Matrix* (1999), 'that there's something wrong with the world... ' Which are commonly reported feelings for trans people. *The Matrix* is full of clues, but only when Larry and Andy Wachowski transitioned to become Lana and Lilly did it suddenly make sense as a trans fable.

During Lana's heroic speech in October 2012 at the Human Rights Campaign gala in San Francisco, she remembered being a boy and staring, bewildered, at her mother, and wondering 'why she cannot see me' as a little girl; and locking herself in a bathroom stall as a teen and weeping, the slip she stole from her sister underneath her gradutaion suit, caressing her frightened body; and writing a suicide note in Burger King 'because I was unable [...] to imagine a world where I would ever fit in.'

But she escaped, like Neo. His old reality collapses, a dream programmed by malevolent cyborgs, and his body finally belongs to him. Meanwhile, Lana talked about how she wanted to 'gain access to other rooms, other worlds previously unimaginable'.

Which somebody might encrypt as 'Follow the white rabbit' – the command that leads Neo on his quest.

Boys Don't Cry (1999) is based on the bleak last days of Brandon Teena, a trans man raped and murdered in Nebraska. Brandon (played by a pixie-ish Hilary Swank in the film) was assigned female at birth but identified as a boy from his mid teens. He fell in love with a girl, Lana Tisdel (dreamy Chloë Sevigny). When they have sex, Lana's eyes roll back in her head – rapturous. She's discovering something scary and sublime. She doesn't know Brandon isn't like other boys.

The spooky scene could be re-scored with trans superstar SOPHIE's track 'Is It Cold in the Water?' (2018). Its singer Princess Mozart's chill voice soars over ecstatic rave synths: 'I've left home [...] I'm falling/Worlds turn to smoke [...] Is it cold', she gasps, 'in the water?'

Ovid writes in *Metamorphoses* that Hermaphroditus, the winged intersex god, was transformed from handsome teen to pretty androgyne when Salmacis, a nymph mad with lust, ravished him in enchanted water. It's all very *Mysterious Skin* (2004): 'Pinning her whole body against him, she clung there and cried: "You may fight as you will, you wretch, but you shan't escape me."' Ovid pictures the scene as a violation of nature: no romance.

A little rewrite...

'Excited by Salmacis' dare, the hot punk Hermaphroditus leapt into the moonlit pool. Goosebumps suddenly in flower all over him, he shivered like a wounded fawn. But clever Salmacis held him tight, and before their bodies oozed together like jelly, she playfully whispered a question in his ear...'

(SOPHIE's debut album *Oil of Every Pearl's Un-Insides* (2018) tells a luscious and disorientating story about how being trans feels and sounds. She conjures up virtual bodies: 'candy boys' and 'pony boys' and 'immaterial' girls. The boundaries between 'organic' and 'artificial' get warped: ASMR squelches; simulations of mirrors shattering; *Rubber Johnny* (2005) elephants shriek. 'Pretending' is a tranced-out score for someone dissociating from the wrong body into a planet far, far away and returning to babble a few alien words. It's scary and it's beautiful. 'I can be anything I want', she sings.)

And then one night I found the chimera sprawled on my bed like Candy Darling. Luminous fluid oozed from her breasts, and when she spoke a choir of demonic voices – heavy metal growls, lost boy sighs, girlish shrieks – came out her mouth, all mixed together. I was bewitched. 'The funny thing is it's *natural*,' she purred, claws glittering, 'this desire to be a strange, new, magical beast. Even haters know it in the toxic waste dumps of their hearts.' The wind quivered in the trees. 'Sometimes, honey, we all look in the mirror', the chimera said, 'and feel like a fucking alien.'

Arca, *Entrañas*, 2016
Matthew Barney, *The Cremaster Cycle* (1994–2002)
Björk, 'All is Full of Love' (1999). Dir. Chris Cunningham
Boys Don't Cry, dir. Kimberly Peirce (1999)
Chris Cunningham, *Rubber Johnny* (2005). Music by Aphex Twin
Donnie Darko, dir. Richard Kelly (2001)
Ghost in the Shell, dir. Mamoru Oshii (1995)
A.M. Homes, 'A Real Doll', in *The Safety of Objects* (1990)
Marilyn Manson, *Mechanical Animals* (1998). Artwork by Joseph Cultrice
Ovid, *Metamorphoses* (8 AD)
Prince, 'If I Was Your Girlfriend', *Sign O' The Times* (1987)
Prince, 'Return of the Flesh', *Camille*, unreleased (1986)
Prince, 'Bob George', *The Black Album* (1987/1994)
Prince, 'Sometimes It Snows in April', *Parade* (1986)
Prince, 'Lovesexy', *Lovesexy* (1988)
SOPHIE, *Oil of Every Pearl's Un-Insides* (2018)
The Brandon Teena Story, dir. Susan Muska and Gréta Olafsdóttir (1998)
The Matrix, dir. Lana and Lilly Wachowski (1999)

NOTES

1. His Royal Purpleness explored a lot of trans feelings in his music, at a time when examples of actual transness in pop culture were more elusive than real-life vampire sects. He switched his given name for an unpronounceable combination of the male and female erotic symbols, and he inhabited a whole carnival of other bodies in his records: Joker, funky imp, Romeo, orchidaceous, *Paris is Burning* femme.

AMROU AL-KADHI

Queer Reclamations: How Drag Splits and Rebuilds the Self

When I first started drag at the age of 19, I experienced a profound fracture. While it liberated me to inhabit a self-constructed feminine alter ego, the process also entailed a sense of splitting. In renouncing my male identity, I simultaneously felt a divorce from my Muslim heritage, as if adopting a queer alter ego severed me from my conservative Middle Eastern upbringing.

I spent my childhood between Dubai, in the United Arab Emirates, and Bahrain, and was raised in a strictly homosocial environment – it was instilled in me that any kind of sexual or gender transgression would have severe social and religious consequences, and I was brought up to be extremely Allah-fearing. As a result, wearing women's clothes and make-up for the first time felt like an active negation of my cultural upbringing. Yes, it was empowering – but it was utterly disorientating too. In inhabiting my authentic, queer identity, did I implicitly have to sacrifice my heritage? Was harmony between the two impossible? In attempting to be authentically queer, did I have to be inauthentic in the context of my own culture? In nearly a decade of drag, my practice has revolved around the ways drag can rupture inherited cultural identities, examining how it splits us, how it renews us.

For *Glamrou* (2016, p. 91), I collaborated with photographer Holly Falconer and Arab stylist and dear friend, Amnah Hafez. We used triple exposure on film to help relay the schizophrenic experience of being in drag as a person of Muslim heritage. In the resulting photograph, which was published in *Cause & Effect* magazine, I attempt to wear a Middle Eastern rug as a dress; yet the mere attempt to create an intersection of my gender identity with my heritage results in a struggle that shatters the self into many different pieces. The very act of drag, for many of us, catalyses the feeling that our identities are unstable. This instability was a surprise to me when I first started my practice. I wholeheartedly believed that costume and make-up would result in feeling at harmony with my queer identity, yet, although moments *in* drag were certainly empowering, the sheer dissonance with my cultural heritage led to the more prevailing feelings of fracture we tried to relay in the photograph.

Drag is as much about self-professing as it is self-obliteration – it's not only a coming into your own, but a coming 'out' of inherited ideas about yourself. And with this can come a lot of friction. In Lyle Ashton Harris's *Josephine #6* (2002, p. 97), we see the artist embodying the image of Josephine Baker, the renowned French-American entertainer and activist who worked in the early twentieth century. Here Ashton Harris collages his own self-portrait with multiple exposures, as if this act of dragging up has shattered his self into multiples. The decision to impersonate Baker – as well as jazz singer Billie Holiday, in the associated series of works *Billie, Boxers, Better Days* (2002) – shows the artist attempting to connect with his black artistic predecessors. But the contexts of the figures he impersonates explain why the image in question is so visually fragmented; Josephine Baker's life and career were inextricably bound up in the acute negrophilia of European modernism, whereby black art was fiercely exoticised and fetishised by the cultural elite – it contributed to her success and popularity, but also to her association with problematic, Western 'types' and stereotypes of blackness. For Ashton Harris, a desire to embody his heritage is brought into conflict with historical Western attitudes toward that legacy, and thus the image cannot sit still.

In attempting to reclaim his own tradition through the lens of drag, Ashton Harris submits his work yet further to the violence of the Western gaze. His desire to impersonate a female rather than male historical black figure reinforces the sense of fracture; in attempting to engage his queer identity with his racial history, the image starts to disappear, just as queer people of colour have long been erased from Western discourse. Drag and gender subversion are often thought to be wholly Western conceits. On learning about drag as a nascent queer artist, I myself had only European and American cultural contexts readily available to me. Mainstream art-historical surveys situate gender subversion in the Western civil rights movements of the 1960s to 1980s, with white performance artists taking centre stage. Late-twentieth-century postmodernism saw a radical deconstruction of gender, race and sexuality in growing artistic practices such as performance art, and it certainly felt like a time of the new. But this is a dangerous misconception. The positing of the West as the inventor of gender subversion equates whiteness and secularism with progressive art forms like drag. It is precisely this equation that can leave drag artists with non-Western and/or religious backgrounds feeling fractured, as if we have to detach ourselves from our cultural heritages in order to be able to express our queer identities.

Missing from popular surveys of drag is the fact that gender subversion has long existed in culturally accepted forms outside the West. In South Asia, the hijra community – sometimes labelled the 'Indian third gender' – have occupied a sacred position within their culture for hundreds, some say thousands, of years. Comprised of intersex, transgender and non-binary Indians, the hijra have been involved in Hindu and Muslim rituals as agents of fertility and blessing, with rich spiritual and social histories. It was only during the British colonisation of the mid nineteenth century, which introduced conservative Western laws and morals into India – such as the 1897 law that made eunuchs illegal – that the criminalisation of hijras and gender nonconformity in India occurred.

In trying to weave together my Muslim heritage and my queer drag practice, I looked to Islam to see if I could find any concealed forms of gender nonconformity. The attitude towards queerness expressed in the way I was raised was punitive, but I wanted to return to the Quran to see if my own specific experience had clouded alternative understandings of my religion. Western narratives portraying Islam as a barbaric, regressive religion had further skewed my perceptions, which is why tying my faith to my gender identity felt so impossible. As it happens, the Quran is teeming with queer magic. I've slowly been able to discover this with the help of London Queer Muslims, a group in which LGBTQIA+ people of Muslim heritage find harmony in the queer possibilities of the Quran. On re-reading the Quran, I was particularly struck by the description of Allah as 'He who shapes you all in the womb as He pleases.'[1] Perhaps Allah themselves could have been the architect of my gender nonconformity?

Sufism is a particular branch of Islam that feels completely hospitable to gender nonconformism. For Sufists, rather than being a monotheistic ruler of all people, Allah is more a non-binary spirit who has their own unique relationship with every single Muslim, taking any shape or form according to the individual. Sufist prayer methods include men wearing skirts and dancing to fuse their own souls with Allah (the famous whirling dervishes). It is a beautifully mystical form of Islam, which undoes patriarchal renderings of Allah as a paternalistic punisher; eighteenth-century female Sufist mystic Rabi'a al-Adawiyya famously referred to Allah as her 'beloved' – no longer a patriarch to be feared, but a spiritual force at one with her female desires. The more research I undertook on the genderqueer practices within the Islamic faith, and the way it accommodates alternative gender perspectives, the more I repaired the seams between my heritage and my queer identity.

Searching through histories to reclaim past contexts as queer is a powerfully healing process. In *Kiss My Genders*, this is pertinently explored in the majestic work of Juliana Huxtable, particularly her *Untitled in the Rage (Nibiru Cataclysm)* (2015, p. 153). Huxtable, who was born intersex, raised male, and now identifies as female, here looks to her obsession with the syncretic religious cult, Nuwaubianism, which incorporates Islamic teachings amongst other beliefs. Although originating in 1960s New York, Nuwaubianism looks to non-Western histories; its followers worship the Ancient Egyptians and pyramids, believe in the supremacy of black people (who are thought to be the descendants of lizard aliens), and dismiss white people as those who belong underneath the Arctic caves. In the image in question, Huxtable presents herself as a goddess-like figure, in a desert landscape, with a green body that makes her look otherworldly. She sits with her back to us while looking to the side, as if she is a being outside our gaze – someone not to be fetishised or exoticised, but to be worshipped and respected from a distance, with her own perspective that we cannot grasp. Huxtable exaggerates her feminine and racial identity with unadulterated power, and she assumes the status of an icon. She places her gender and racial identities within an alternative narrative that undoes reductive Western imaginings; here, she is in charge, making the viewer feel 'other'.

American photographer Peter Hujar's work *Ethyl Eichelberger as Nefertiti (III)* (1979, p. 151), shows a queer performance artist similarly occupying the persona of the Ancient Egyptian queen. Eichelberger was a notorious East Village drag performer, actor and playwright in 1980s New York who wrote, starred in and produced over 30 solo drag performances based on the lives of great women of history, literature and myth, including Medusa, Lucrezia Borgia and Medea. In Hujar's photograph, we see Eichelberger standing barefoot and frail, performing the role of historical royalty with a moving queer fragility. The costume seems to be improvised and the setting is sparse, but it is a proclamation that queer people deserve their place in grand historical narratives, and that we can create new ones for ourselves at any given moment.

I have personally been able to construct a fresh narrative out of the rubble of my previous ones. Being a queer person as well as one of Muslim heritage once felt like a treacherous juncture, an intersection of identities that could only result in a car crash. My own childhood understanding of Allah as someone who would punish me for my gender nonconformism made me feel at odds with my faith every time I wore a dress. But through a radical process of re-reading the Quran, I've been able to undo my own childhood teachings, as well as unlearning contemporary Western notions of Islam as regressive. Now my experience in drag entails, not a sharp pang of fracture, but instead a magical harmony between my heritage and my queer identity. For the power of drag is not only that of the new – it is also how it rediscovers the old, with boundless potential.

NOTES

1. M.A. Abdel Haleem, *The Qur'an: A New Translation* (Oxford: Oxford University Press, 2016), p. 34

MANUEL SEGADE

To Strike a Pose is to Pose a Threat

Identity is an endless, ever-unfinished conversation.
Stuart Hall[1]

So it is better to speak
remembering
we were never meant to survive.
Audre Lorde[2]

Someone asked you in an interview, 'What's the nastiest shade you've ever thrown?' And you said, 'Existing in the world.'
Che Gossett in conversation with Juliana Huxtable[3]

Bodies are the agents of history – the ultimate historiographic tool. History is somatic, a choreographic series of gestures arranged to be read in a certain order. Communities always identify through similarities of movement rather than the sameness of bodies. Gestures are learnt, legitimised, codified. They are attributed to a gender, a race, a class, and naturalised within historically defined social spheres. Poses, on the other hand, dismantle the language of appropriate gestures: a pose is not simply a gesture, but a radical gesture. To strike a pose is to draw on the existing code as a set of samples available to bodies, which embody them as events on each occasion, taking apart and reassembling the relationships forged by history. To strike a pose is to become aware of how a body makes history. In other words, posing is history's flesh against the grain.

To strike a pose is to pose a threat.[4] Poses allow us to read the choreographic phrases of dissent,[5] the microhistories that expose twists, turns and repetitions – they are history dancing. Just as anarchist Emma Goldman refused to be part of a revolution in which she could not dance, poses struck in radical performance are a kind of danced micropolitics that threatens hegemonic readings.[6] So-called radical gestures discriminate, critique and shift, like embodied signs drawing attention to the failure of the oppressive systems that subjugate them: the pervasive codification of the choreographies enshrined by the heteropatriarchy, racism and classism. Every time a body strikes a pose – makes a radical gesture – an epidemic of differential signification is unleashed. An affective contagion spreads through affected bodies and contaminated poses, expanding the possibilities of forms of life – bringing to life intersectional forms of dissent that existentially enable themselves as well as many other bodies.

The grand narrative of history – monologic, Western, white, male and at least middle class – has been challenged, criticised and reconstructed by postmodernist thinkers, feminisms and queer theory, postcolonial and decolonial thought since the end of the 1960s. Parallel to, or together with, this reconstruction of history into a series of interconnected stories, emerging forms of new artistic behaviour also instigated a fundamental critique of the uses of art. This political revolution in the field of representation gave rise to what we now know as contemporary art: a conceptual, critical, emancipatory tradition that has taken a stance against perpetual progress and against the conventional, teleological historical narrative.

Recent researchers such as Eve Meltzer have reframed the conventions of the history of conceptual art by introducing affect.[7] Meltzer writes that, while the system of structuralist thought – pioneered by thinkers like Roland Barthes and Claude Lévi-Strauss – allowed the emergence of new methodologies in art, structural theory also had collateral effects, creating a space for feeling. Social theorist Brian Massumi describes affect as 'the gaps between positions on the grid'.[8] Without affect, no ideological or interpretative system can exist, Massumi argues; it forms the connective tissue or, rather, the functional void between organs in the body ideological. The New Left in the 1960s and Marxism – both of which appeared obsolete a few years ago, but have been restored to relevance in today's times of crisis – used Fredric Jameson's maxim 'History is what hurts', which is apposite here.[9] The hurting he refers to is experienced in the social body, a necessarily affective body formed by the convergence of a sum of minorities, who cannot easily gain political parliamentary representation and thus operate differently.

Aware of the critical power of representation, artistic practices in the conceptual tradition brought history into contemporary art through stories about forms of life: the affective narratives that sprung up among bodies in May 1968; at the Stonewall riots in 1969; in the first generations of feminist artists in the art world; during the last gasps of the fight for independence in the countries that were part of Europe's colonial empires. Affect and being affected is what weaves individuals into the events of history and, as such, it is the sociological genesis of the artistic practices that come under the umbrella of the selective genealogy of contemporary art. It is not a trend, a preference or a political choice: the affective radicality that speaks through bodies as they strike a pose is the crux of the construction of a shared history. This is the history of belonging to a field of knowledge – contemporary aesthetics – that evolves as an ever-expanding dissident social sphere: in gender theory, decolonial thought and the critique of the social class system.

Critic Elizabeth Freeman uses the term 'chronopolitics', describing the present as a hybrid and positing a conception of conventional time as a form of power and oppression that can be criticised and transformed to allow marginalised positions to produce new forms of chronology. She writes that this concept of time 'admits that contact with historical materials can be precipitated by particular bodily dispositions, and that these connections may elicit bodily responses, even pleasurable ones, that are themselves a form of understanding. It sees the body as a method, and historical consciousness as something intimately involved with corporeal sensations.'[10] Up against the productive time of neo-liberal capitalism and of the reproductive heterosexual couple, Freeman explores alternative relationships between body and time, between the dissent produced by differential affects and new social forms. As empowered gestures, poses are a form of chronopolitical expression, collapsing the time of Western rationality and thus opening a dialogue among many bodies, in which each pose is a vector that expands its own potential for both relating and taking distance. To strike a pose is to appropriate the gesture of another – an earlier gesture, from an earlier moment – to non-synchronously mimic another body, for a moment. Following Freeman's thinking, a drag queen can come up into the scene to play Madonna and five minutes later come back as Dalida or Aretha Franklin. All those consecutive performances are forms of time travel that disrupt linear time.

This is what lies behind the current importance of the performativity of bodies that exceed the norm: bodies that are storming the programming of independent spaces and museums, reclaiming a place in the public eye in contexts where that was previously impossible. Rather than a passion for the exotic, interest in these bodies is a way of considering the importance of these minorities from the point of view of the transformation of collective life. The need to experience dissident modes of subjection was already noted in the 1980s by exiled scholars from the geopolitical South, such as Néstor Perlongher, who wrote:

What is interesting about these minorities is that they open 'points of flight' for the implosion of a certain normative paradigm of social personality [...] These processes of marginalisation, of flight, in differing degrees, release becomings (molecular particles) that cast the subject adrift along the margins of the template for conventional behaviour.[11]

Poses do not reside in bodies: they are a dialectic interplay of representational, technological and social forms with overlapping histories. This is what makes it possible, through art, to insert history back into experience as event. Bodies connect events that turn history into a present awaiting reconstruction: not history to be relived, but to be detected in representation, like an existing image in a memory that may or may not be ours, but is certainly shared. As Baruch Spinoza wrote, 'No one knows what a body is capable of.'[12]

One example of what a body can do is found in the story of Joan Jett Blakk. Born in Detroit as Terence Smith, she began performing as a drag queen in 1974, a period in which the patriarchal masculinity inherited from first-generation leaders of the civil rights movement had become the norm. As sociologist Michelle Wallace writes, 'The black man of the 1960s found himself wondering why it had taken him so long to realise he had an old score to settle. Yes, yes, he wanted freedom, equality, all of that. But what he really wanted was to be a man.'[13] In the mid 1980s, Terence Smith co-founded Queer Nation Chicago, an activist group formed by members of the direct action group ACT UP (AIDS Coalition To Unleash Power) to educate and raise awareness of the AIDS crisis and sexual politics. In 1990, Smith took up the *nom de guerre* Joan Jett Blakk and decided to run for mayor of Chicago. Her campaign – a full-blown camp performance – raised the profile of political views and subjectivities that were excluded from representation in the mainstream public sphere. In 1992, this African-American drag queen ran for president as part of the Queer Nation Party, under the memorable slogan 'Lick Bush in '92!' Despite the seemingly tongue-in-cheek tone of the campaign, her electoral programme was a direct response to the urgent challenges raised by the AIDS crisis at its worst, pointing out that 'the US is the only industrialised nation without a national health care policy.'[14] In interviews, Jett Blakk claimed she represented the Blakk Pantsuit Party, with slogans like 'Let's put the CAMP back into campaign' and 'I want to make America beautiful again', and election promises such as having Dykes on Bikes patrolling the borders for national security.

Jett Blakk's 1992 presidential campaign poster (p. 157) is an exemplary radical gesture. The portrait, by photographer Mark Geller, recreates an iconic image of Dr Huey Percy Newton – who co-founded the Black Panther Party with Bobby Seale in 1966 – except the rifle and the spear of the original are replaced here by a plastic machine gun. Jett Blakk is impenetrable, de-identified by her sunglasses and by the sinewy arm holding the toy. At the same time, the Afro wig, the earrings, the lip gloss and the crossed legs connect transvestite and black demands. As the slogan says, 'Joan Jett-Blakk for President. By any means necessary.' This catchphrase was also an appropriation: on the lips of Malcolm X, it had legitimised the use of violence to defend the black community from racist attacks. Behind the apparent frivolity, however, the image is actually a bitter queer political gesture: a reminder of dissident life, of a minoritised existence. Jett Blakk's portrait is an ironic dissemination parodying a kind of masculinity that can exert power over dissident bodies. The campaign poster was a staged representation of a political conflict – violence crossing Jett Blakk's black, gay, drag body, in what academic José Esteban Muñoz called a historically dense queer gesture.[15] The performed candidature was a voluntary act of affirmation of survival, and thus a response to collective grief. Radical gestures are built on the dead, as a form of cross-gendered public mourning.

In their relationship to the choreographic phrases that they appropriate, radical gestures – threatening poses – perform a time frame that falls before the performer's death and after the dead that they embody. As academic Dagmawi Woubshet put it:

Mourning takes on a form commensurate with its occasioning, and in the early era of AIDS that form assumed an expression of compounding loss, blurring the line between the subject and the object of mourning, between the death-bound who are mourning and the dead who are mourned. Reckoning with reflexive and multiple losses, this form resists closure, insisting on repetition and extension to account for the mounting past and pending losses.[16]

It is in relation to this constantly embodied constellation – in the dialogue between living and dead bodies – that writer and artist Morgan M. Page recently raised a matter that is key in a time dominated by global governmental conservatism. More research, he writes, 'may be needed to confirm the link between periods of media visibility for trans people and increased levels of physical and legislative violence against them, but from what I have observed through my historical research, the two seem to follow hand in hand.'[17]

The term 'social choreography' is useful here as a promise for the coordination of the discursive forces that gesture from dissident bodies. Andrew Hewitt frames the notion within a tradition of thought on social order that draws on the field of aesthetics, applying it directly to the level of the body. Social choreography, Hewitt writes, 'serves as a cultural trading post where aesthetic norms (in the more limited sense) are tried out for the social formations they might produce, and at which new types of social interaction are forged into new artistic forms.'[18] Or, to put it another way, activism may emerge from social, embodied acts of artistic experimentation, and vice versa. This notion may make it possible to connect radical gestures – embodied intersectional critique – as an unprecedented social force. In reference to the terrorist attack at Pulse nightclub in Orlando in summer 2016, writer and activist Che Gossett wrote:

Anti queer/trans necropolitical violence is about stopping the pulse of queer and trans of color life/worlds and the club was a target because the club is a flashpoint for eroticopoliticised desire. Queer and/or trans nightlife has always been about survival and creating temporary autonomous and temporary fabulous zones that are as much affective – a structure of queer and trans feeling – as material in its electric choreography of bodies.[19]

There lies the power of poses and their still unexplored possibilities of interference and contagion – the ceaselessness of gestures appropriated from one body to another, multiplying like a virus. There lies also the true genesis of new forms of life, the hope that contemporary art institutions may become spaces for new commons and under-commons yet to be invented – hope for a critical hedonism that allows the exponential explosion of subjectivities in a prodigious complexity that eliminates any chance of going back. Because, unfortunately, as artist Hannah Black writes in her comment on Brexit, 'The end of the world is a fantasy but death is still real.'[20]

According to a popular American saying often attributed to Mark Twain, 'history does not repeat itself, but it often rhymes.' Striking a pose renews this cyclical choreography, making us aware of the possibility of rhyming to a different rhythm and the opportunity to change the course of history. When a pose is struck, a threat is posed. In reference to dancing together, to the social choreographies in which these poses – these radical gestures – are simply the stopping positions of other forms of life, Muñoz wrote:

Dance, like energy, never disappears; it is simply transformed. Queer dance, after the live act, does not just expire. The ephemeral does not equal unmateriality. It is more nearly about another understanding of what matters. It matters to get lost in dance or to use dance to get lost: lost from the evidentiary logic of heterosexuality. For queers, the gesture and its aftermath, the ephemeral trace, matter more than many traditional modes of evidencing lives and politics.[21]

NOTES

1. Stuart Hall, interviewed in the film *The Stuart Hall Project*, dir. John Akomfrah, 2013, 103 min

2. Audre Lorde, from 'A Litany for Survival', in *The Black Unicorn: Poems* (New York, London: W.W. Norton, 1995 [1978]), p. 32

3. Che Gossett in conversation with Juliana Huxtable, 'Existing in the World: Blackness at the Edge of Trans Visibility', in Reina Gossett/ Eric A. Stanley/Johanna Burton (eds.), *Trap Door: Trans Cultural Production and the Politics of Visibility* (Cambridge, MA: The MIT Press, 2017), p. 39

4. 'To strike a pose is to pose a threat' is a quote from American cultural theorist Craig Owens, who was part of the group that formed around *October* journal and introduced the allegorical impulse in postmodernist thought on representations. He died in 1990 from AIDS-related complications. The sentence paraphrases theorist Dick Hebdige's ideas on youth subcultures. Craig Owens, 'The Medusa Effect, or, the Spectacular Ruse', in *Beyond Recognition: Representation, Power, and Culture* (Berkeley: University of California Press, 1992), p. 198

5. In dance, a phrase is a brief sequence of movements linked together to create a distinctive pattern.

6. Emma Goldman, 'If I Can't Dance, I Don't Want to Be Part of Your Revolution', in *Living My Life* (New York: A.A. Knopf, 1931)

7. Eve Meltzer, *Systems We Have Loved: Conceptual Art, Affect, and the Antihumanist Turn* (Chicago: University of Chicago Press, 2013)

8. Quoted in 'An Inventory of Shimmers' [introduction], in Melissa Gregg/Gregory J. Seigworth (eds.), *The Affect Theory Reader* (Durham, NC: Duke University Press, 2010)

9. 'History is what hurts, it is what refuses desire and sets inexorable limits to individual as well as collective praxis, which its "ruses" turn into grisly and ironic reversals of their overt intention. But this History can be apprehended only through its effects, and never

directly as some reified force. This is indeed the ultimate sense in which History as ground and untranscendable horizon needs no particular theoretical justification: we may be sure that its alienating necessities will not forget us, however much we might try to ignore them.' Fredric Jameson, *The Political Unconscious: Narrative as a Socially Symbolic Act* (Ithaca: Cornell University Press, 1981), p. 102

10. Elizabeth Freeman, *Time Binds: Queer Temporalities, Queer Histories* (Durham, NC: Duke University Press: 2010), p. 96

11. Néstor Perlongher, *Prosa Plebeya* (Buenos Aires: Excursiones, 2013), p. 84 (translation author's own)

12. Spinoza's phrase became a leitmotif in Gilles Deleuze's work on the critique of identity, and a key element in the books he wrote with Félix Guattari: *L'anti-Oedipe* (Anti-Oedipus, 1972) and *Mille Plateaux* (A Thousand Plateaus, 1980). Baruch Spinoza, *Ethics*, III, Proposition 2, Scholium, in Edwin Curley (ed.), *The Collected Works of Spinoza* (Princeton, N.J.: Princeton University Press, 1985), translation author's own.

13. Michelle Wallace, *Black Macho and the Myth of the Superwoman* (New York, London: Verso, 2015 [1978]), p. 30

14. Joan Jett Blakk in conversation with the author, 2017

15. 'By historically dense queer gesture, I mean a gesture whose significance and connotative queer force is dense with antinormative meanings.' José Esteban Muñoz, 'Gesture, Ephemera, and Queer Feeling: Approaching Kevin Aviance', in *Cruising Utopia: The Then and There of Queer Futurity* (New York: New York University Press, 2009), p. 198

16. Dagmawi Woubshet, *The Calendar of Loss: Race, Sexuality, and Mourning in the Early Era of AIDS* (Baltimore: John Hopkins University Press, 2015), p. 146

17. Morgan M. Page, '*One from the Vaults*: Gossip, Access, and Trans History-Telling', in Gosset/Stanley/Burton (2017), p. 143

18. Andrew Hewitt, *Social Choreography: Ideology as Performance in Dance and Everyday Movement* (Durham, NC: Duke University Press, 2005), p. 23

19. Che Gossett, 'Pulse, Beat, Rhythm, Cry: Orlando and the Queer and Trans Necropolitics of Loss and Mourning', Verso blog, 5 July 2016 [www.versobooks.com/blogs/2747-pulse-beat-rhythm-cry-orlando-and-the-queer-and-trans-necropolitics-of-loss-and-mourning, accessed 29 January 2019]

20. Hannah Black, 'Go Home: Brexit, Racism, and the Fantasy of White Working Class Ignorance', in The Towner, 4 November 2016 [www.thetowner.com/brexit-bracism/, accessed 29 January 2019]

21. Muñoz (2009), p. 76

[second transfeminist tract / i]

NAT RAHA

galore in staying wake trill soft us
upon each suggest
to consider in pleasure
≠ before you/i draw sensate / quiet
streams to skin composed
&& arms around the dress ,,
pressing tangent/ temples & cheek\bone
\degrees 120 across neck in kiss:::y/ our/s
sweet to musculature paths across\
that we invent passion here
in critique of universalisms,,,
that the labour to keep selves in
challenge of particulars our divergent bodies experience,,,
that to give hands // lips public to each
gains the signifier lesbian & politics is not a given,,,
that our genders socially contingent
& evolving in critique of the same,,,
that *inflammatory homosexual* is bracer rouse necessary
of desires we work to externalise from relational our;;

designation to us slipping enunciate relation adjective
accrued social form as image particular;
whereas *dyke bi punk riot drone sonics* does not
circulate the wealth does not in mainstations we
speak in thrills relative /// by

flesh temperate for arms softkiss before
timepolotik construes AM upon plural
that we will be tired in hours free from our wage work /
left to domestics
,, you holding& close \ shoulder to
button print resist psychic death

RENATE LORENZ

7 Methods of a Freak Theory of Contemporary Art

Following the stagings, narrations and performances of the historical freak show, I would finally like to trace the question of what it might mean to propose not (only) a *queer* theory but a *freak* theory of art. How can a theory be and act 'freaky'? How can it 'laugh rather than argue'? Through seven methods of a possible freak theory, I would like to propose some reflections about how the dual account of the historical freak shows – the exhibition of and staring at 'other bodies' on the one hand and the corporeal practices beyond a logic of norm and deviation on the other hand – produce a theory that is embodied *and* at the same time acts with a certain distance to the body.

1ST METHOD: FREAK KNOWLEDGE
(The Production of Knowledge Is Placed in Other Hands and Pursued by Dubious Means)

One challenge for freak theory is that it is confronted with knowledge about bodies and bodily practices produced by so-called specialists, for instance scientists, legislators, judges, doctors and educators. Certain people become authorised to speak the truth not only about themselves but also about others. People who obviously do not fit in with the body ideals of their time are excluded from this truth production in a particular way. The historical freak shows were dealing with just such a process of power-knowledge production, transferring it into show business, an area that has not generally been granted the authority to produce knowledge. Correspondingly, in freak shows there was usually one central person, called 'the professor,' who spoke about the freak performers, their presentations, and their biographies. This speech was referred to as a 'lecture'.[1] The professor claimed that the stories were 'the truth.' The narratives provided a scientifically authorised explanation for, to take one example, the black beard of the bearded lady. Perhaps, it was said, the bearded lady's mother had been taken by surprise in her house by a puma while she was pregnant. There were frequent references in such narratives to science, scientists and scientific organisations.

Moreover, many freak performers gave lectures about themselves. Since the professor or performer was supposedly telling 'the truth,' which nonetheless quite obviously contained fictional elements, they and the audience would sometimes laugh about discrepancies in the performed statements. Laughing thus became part of the production of knowledge – a phenomena that undermined the opposition of 'truth' and 'lies' and turned the staging of bodies into an intersection between the most diverse elements from the fields of science, mythology and literature, and into a field of possible contestation. So the freak production of knowledge practiced here claimed to be 'true,' with a twinkle in the eye, thus thematising its means and manner of production.

If we follow this method, a freak theory undermines a logic of norm and deviation in that it produces or confirms the norm by deploying highly unstable narratives about the 'other,' so that a kind of pleasure arises precisely from the *instability* of the narrative. David Hevey has characterised processes that participate in critically constructing a dichotomy between 'freak' and 'normal' as 'enfreakment,' a process that we might say is accompanied by an 'en*drag*ment.'[2] The appearances present conspicuous bodies but as a performance: a visualisation of bodies that in a certain way fictionalises and unsettles these bodies, thus coming into a deviant and ambivalent relationship to norms, destabilising and contesting these norms, or even abandoning them.

In the freak shows there were different types of narratives used to present the freaks in the lectures. One type of story presented the freak performer as superior and especially talented. Their social position, talent, family, or special bodily skills were invented or exaggerated. These freak performers were given important titles like 'captain,' 'general,' 'prince,' or 'king.' Since Europe was highly prized in the US, the freaks often came from Europe, and above all from England. They were – according to the story – highly educated, spoke several languages, and had aristocratic hobbies like writing history or painting.

In another story type, the 'mode of the exotic,' the origin of the freak performer was shifted to some foreign and exotic location. So, for instance, it was claimed that someone born in Ohio or Brooklyn instead came from Borneo. Other shifts, inventions, or exaggerations referred to details of history in order to emphasise the exoticism of the performers and their culture. For instance, they would mention cannibalism, human sacrifice, bounty hunters, polygamy, unusual clothing, or dietary customs that US Americans and Western Europeans found repulsive, for instance eating dogs or insects. Both types of narratives clearly referred to colonial history and to the construction of a supremacy of the US and Europe and their 'superior' cultures. This logic then gave the US and Europe the mandate to colonise the 'uncivilised' peoples of other lands and their sometimes desired, other times feared exotic cultures. Pictures from imperial journeys and colonial research often supplied the details of the 'exotic type' narratives.

The presentation of the freak performers in terms of exceptional education or exoticism is thus based on social hierarchies and their associated ideas and fantasies. The production of knowledge in the freak shows resorted to this visual archive of deprivileging and excluding – to 'ideals' as well as to images of the 'other' that were then reapplied. We could nonetheless ask whether these presentations did not also manage to cast doubt on the objectivity of the knowledge about 'savage,' non-Western bodies that was being constructed by dubious experts and exaggerated, fabricated, or ironic stories? And whether these presentations made the social meaning of a particular education a subject of reflection and even of mockery through affirmative-critical strategies, as well as through ridiculing the system of 'tribute' inherent in titles by giving them out quite at random? The embodiments of the freak performers were associated with the socially approved system that short-circuited difference with hierarchy. But this was applied in such a 'wrong' way that both the classification of the bodies presented as well as the so-called scientific method of classification could not be maintained.

2ND METHOD: THE PRODUCTION OF FREAKS AND DUPES
(The Social Construction of Inside and Outside and the Shift of the Rules of Intelligibility)

During the freak shows, as Robert Bogdan has noted, a feeling of camaraderie and a similar view of life was shared between the show-people, the hosts of the show and the 'human oddities.'[3] Humanity was, according to Bogdan, divided into two groups: those who 'are there' (that is, in the entertainment industry) and those who are 'not there.' The construction of these two groups was supported by a common language, a shared lifestyle, insider secrets and jokes about the outsiders.

In some cases, these outsiders were cheated by manipulated gambling schemes or by pickpocketing. Those that did not belong were the ones who were taken in, either by the lies on offer and the manipulated bodily presentations or by theft. The construction of groups at the freak show were thus not based on presumably 'natural' characteristics or differences – not on bodily or mentally 'being-other' – but instead on particular abilities in which the freak performers were the side with the advantage.

In her discussion of 'passing' as performance,[4] Amy Robinson explains that this performance need not necessarily be understood as a strategy of identity politics.[5] What is much more pertinent is the social function that it has for the production of culturally recognised knowledge. The 'deceiver' and the 'insiders,' who observe and recognise the deception, form themselves into one group that understands procedures and operations to which the dominant society has no access. The question here, according to Robinson, is not really about whether it is true or whether anyone actually possesses such a special ability. The claim alone is a socially productive practice. When a group shares a certain field of knowledge (thus becoming an insider group), those who 'do not understand' or are deceived, the so-called 'dupes,' are in Robinson's model those who are excluded from this knowledge. A social constellation arises in which the rules of intelligibility – the rules of what can be spoken and who can speak – are shifted. Those who belong to the dominant social groups and who usually set the rules of knowledge are here excluded from the position of knowledge. The dupes, the now non-knowing, are constituted as *other*. The deceivers and the insiders, who share their exclusionary knowledge, then take over the usual function of a majoritarian group. A certain economy of representation is thus turned on its head; the social constellation is shifted at the same time as it remains open to new shifts.

When our attention is focused on such a triangular arrangement, it becomes clear that the deceiver and the insiders can make practices and images intelligible that are not legible within the hegemonic cultural conventions represented by the dupes. In relation to bodies, the focus is shifted from the *identity* of bodies to their *legibility*. It poses the questions: For whom does a body become legible? Who sets the rules of intelligibility? This, as Robinson argues, is exactly where authority lies for the 'deceiver' and the members of the insider group. For two concurrent methods of recognising and acknowledging are taking place. While the dupe can only see the assumption of a place – here that of the 'freak' – those belonging to the insider group are in the position to observe the crossing from one place to another, and to see how a person is created as a 'freak' by means of a performance. This perception is something from which the dupes remain excluded. It shifts, again according to Robinson, the rules of intelligibility, allowing for a challenge to the hegemonic rules of recognition represented by the dupes.[6] Instead, the (so far) hegemonic reader is subordinated to the interpretative authority of the insider group. In this way, as Sue Ellen Case articulates it, passing is rather when 'a strategy of appearances replaces a claim of truth'[7]. As Robinson summarises, this represents a new model of how someone can maintain a position of power and presence in the Western order of truth. Therefore, the freak performance can be viewed as a practice of self-empowerment, intervening without authorisation into the construction and understanding of one's own body.

The freak performances can, however, be distinguished from the performance of 'passing,' for the dupes are constantly being given the chance to understand or at least to guess that they are being deceived – that they are seeing a 'show.' For the dupes (the hegemonic group), pleasure lies in the instability passing through them that contains the possibility that even their own bodies and their social positioning might be exposed to a similar destabilisation. Therefore, even if it is only the insider group that completely 'knows' that this is all about drag (a calculated performance) and fully recognises the processes of production (thus landing in the position of the 'knowing'), nonetheless 'objectivity,' 'truth,' and the 'reading of bodies' is also cast into doubt for the dupes. In this process, therefore, not only are the positions of 'knower' and 'object of knowledge' switched, as Robinson describes it, but the methods and categories of knowledge production and the 'reading' of bodies can also be disputed. This, of course, is a process that noticeably pulls the rug of certain knowledge out from under the feet of the dupes.

3RD METHOD: FREAKY MULTIVALENCE (A Figure of Difference Is Produced that Refuses to Be Categorised, Immobilised, or Exhausted Through Understanding)

The freak shows were populated by freak performers who were supposedly born with a particular physical or mental quality, be it skin color, a particular kind of hair growth such as that of the 'bearded ladies,' or many other things that would later be designated as 'disability' or 'illness.' Then there were those who had supposedly inherited such a quality later in life because they fell ill or lost a body part. Finally, there were also the so-called novelty acts: those who gave special performances such as sword swallowers or snake charmers.

Later, for example in the 1970s, the name 'freak' also transformed into a name for social practices that called for the right to laziness or alternative economies. The term 'freak' has been used to collect the most diverse ways of taking on or producing a certain distance to dominant norms or to the normalising practices of white, heterosexual, masculine or feminine US Americans or Europeans without this difference in turn producing a unified and recognisable category. I would like to refer to such performance as 'radical drag.' These freak performers do not only exhibit embodiments that resist dichotomous descriptions according to gender, sexual or other categories. They are often also exhibited as dysfunctional or incompatible with social and economic demands, or they maintain abilities quite other than those normally recognised. Rosemarie Garland-Thomson understands the 'freak' as an icon of general embodied deviance that can affect gender, race, sexual orientation or ethnicity. She thus refers to this figure as 'multivalent'.[8] The designation 'freak' therefore also makes it possible to connect different representations of sexuality and gender with other axes of power and discourses, for instance with a discussion of racism, disability, or a critique of capitalist economies.

4TH METHOD: FREAK EMBODIMENT
(Staged Freaks, Fake Freaks and Freak Subjectification)

The visual representation of difference often touches on questions of visual evidence. It calls up the notion that the bodies that are shown are legible. The presumed legibility of visual representations of the body was and is the foundation of various strategies of 'otherings,' for criminalising or pathologising, for instance. Allan Sekula has examined how the photographic portrait in particular is a form of depiction that claims to say something about the person depicted, especially about his or her personality.[9] Photography is a technology that was already being used for police surveillance as early as the nineteenth century. It began, as Sekula notes, 'to establish and delimit the terrain of the *other*, to define both the *generalised* look – the typology – and the *contingent instance* of deviance and social pathology'. In Paris, Jean-Martin Charcot had a photo studio set up in the Salpêtrière Hospital in order to manufacture portraits of hysterical woman.[10] In the context of colonial history, photography was used to fit the 'family of man' into classification systems, to become acquainted with it, and to understand it.[11]

The invention of photography gave rise to the idea that there is such a thing as a photographically represented body. This truth claim was also the foundation for photographic portraits of the freak performers, which already in the second half of the nineteenth century were being sold outside the shows as a kind of autograph picture. These photographs were carefully staged in terms of lighting, backdrops, costumes and hairstyles. For instance, the bearded lady Annie Jones, whose portrait is the basis for the film *N.O. Body* (2008), wore long Victorian dresses in the photographs, emphasising the contrast between her feminine dress and her masculine beard. Other bearded ladies were shown alongside their husbands to stress the deviation from the usual family portrait, or a very short man was placed next to a very tall one. The presentation of freaks thus touched on a performance involving operations such as displacement, exaggeration and exoticisation. The stagings went so far as to 'fake' the particular qualities of certain freaks, such as a man with a second, smaller head on his forehead, who was presented with the claim that this head could speak until he was 20 years old.[12] Or at least, it was not always known precisely whether certain talents and oddities were a fake or not. The appeal lay, as in the 'lectures,' precisely in the uncertainty and the destabilisation associated with it.

5TH METHOD: THE FREAK ECONOMY
(Reworking Capitalism)

Rosemarie Garland-Thomson has pointed out that the changes in production, work and technology referred to as 'industrialisation' redefined the relation to the body.[13] The growing significance of factories and machines in the nineteenth century led, according to Garland-Thomson, to a high valuation of bodies that were capable of following predetermined temporal divisions, of linking up with machines, and of being efficient. Practices such as standardisation, mass production, and work with exchangeable parts led to the advancement of 'sameness' (not equality) as a cultural value.

In the economy of the freak shows, which was developing at the same time, the bodily features that were emphasised and exhibited through performance were precisely those that were in no way consistent with the industrial demands of sameness. As J.K. Gibson-Graham stresses in her book *The End of Capitalism (As We Knew It)* (1996), various economies always exist alongside one another that follow different or even contradictory rules.[14] Capitalism can thus neither be approached as a uniform whole, nor should the alternative economies be overlooked. Freak economies thus definitely arose with industrialisation and were consistent with the capitalist theory of surplus value in that an entrepreneur, usually P.T. Barnum, drew off the surplus value of the freak performer's work, availing himself of a niche and exploiting bodies that fell outside the demands of industrialisation. At any rate, it was also possible that those who had neither found work in industry nor in the household could here obtain both wages and social recognition. A few of the freak performers even became 'celebrities.' Their biographies elicited great public interest and they could, as in the case of the bearded woman Annie Jones, attain a sizeable income.

The question arises as to whether the integrative processes of current economies were foreclosed here. Today, according to Antke Engel, we can recognise an increasing appreciation and integration of difference.[15] Cultural images of hybrid, flexible and ambivalent identities have been proposed as the epitome of successful, creative individuality, and new hierarchies have been opened up in relation to those who cannot be evaluated or exploited in the same way. We must critically ask, then, whether a (freak) performance disturbs the processes of hierarchisation and ostracism via economy or can even produce other economies? On the one hand, economies also arose in the context of the freak shows that cannot be sufficiently described by the keyword 'capitalism,' such as those of theft, which disregards the capitalist category of private property. On the other hand, the freak shows produced bodies that, to borrow a term from Robert McRuer, were perceived as 'transgressive' and as such, despite possible economic success, enduringly brought images of bodies into the public eye that could not be associated with any similar success in other social fields.[16]

McRuer derives his discussion of the 'transgressive' as an economic-critical method from a debate about visualisation that was sparked by Garland-Thomson's texts about photographs of differently abled people.[17] Garland-Thomson distinguishes in the visual rhetoric of (photographic) representation of difference between four modes: the 'wondrous mode' that represents subjects as special and admirable despite their deviation; the 'sentimental mode' that elicits pity; the 'exotic mode' that exhibits deviation ('which makes disability strange and distant – a freakish or perhaps transgressive spectacle');[18] and the 'realistic mode' that minimises deviation and reduces the distance between observer and observed. Garland-Thomson assesses the 'realistic mode' as particularly promising, since this one would make it possible for people with deviations to be integrated into work and consumption.

Despite his esteem for Garland-Thomson's theoretical work, McRuer sharply criticises this assessment since it offers a narrative of progress and is meant to line up with the demands of neoliberal economy instead of, on the contrary, paving the way to changing these demands – a way that would no longer privilege certain bodies and exclude others. He makes a case for the 'exotic,' or as he would prefer to call it, the 'transgressive mode' – a mode that would block any integration and any subdivision into norm and deviation. As an example of this mode, he takes up the work of the performance artist Bob Flanagan, who in the 1990s used his cystic fibrosis as well as his interest in sadomasochistic practices as the starting point for his performances. Flanagan's self-representation does not seek to solicit pity nor is it geared toward 'normality.' According to McRuer, Flanagan's works seem to say: 'Look at me: I am like you [...] maybe. But we're not like the others and we might, you and I, be able to imagine something other than, different from, or beyond all of this.'[19]

6TH METHOD: FREAK HETEROTOPOLOGY
(Making Use of the Productivity of Space)

In her book *The Ugly Laws: Disability in Public* (2009), Susan Schweik analysed a set of 'ugly laws' that were in force not only in the US, but also in Europe and Asia throughout the nineteenth century.[20] According to these laws, which sought to regulate appearance and behavior in public, freaks shows were places where people with bodily particularities were not only exhibited but also shut away. In Michel Foucault's terminology, such a place is a 'heterotopia' – an 'other' place – that is nonetheless not outside the world. Heterotopias are permeated with power relations and this determines their relationship to other spaces. In contrast to utopias, heterotopias are real and efficient places.[21] As examples of heterotopias, Foucault names hospitals, nursing homes, barracks and ships. Heterotopian space is not opposed to other space, like private space is to public space, for instance, or like the space of leisure is to the space of work. Instead, it is a space with the particular quality, according to Foucault, of having to do with all other spaces and relations while at the same time being quite different from them.

According to Foucault's classification, we could designate the freak show as a 'heterotopia of deviation' in which individuals are found whose behavior deviates from the norm, such as psychiatric clinics or prisons.[22] The problem with Foucault's term 'heterotopias of deviation,' as I see it, is that he reaffirms the relation of norm and deviation, which is here spatially established, instead of stressing the capacity of heterotopia to shift this relation or even reverse it. I think, for example, of the well-known film *Freaks* by Tod Browning (1932) in which the main character, who is exhibited because he is considered very small, lives in a tiny circus wagon. The size of the wagon is such that it causes his so-called 'normal sized' colleagues to appear inappropriately large – as non-normal or non-standard. A freak theory could thus propose a heterotopian space that would emphasise this capacity to produce one's own measure, one's own ideas of evaluation, one's own aesthetics and logics. Admittedly, these are not independent of the power relations from, in, and against which they arose. They are nonetheless in the position of transforming, at least momentarily or fragmentarily, the relation between norm and deviation, and thus of functioning themselves as dominant, as hegemonic, and as determinant for the production of knowledge, intelligibility and forms of representations.

Foucault concludes his short lecture with the claim that every heterotopia has a certain function that it takes on in relation to the rest of space. So the question arises, what social function could the freak show have? For the social relations of power that lead to 'enfreakment' are here constantly present and are repeated in the relationship between spectators and performers. Nonetheless, a space is created on the basis of the largest possible distance from a set of excluding norms. This distance makes it possible that the function of the space confirms the norms for the spectators (who perceive themselves as 'normal' in contrast to the freak performers), but that the distance is also desired by them. Identification with norms is thus deferred or shifted; the desired distance offers not only a spatially (and temporally) restricted alternative to certain social norms, but perhaps also makes it possible to install new ideals. A freak theory produces queer-artistic heterotopias, for instance in an exhibition space or a cinema, that are possibly in the position to oppose a re-introduction of the ugly laws, as Susan Schweik has discussed. Schweik speaks of the 'vestiges' of the ugly laws, as they can be seen, for instance in current practices of privatisation and exclusion in public space where access is more and more regulated.

7TH METHOD: FREAK HETEROCHRONY
(Appropriating the Productivity of Time)

Much as the freak show can be considered a heterotopian site, it also produces its own time. Biographies are introduced that offer alternatives to a heteronormative biography in which youth and education is followed by childcare and wage labor. The stage props often connect bodies to another time period, for instance to antiquity. Compliance with a normative ideal is only rarely staged, as for example at the wedding of the famous freak performer Charles Stratton (stage name Tom

Thumb), which was met with great interest in 1883 and was reportedly attended by more than 2000 guests. Not only did the biographies presented occur differently, often very spectacularly and full of magnificent incidents, but also, for instance, personalities were presented that were said to be 170 years old, or consistencies were presented with and in continuation of colonialist ideas of inhabitants of places 'where time stood still.' The time of the freak show is thus not that of capitalist progress; there is no modern temporality of any 'meanwhile' possible here that would ensure that the unity of a nation or the ideal of capitalist economy would be processed in various places at the same time.[23] Corresponding to Foucault's notion of heterotopia, we could also speak of a 'heterochrony': of a time that is not independent of the power relations that structure our understanding of time – for instance of 'backwardness' in the colonies – but that nonetheless establishes its own rules that intervene in the dominant temporality.

FREAK THEORY

All of the methods presented here – of a dubious production of knowledge; of shifting the rules of what is intelligible; of non-identitarian, non-unified, and staged embodiments; of experimenting with economies; and of interventions in space and time – inspire a theory that produces interventions in norms and normalities. Freak theory is thus not a theoretical practice that stands outside social power relations. Rather, it is a practice that co-produces inventions and images – that offers alternatives to social power relations that are more and different than critiquing, 'reworking' or subverting social norms. The freak theory of art is thus 'in drag.' It uses the contemporary language of poststructuralism and queer theory and at the same time the language of the freak show. In this way, queer theory becomes a performer who takes up contact with an earlier language and sounds out its potentials for denormalisation and dehierarchisation – a practice that I designated more precisely as 'transtemporal drag.'

NOTES

1. Robert Bogdan, 'The Social Construction of Freaks', in Rosemarie Garland-Thompson (ed.), *Freakery: Cultural Spectacles of the Extraordinary Body* (New York, London: New York University Press, 1996), pp. 23–37

2. David Hevey, *The Creatures Time Forgot: Photography and Disability Imagery* (New York: Routledge, 1992), p. 53

3. Bogdan (1996), p. 30

4. Amy Robinson, 'It Takes One to Know One: Passing and Communities of Common Interest', in *Critical Inquiry*, Vol. 20, No. 4, Summer 1994, pp. 715–33

5. A queer-theoretical critique of identities such as 'being-lesbian' or 'being-gay,' 'being-man' or 'being-woman,' is well known. If an identity is claimed, the process of differentiating is halted, power relations associated with it are rendered unrecognisable, and the identity appears to be stable, coherent and independent of everything that it is distinct from. Identities furthermore require criteria of who belongs and who does not. They are often naturalised by claiming that a person who belongs to a named group has certain characteristics. Yet, even critics of identity politics themselves constantly exhibit difficulties in addressing power differences and different experiences when the construction of groups is entirely rejected.

6. Robinson (1994), p. 730

7. Quoted in Robinson (1994), p. 730

8. Garland-Thompson (1996), p. 10

9. Allan Sekula, 'Der Körper und das Archiv', in Herta Wolf (ed.), *Diskurse der Fotografie: Fotokritik am Ende des fotografischen Zeitalters* (Frankfurt am Main: Suhrkamp, 2003), pp. 269–337

10. Georges Didi-Huberman, *Invention of Hysteria. Charcot and the Photographic Iconography of the Salpêtrière* (Boston: MIT Press, 2004)

11. Anne McClintock, *Imperial Leather: Race, Gender, and Sexuality in the Colonial Contest* (New York: Routledge, 1995), p. 124

12. Robert Bogdan, *Freak Show: Presenting Human Oddities for Amusement and Profit* (Chicago, London: The University of Chicago Press, 1988), pp. 84–85

13. Garland-Thompson (1996), pp. 11–12

14. J.K. Gibson-Graham, *The End of Capitalism (As We Knew It)* (Cambridge and Massachusetts: University of Minnesota Press, 1996)

15. Antke Engel, *Wider die Eindeutigkeit Sexualität und Geschlecht im Fokus queerer Politik der Repräsentation* (Frankfurt am Main: Campus Verlag, 2002)

16. Robert McRuer, *Crip Theory. Cultural Signs of Queerness and Disability* (New York: New York University Press, 2006), p. 171

17. Garland-Thompson, 'Seeing the Disabled: Visual Rhetorics of Disability in Popular Photography', in Paul K. Longmore and Lauri Umansky (eds.) *The New Disability History: American Perspectives* (New York: New York University Press, 2001)

18. McRuer (2006), p. 171

19. Citation from McRuer's discussion of Roland Barthes's *Mythologies* (1957). The production of myths, according to McRuer, consists of 'routinising and making something seem ordinary' (McRuer (2006), p. 180). Barthes imagines the images saying: 'Look at me: I am like you'. (Ibid.).

20. Susan Schweik, *The Ugly Laws: Disability in Public (The History of Disability)* (New York, London: New York University Press, 2009)

21. Michel Foucault, 'The Utopian Body' in Caroline A. Jones (ed.), *Sensorium: Embodied Experience, Technology, and Contemporary Art* (Boston: MIT Press, 2006)

22. Ibid., p. 12

23. Benedict Anderson, *Imagined Communities: Reflections on the Origin and Spread of Nationalism* (London, New York: Verso, 2006); Homi K. Bhabha, *The Location of Culture* (New York: Routledge Press, 1994), p. 199

Text originally published in Renate Lorenz, *Queer Art. A Freak Theory* (Bielefeld: Transcript, 2012), pp. 161–72. Bibliographic notes have been abridged.

Glory

TAREK LAKHRISSI

I've seen waters

•

my body was not here

•

i thought i was a ghost

•

but i was glory glory and glory

Ajamu

82 – 89

amrou al-kadhi + holly falconer

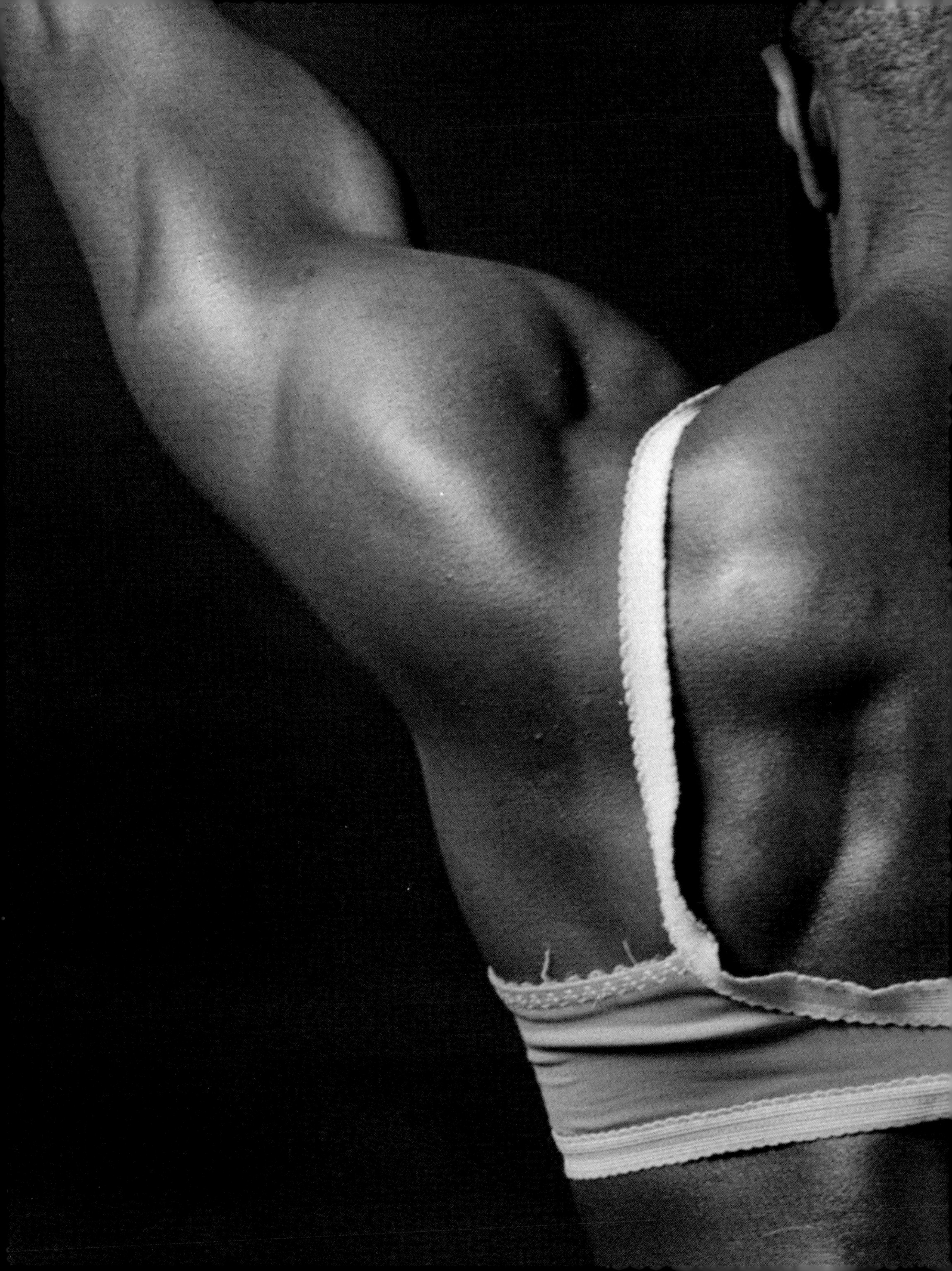

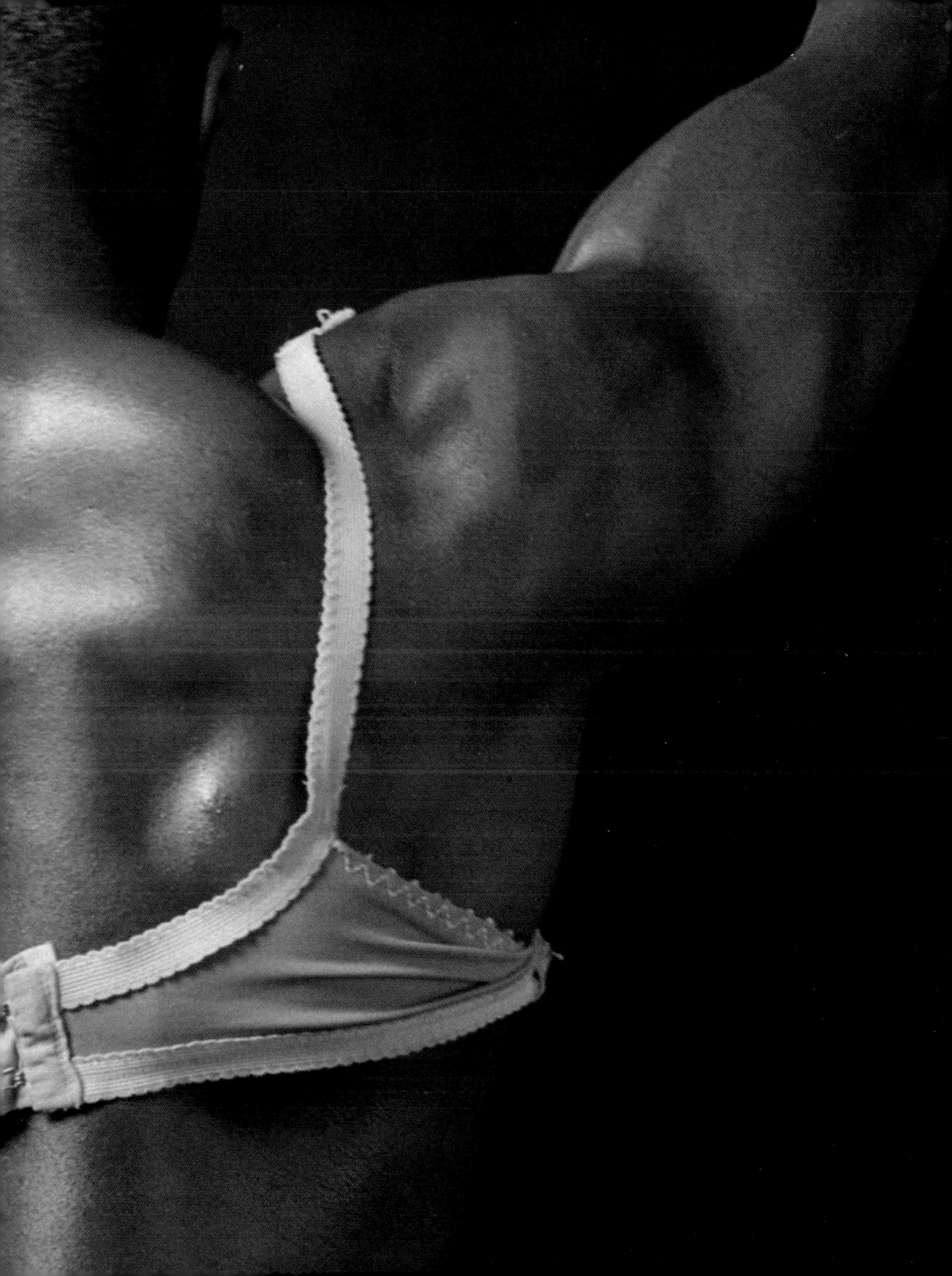

AJAMU

Cock and glove, 1993

Katchi Kwok, 1990

Previous

Body builder in bra, 1990

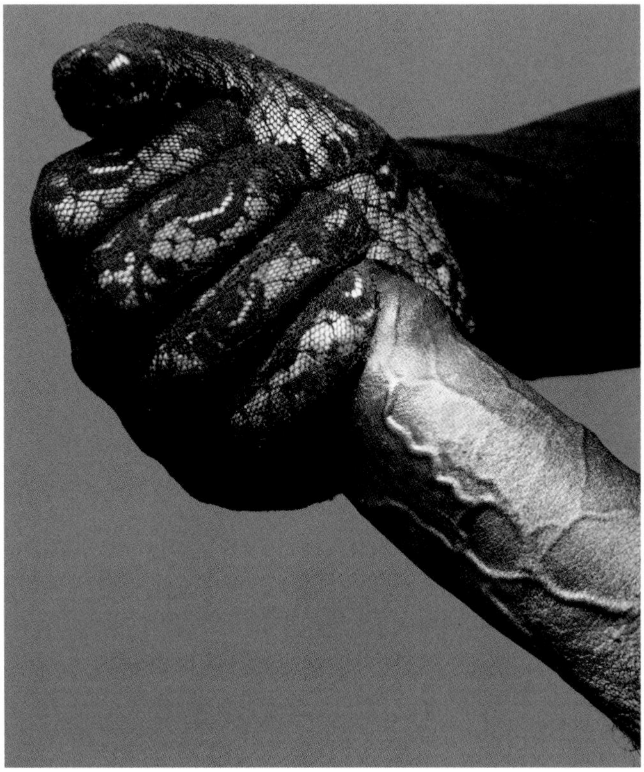

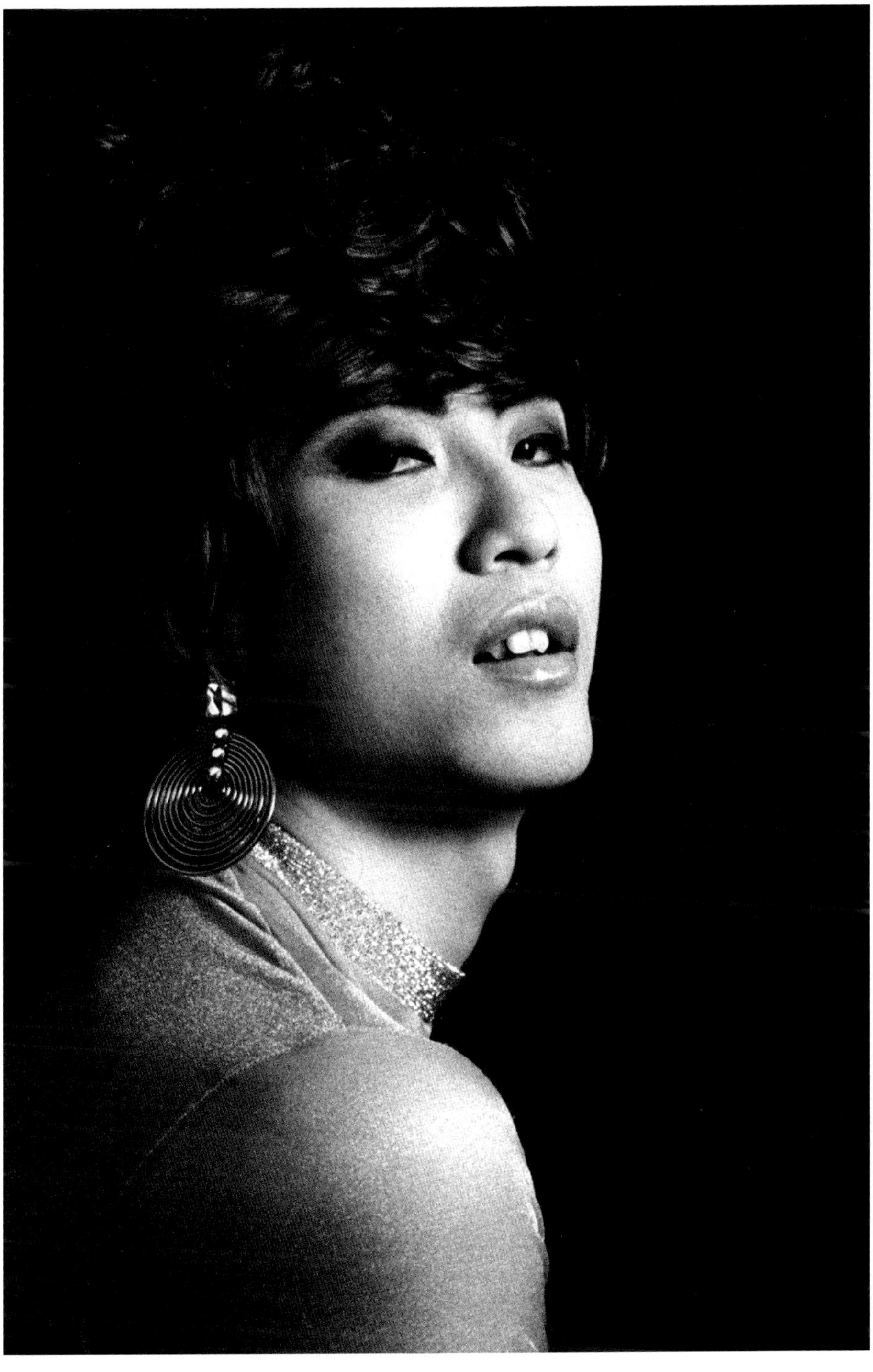

AJAMU

Man in gloves, 1993

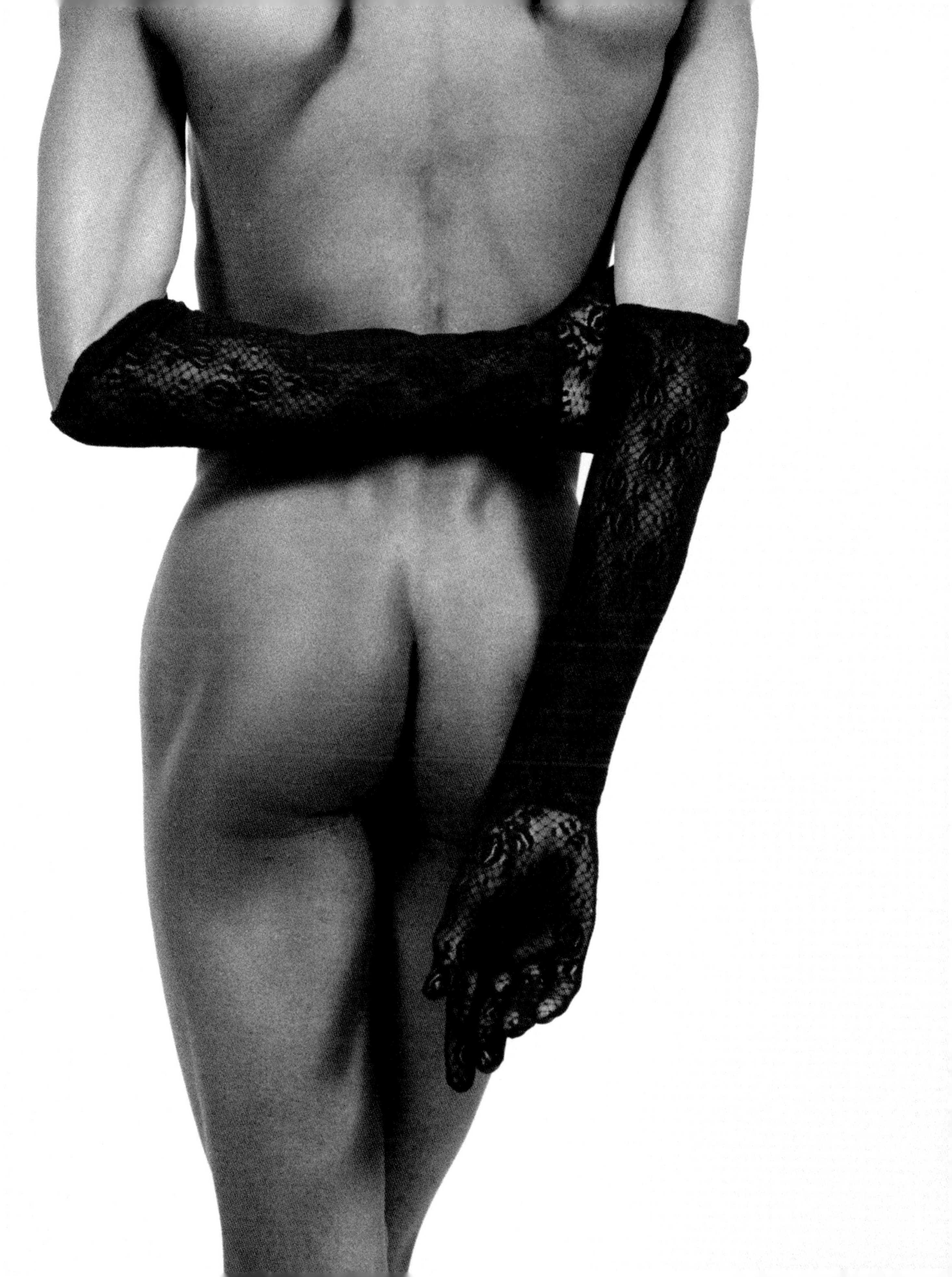

AJAMU

Heels, 1993

Feet of Duane Cyrus, Dancer, 2015

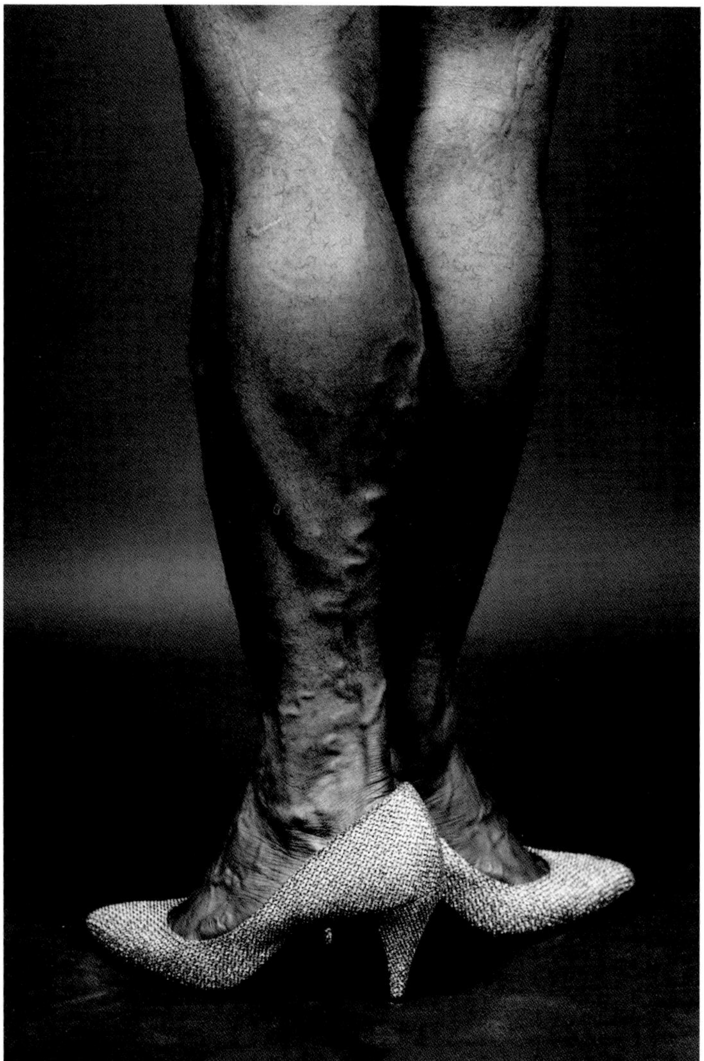

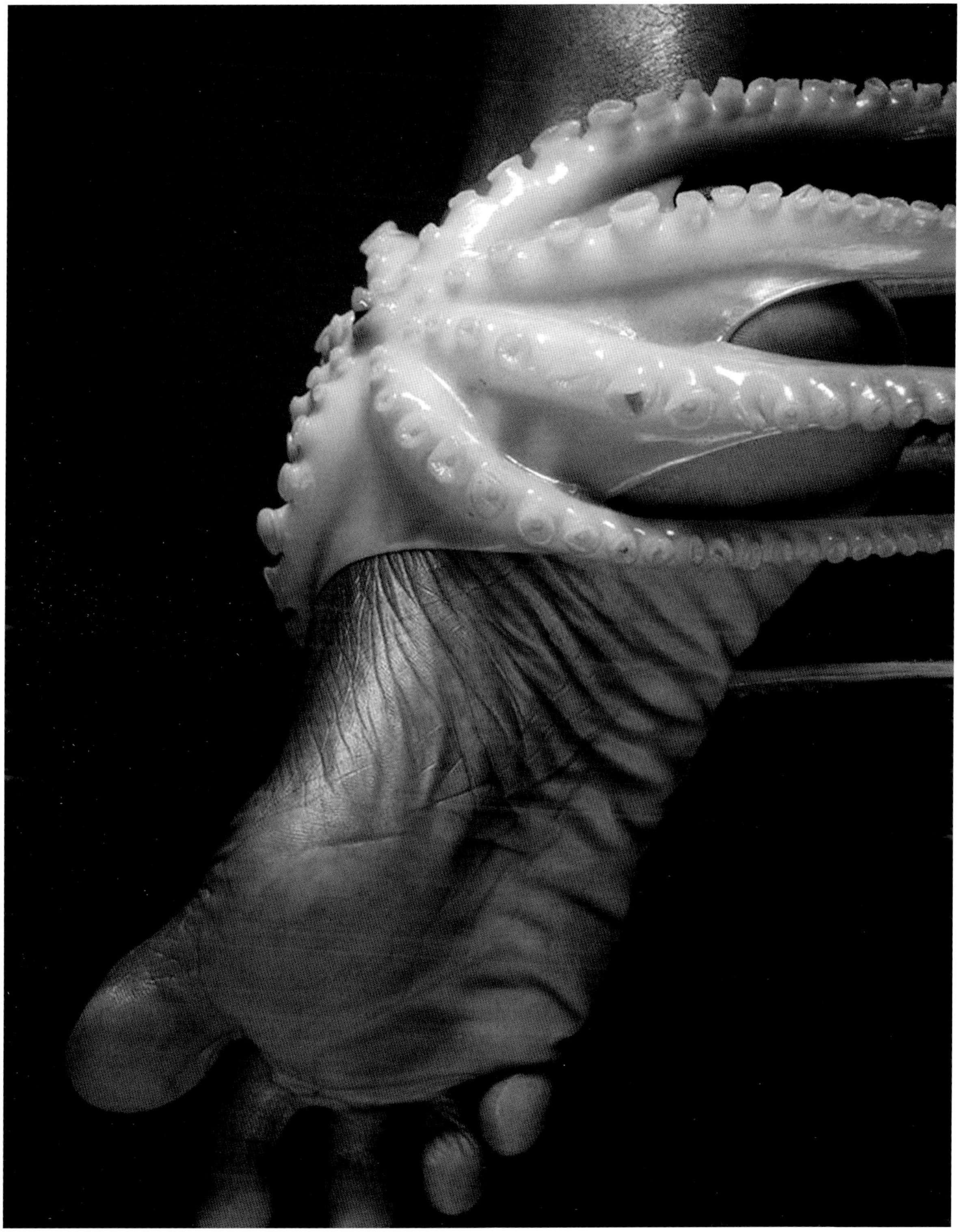

AMROU AL-KADHI
AND
HOLLY FALCONER

Glamrou, 2016

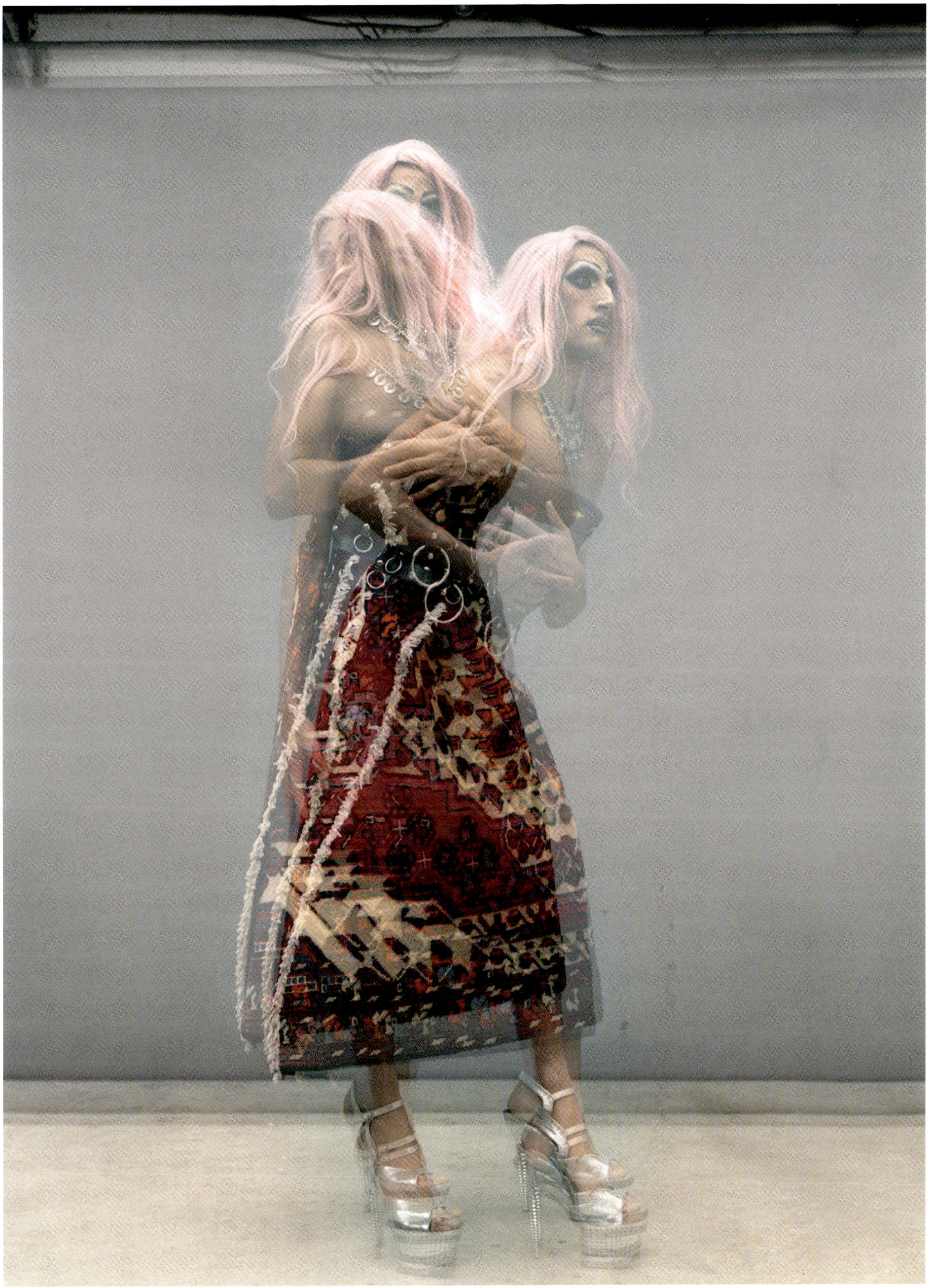

Lyle Ashton Harris

94 – 97

Sadie Benning

98 – 99

Nayland Blake

100 – 01

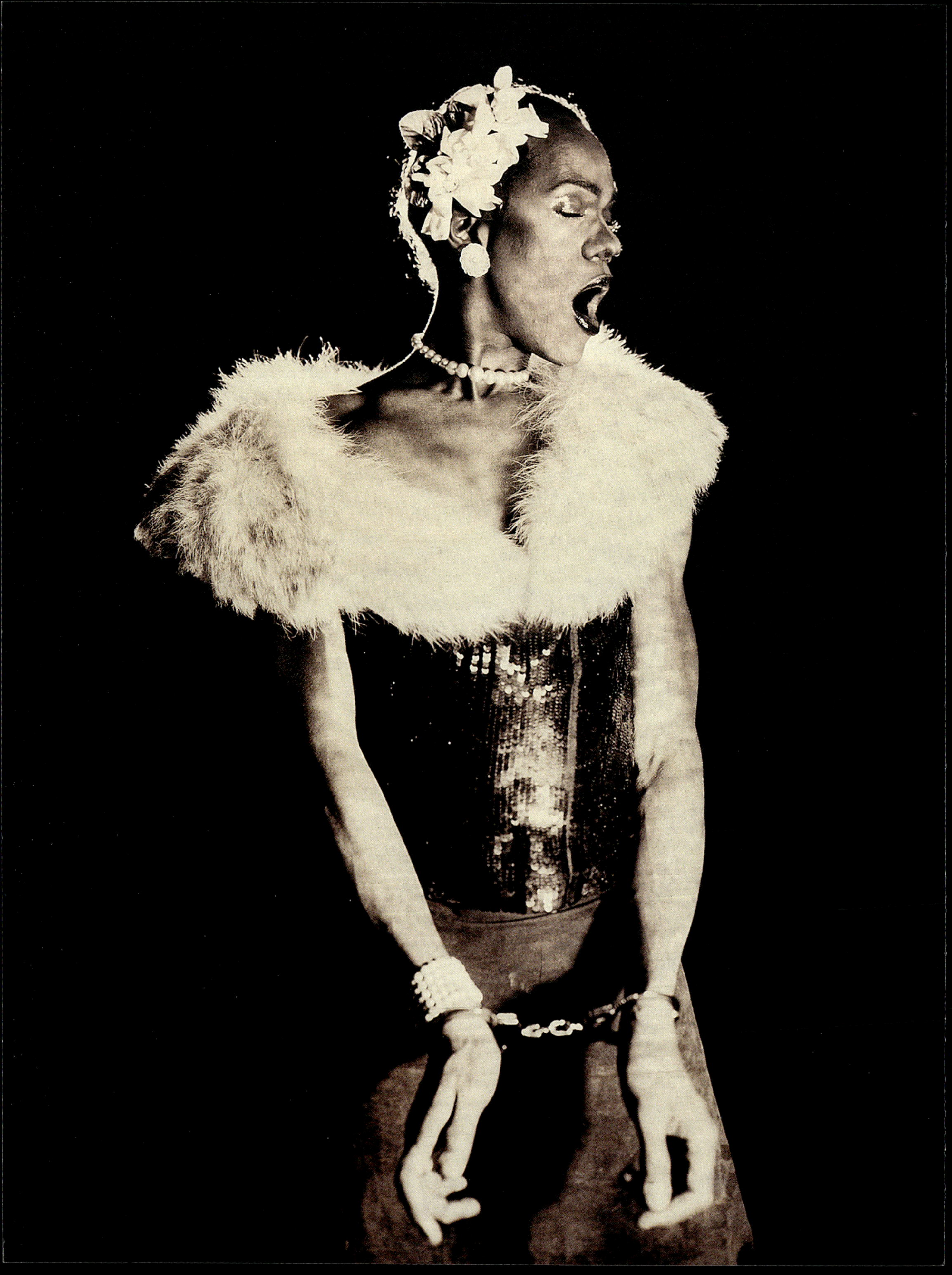

LYLE ASHTON HARRIS

Billie #1, 2002

Blue Billie, 2002

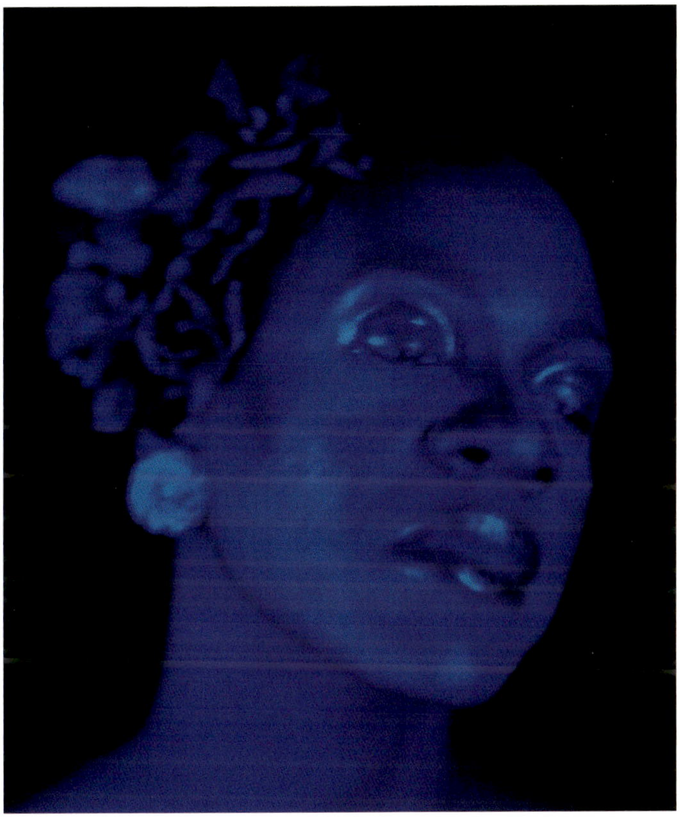

LYLE ASHTON HARRIS

Billie #4, 2002

Josephine #6, 2002

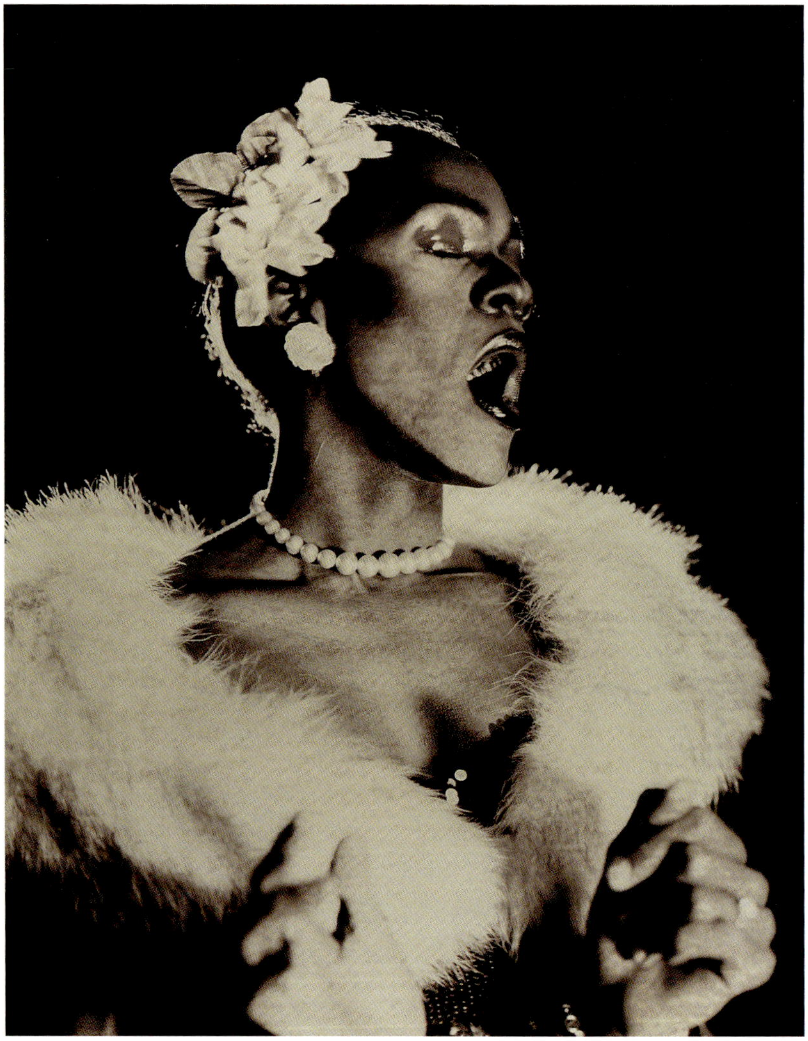

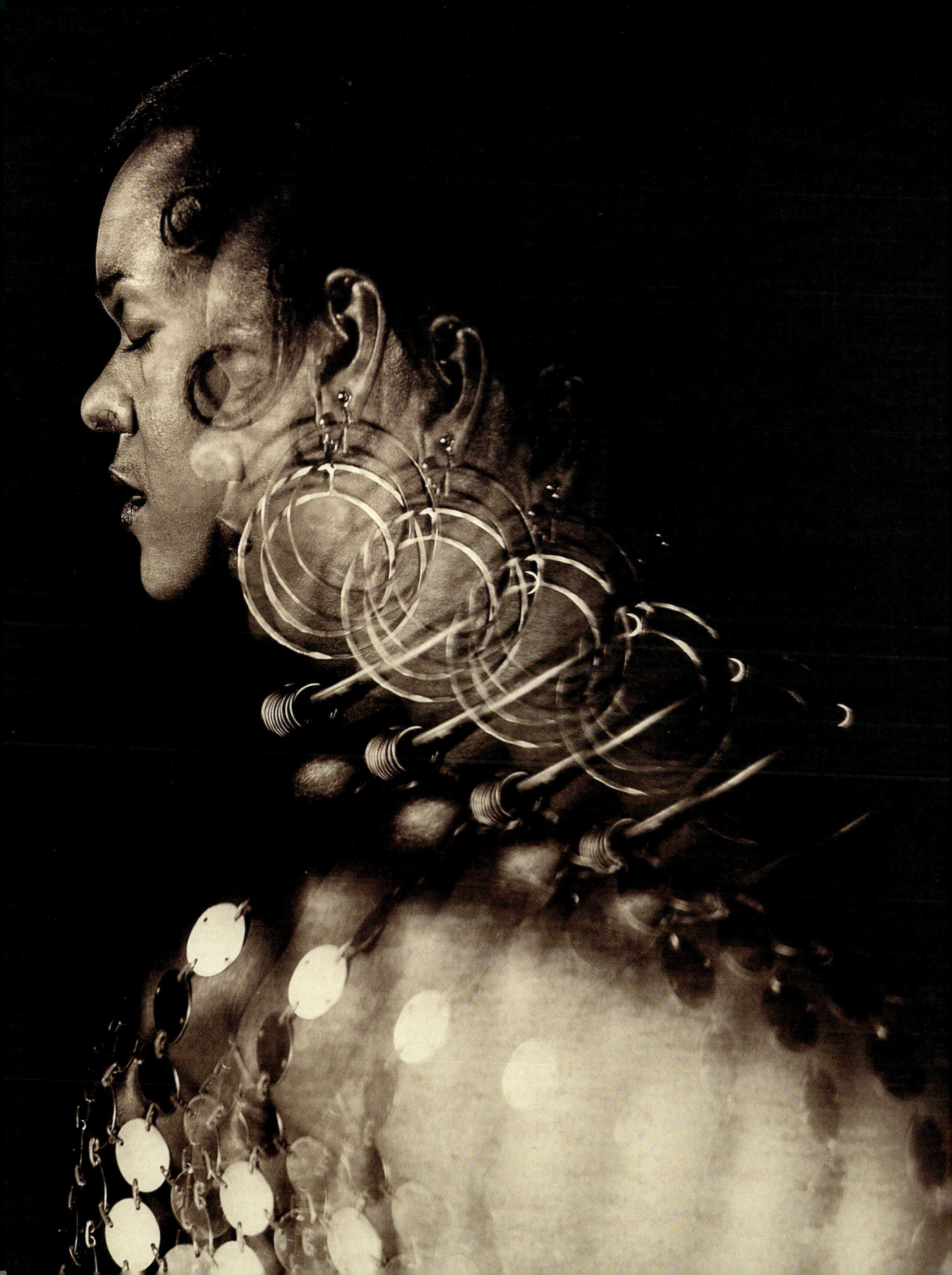

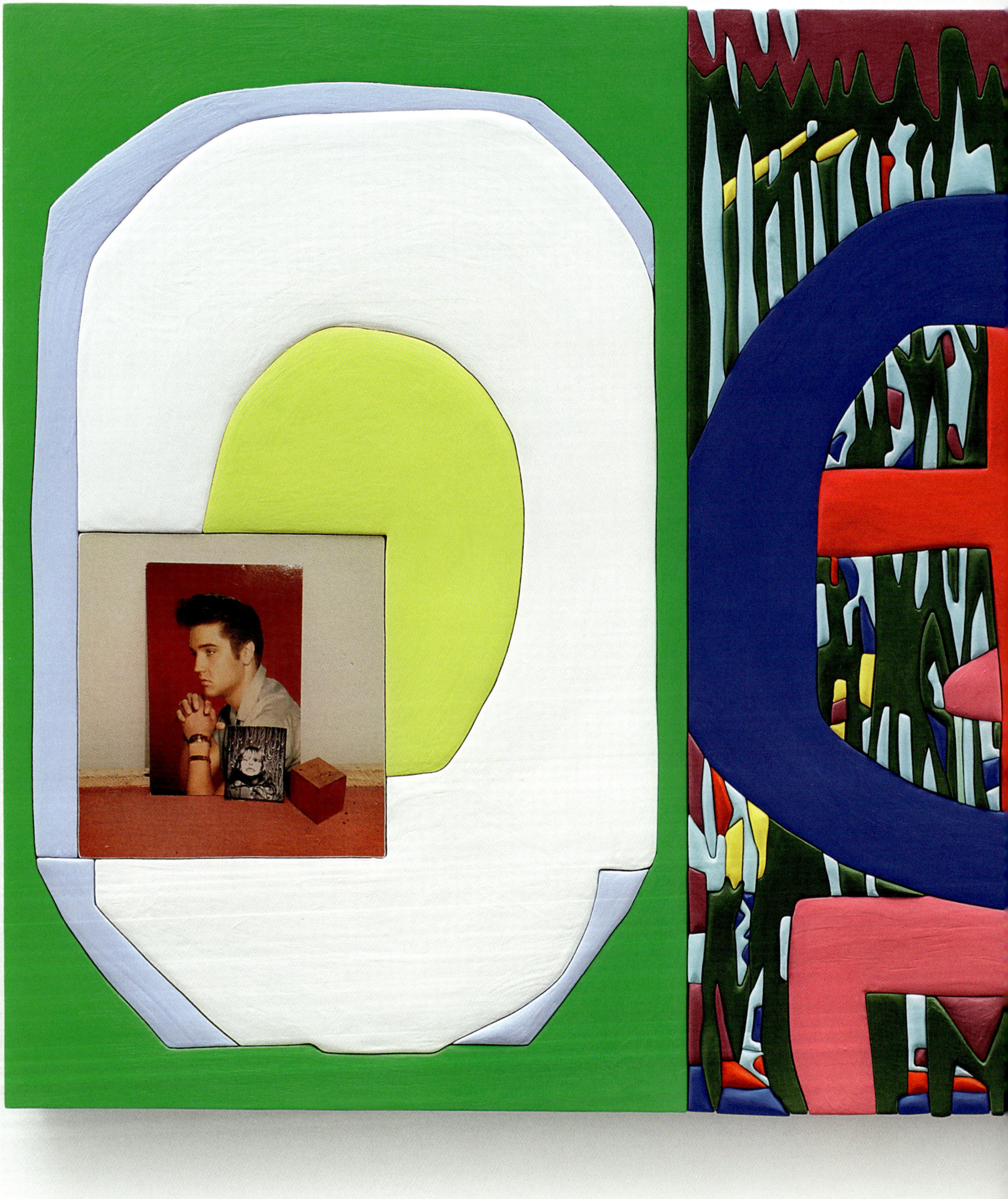

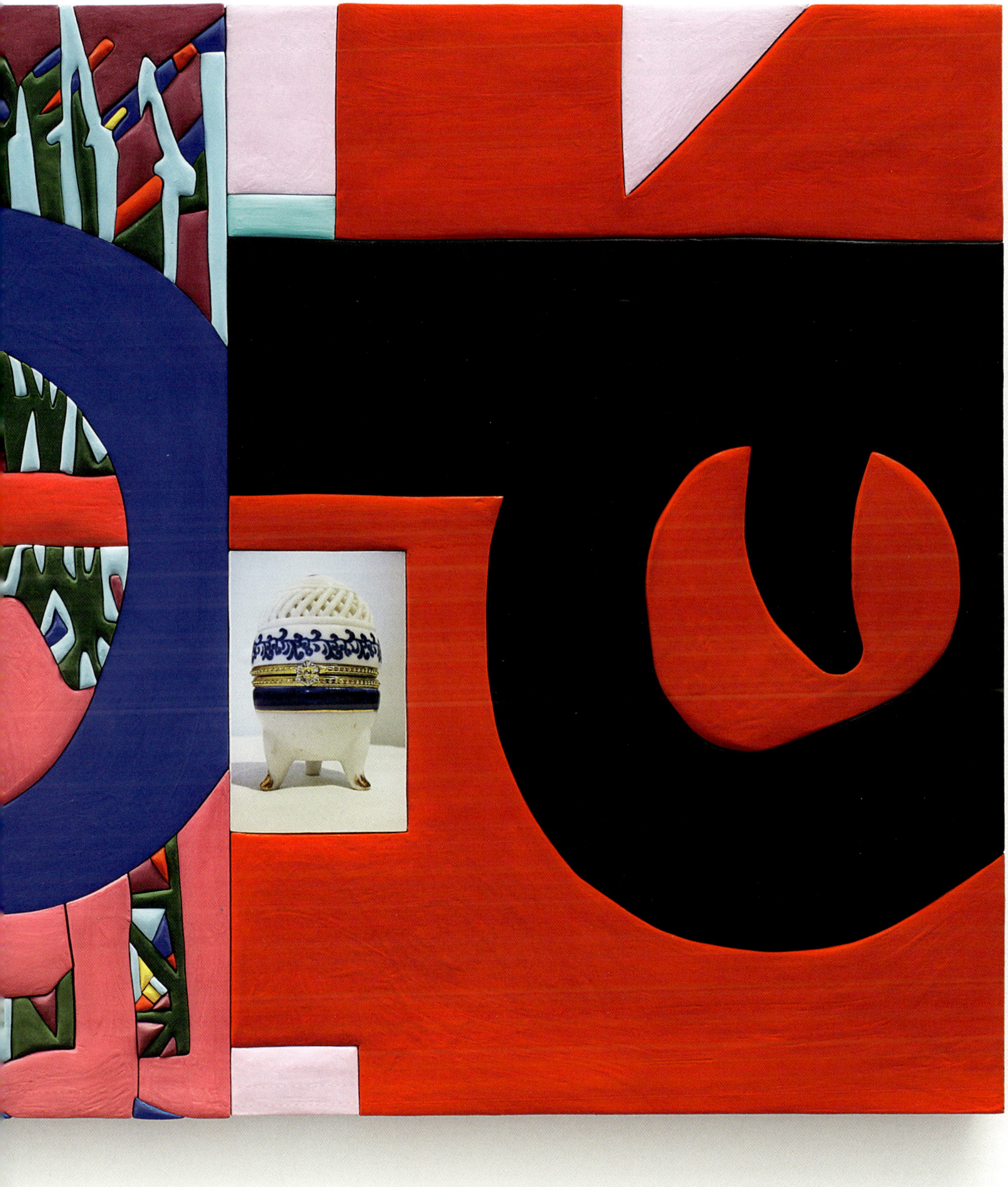

NAYLAND BLAKE

The Big One, 2003

Rabbits of different sizes, shapes and forms have appeared in Nayland Blake's performance, video and sculptural work – as well as drawings and works on paper – since the early 1990s. In Blake's words, these rabbits function as 'iconographic surrogates' and recall figures from popular culture, including the irrepressible Bugs Bunny; the six-foot-eight-inch 'invisible' white rabbit in the cult film *Harvey* (1950); and the quick-witted 'trickster' Brer Rabbit from the *Uncle Remus* folk tales (1881). For Blake, these rabbit surrogates relate to the stereotype of homosexual promiscuity, the artist's own mixed-race heritage, and broader issues around gender, identity and sexuality. Blake's rabbits have often taken the form of costumes worn by the artist during performances. *The Big One* (2003), a giant white-fabric rabbit suit displayed spreadeagled on the gallery floor, is too big for anyone to conceivably wear. Physically dwarfing the viewer, it is intended to function more like an environment than a sculpture.

Previous

SADIE BENNING

Gun Egg, 2017

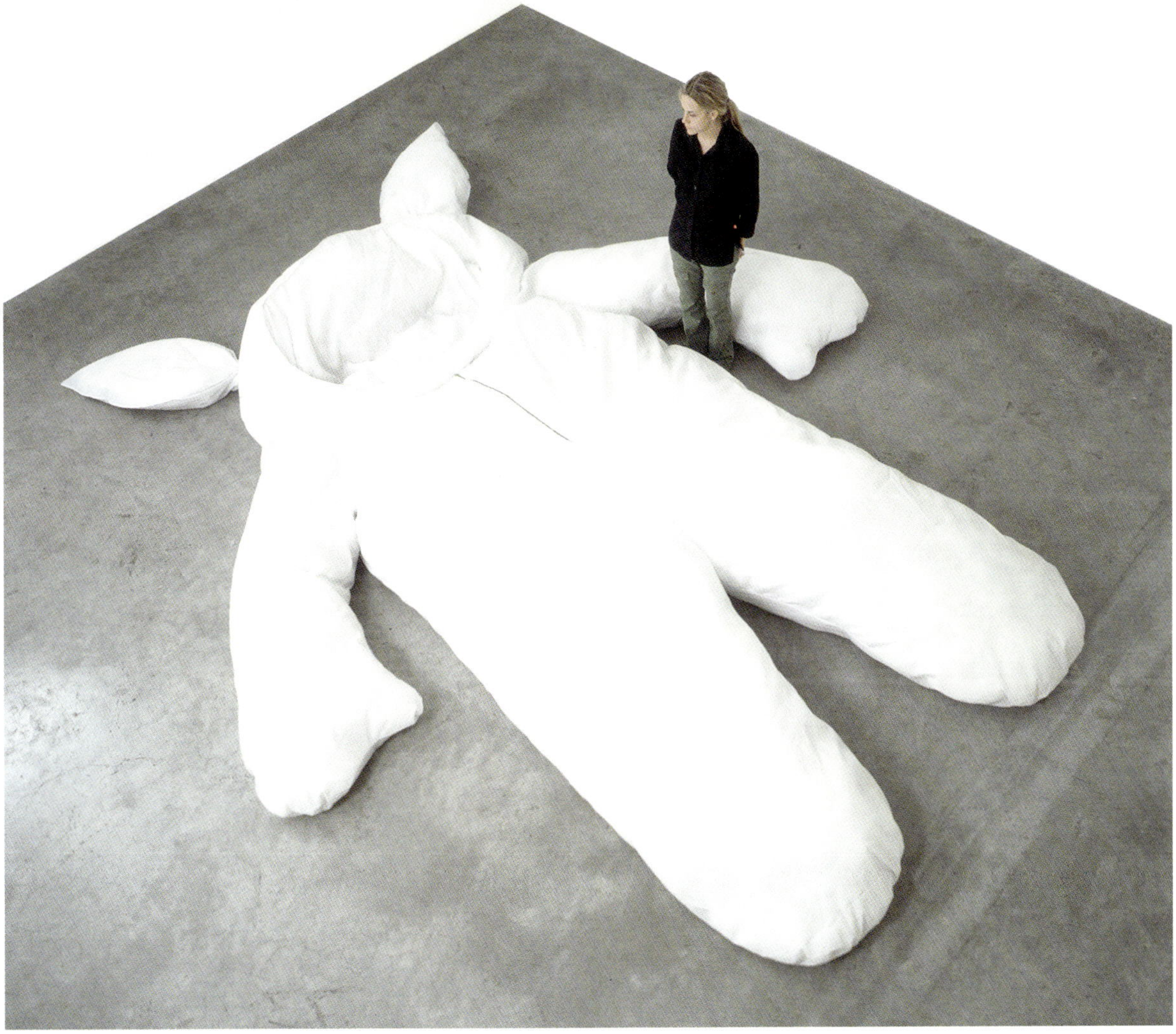

Pauline Boudry / Renate Lorenz

FLO BROOKS

108 – 13

LUCIANO CASTELLI

114 – 17

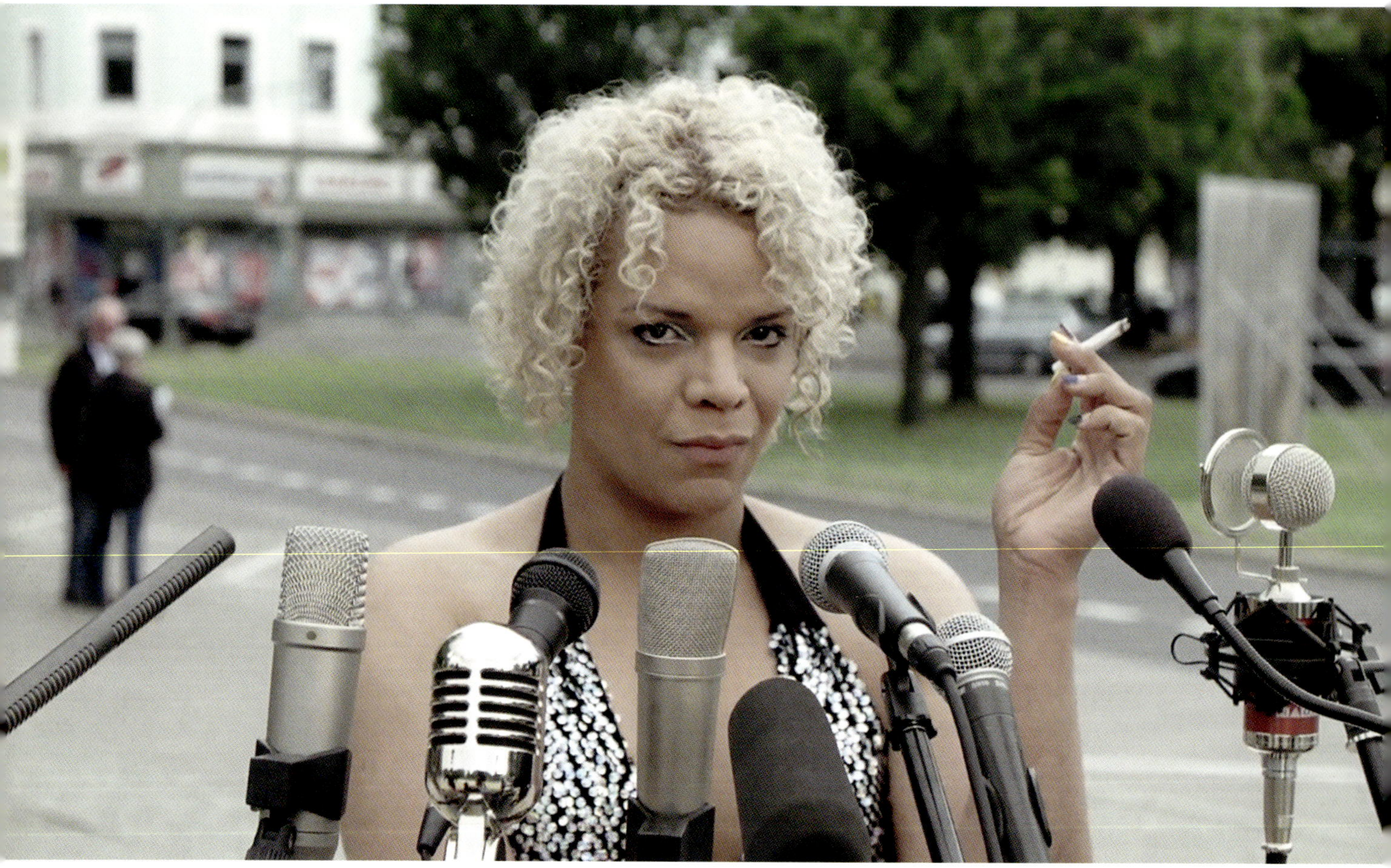

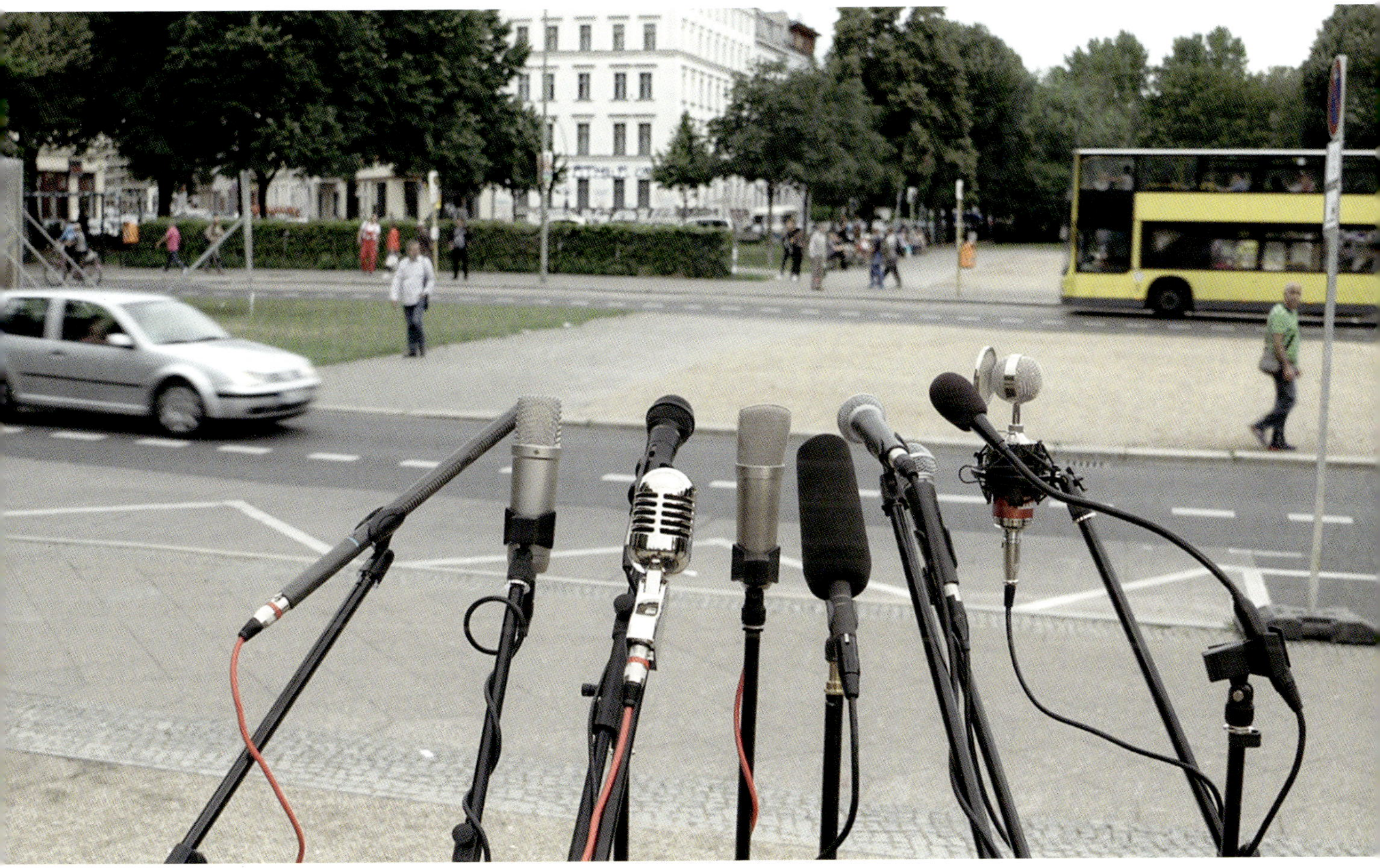

PAULINE BOUDRY /
RENATE LORENZ

Silent, 2016

In their video works and installations, Pauline Boudry / Renate Lorenz often revisit or restage existing artworks, scores, songs or performances. In *Silent* (2016), musician Aérea Negrot performs John Cage's famous work *4' 33"* (1952), a score conceived for any instrument, in which performers are instructed not to play for the duration of the piece. Negrot's performance of Cage's work takes place in a public square in Berlin, Oranienplatz, which between 2012 and 2014 was the site of a refugee protest camp. Boudry / Lorenz are interested in the ambiguity of silent acts, which could either be 'a violent experience, as in being silenced, or a powerful performative act of resistance'. In *Silent*, they attempt to find a way to address violent acts without reverting to the 'language of urgency' employed by the mainstream media.

Previous, stills

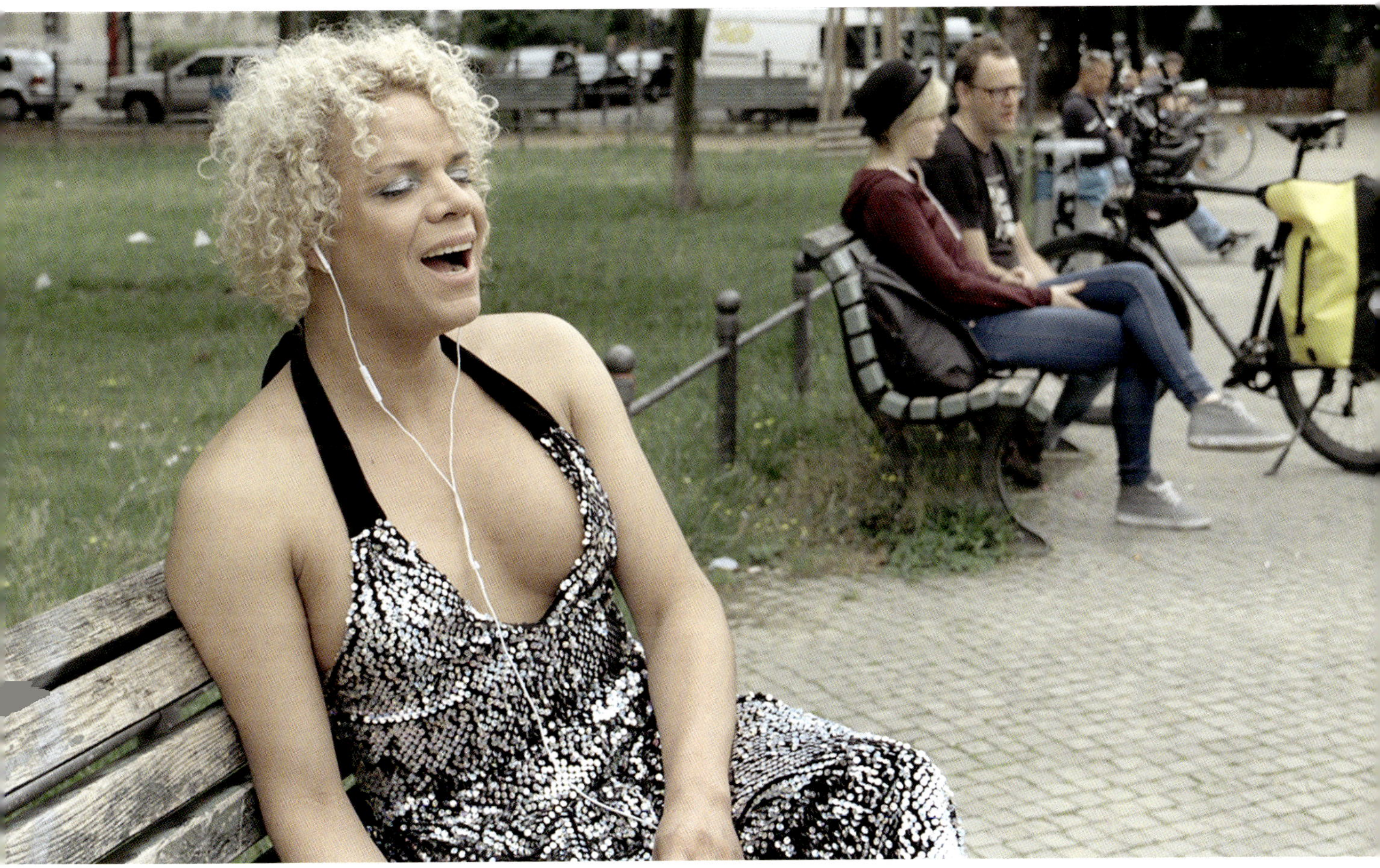

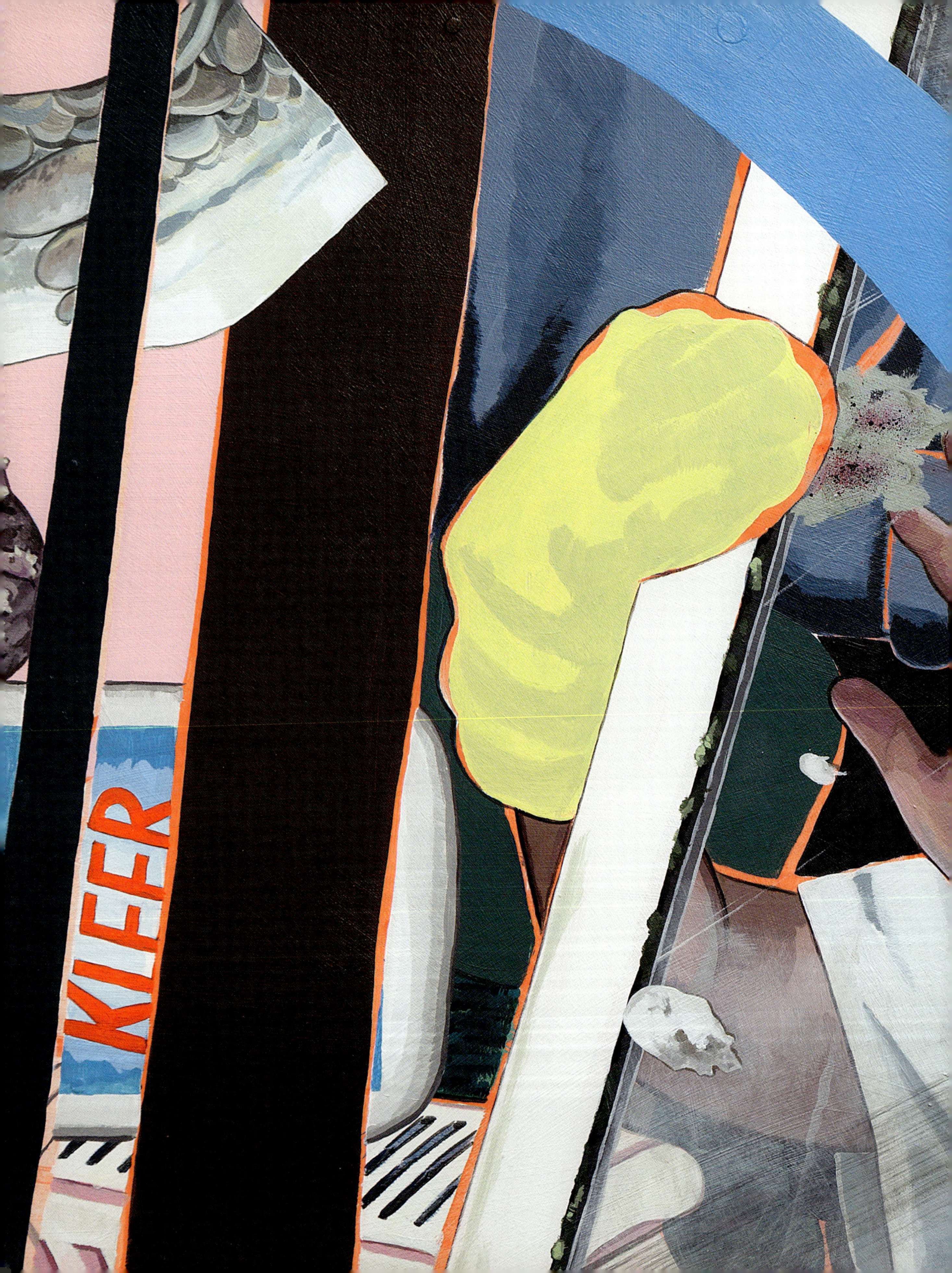
KIEFER

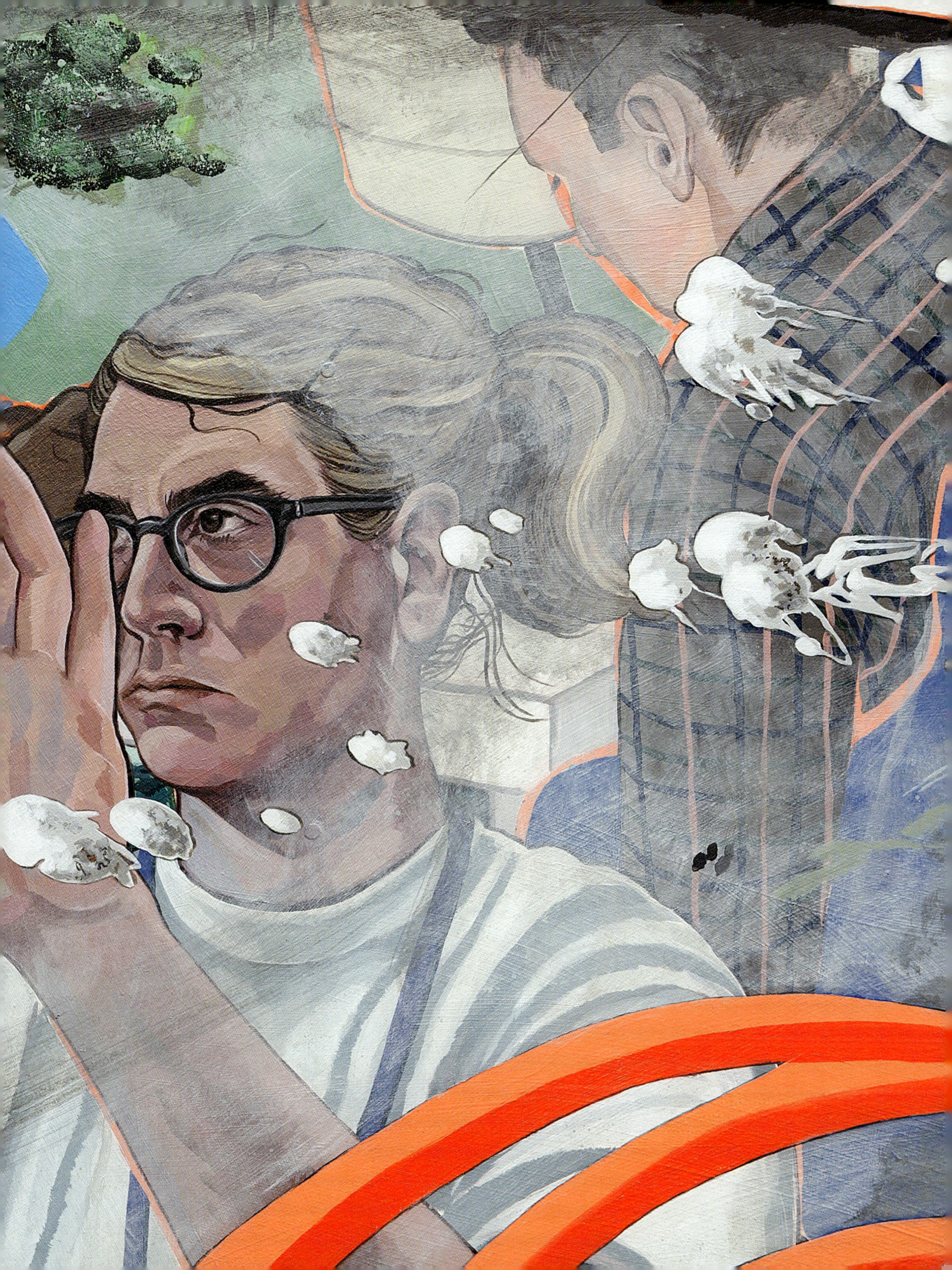

FLO BROOKS

YessSIR! Back off! Tell me who I am again?!, 2018

Flo Brooks untethers scenes of everyday life from space and time in a process that he describes as 'transing'. In the series of paintings *Scrubbers* (2018), Brooks depicts a team of cleaning contractors at work in different locations, including a gym, therapy room and public toilet: environments designed, in the artist's words, to 'clean, conceal and correct'. Armed with an array of toxic products, the cleaners labour tirelessly against dirt and grime. But we are also shown what is hidden beneath visible surfaces: substrata of accumulated waste, clogging pipes and blocking air vents so that they barely function. Like architecture, our bodies have outsides and insides, visible and invisible planes and are subject to intensive regulation in the name of health and hygiene. Brooks' paintings are rich with visual puns and playful bodily metaphors which, in his words, 'evoke a kind of transness and queerness, provoking and belittling symbols of normativity associated with gender and sex'.

Previous, detail

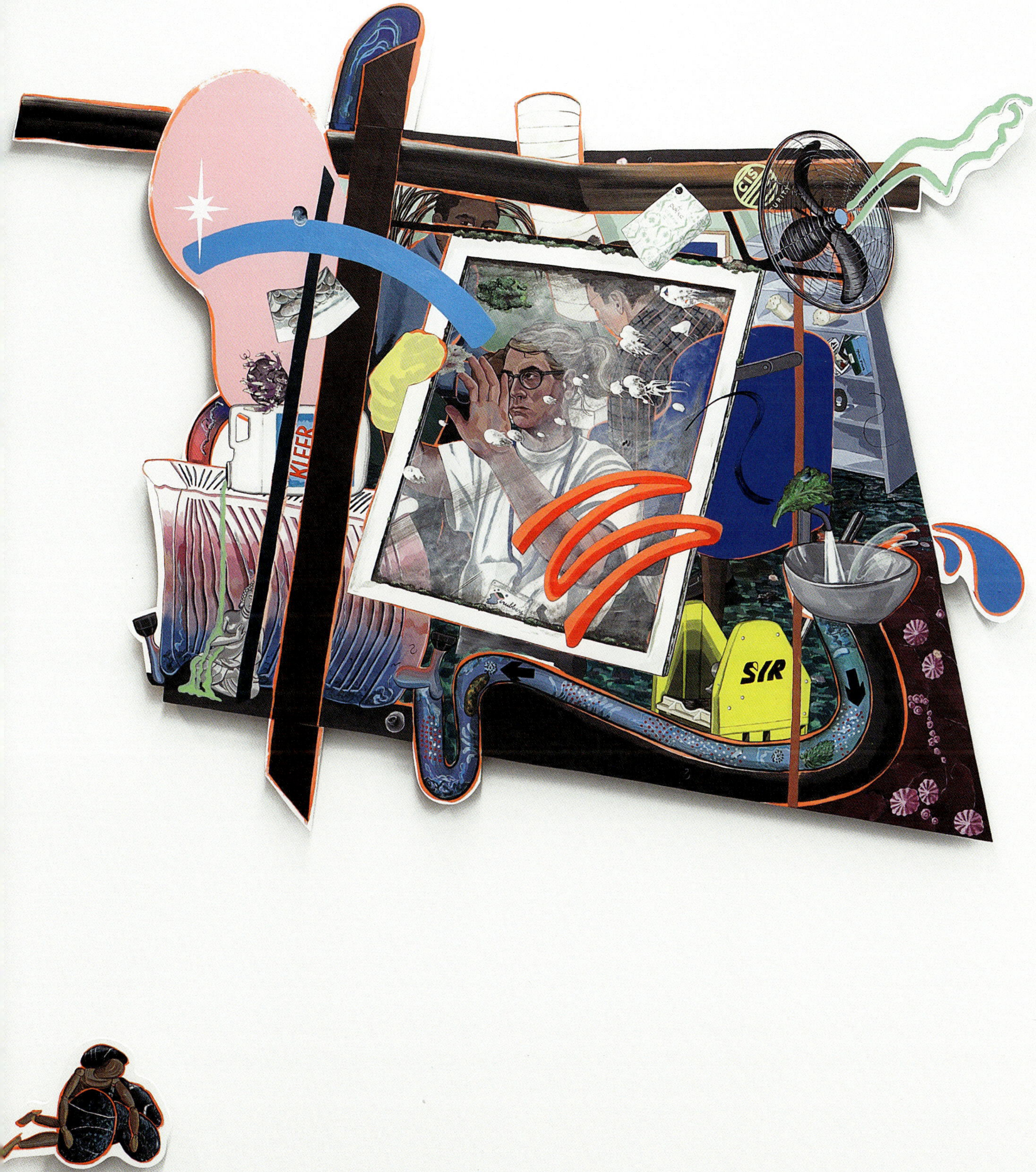
KIFER
SIR

FLO BROOKS

U Bend but it's still a trap, 2018

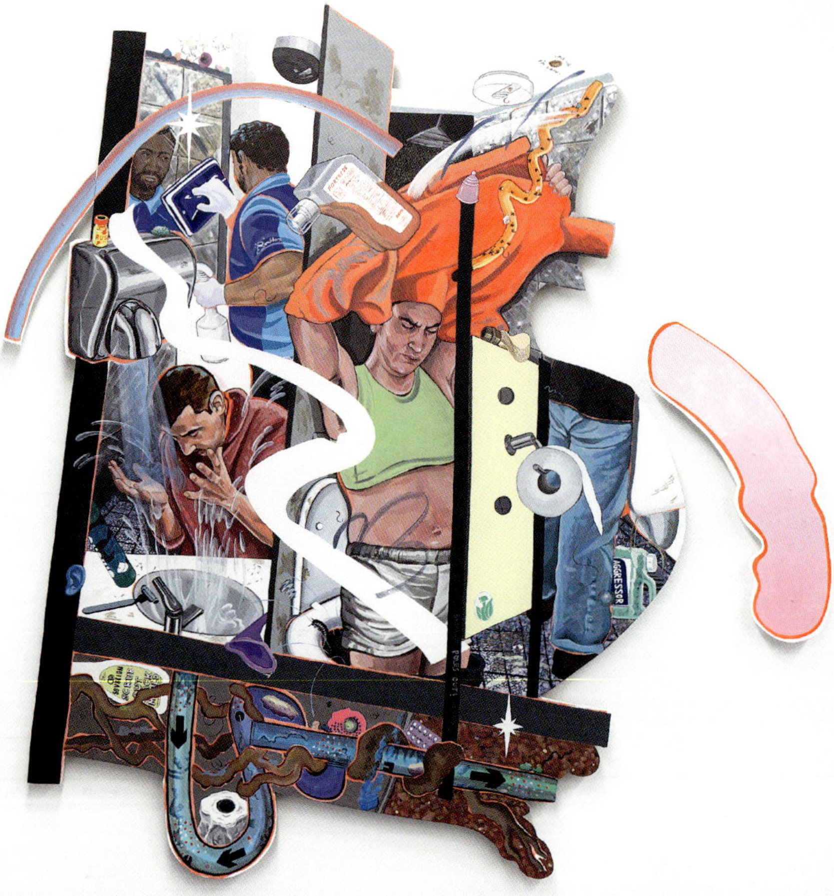

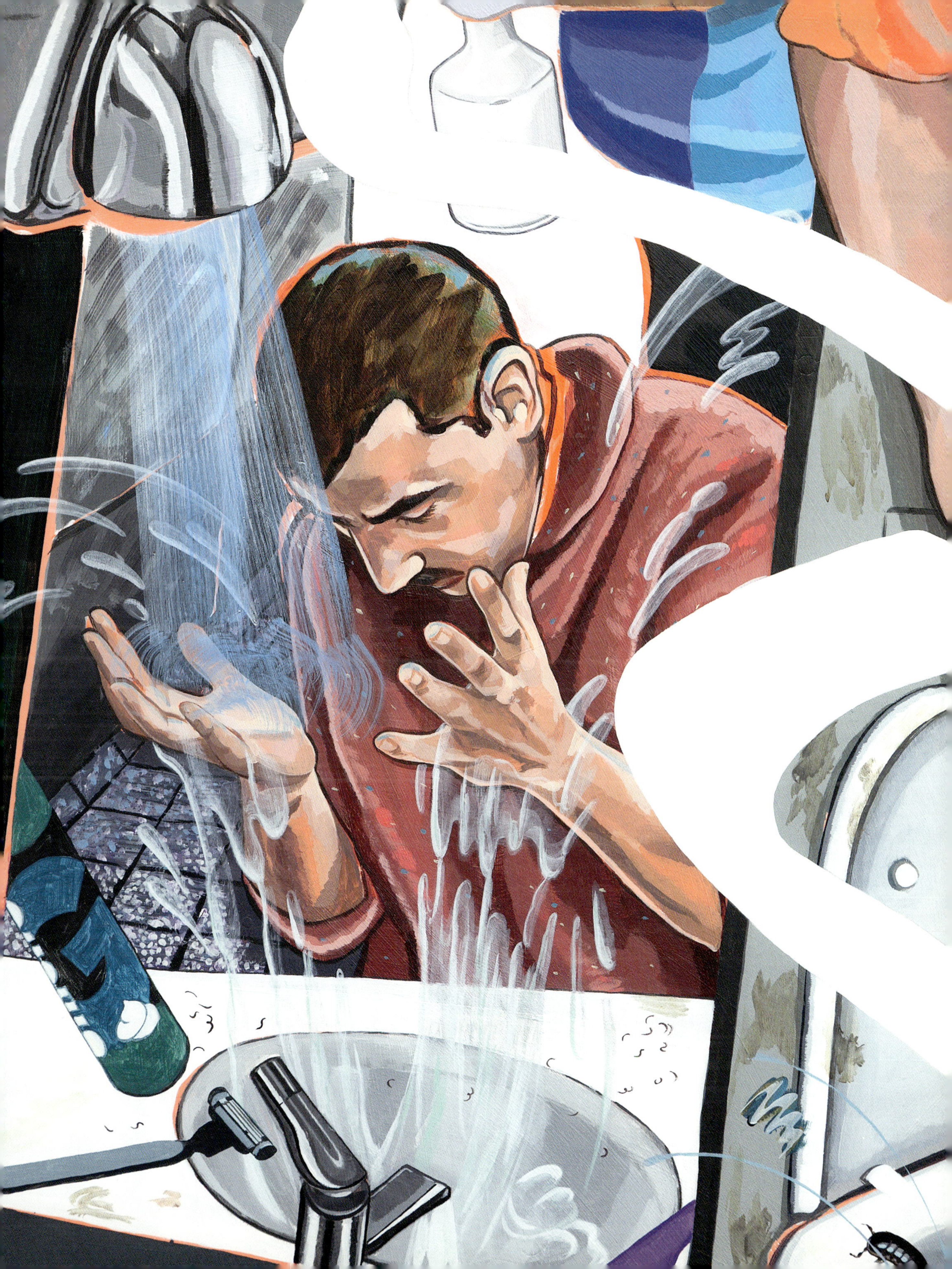

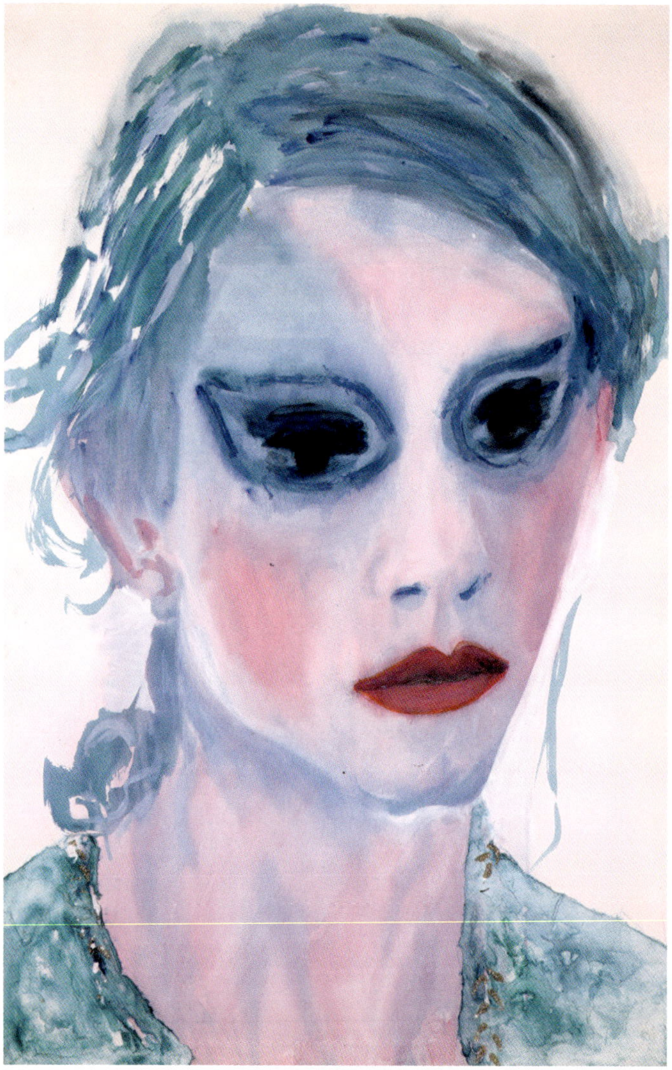

LUCIANO CASTELLI

Lucille Self-portrait, 1973

Golden Record 3, 1974

Overleaf

Self-portrait, 1975

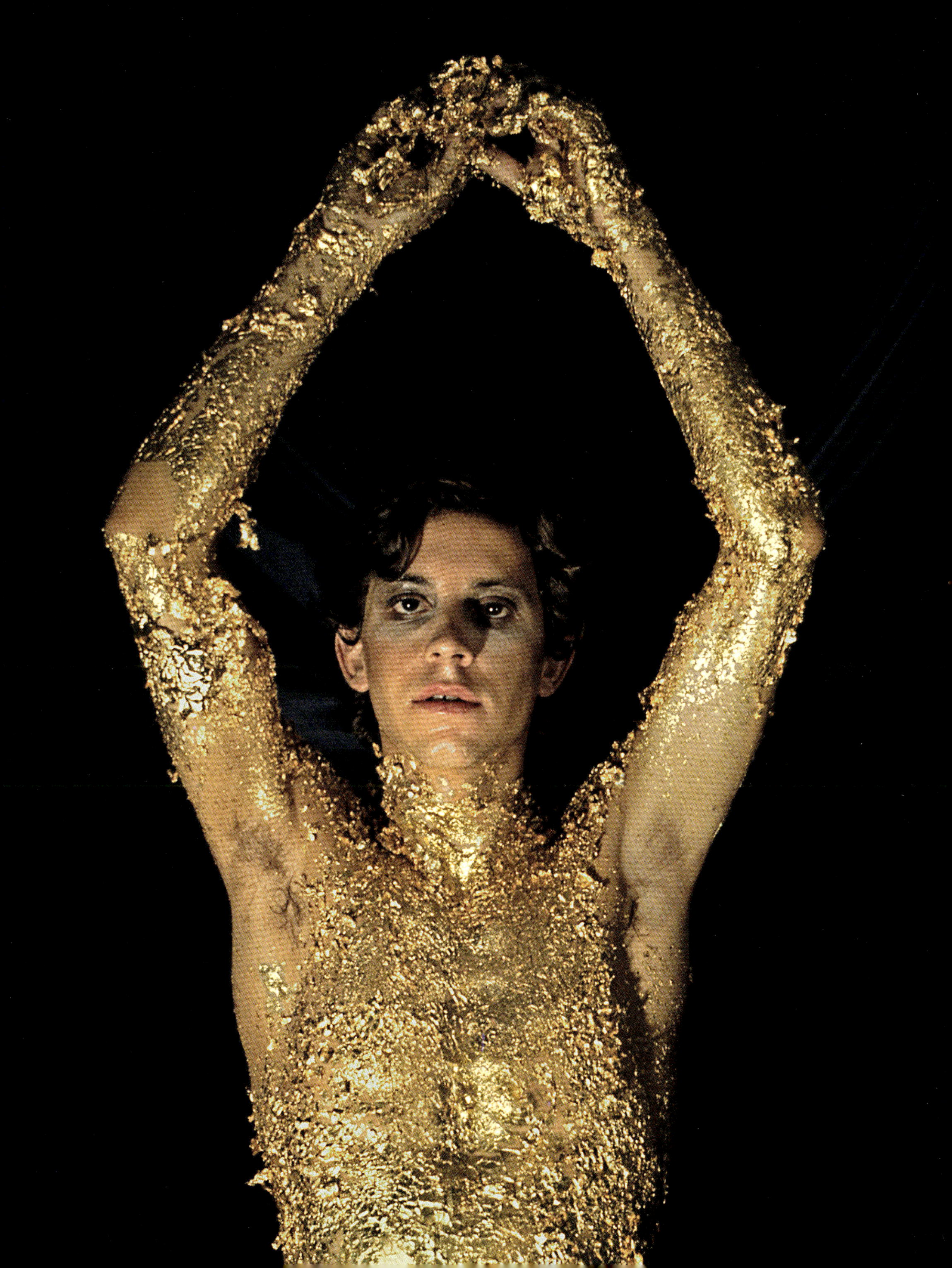

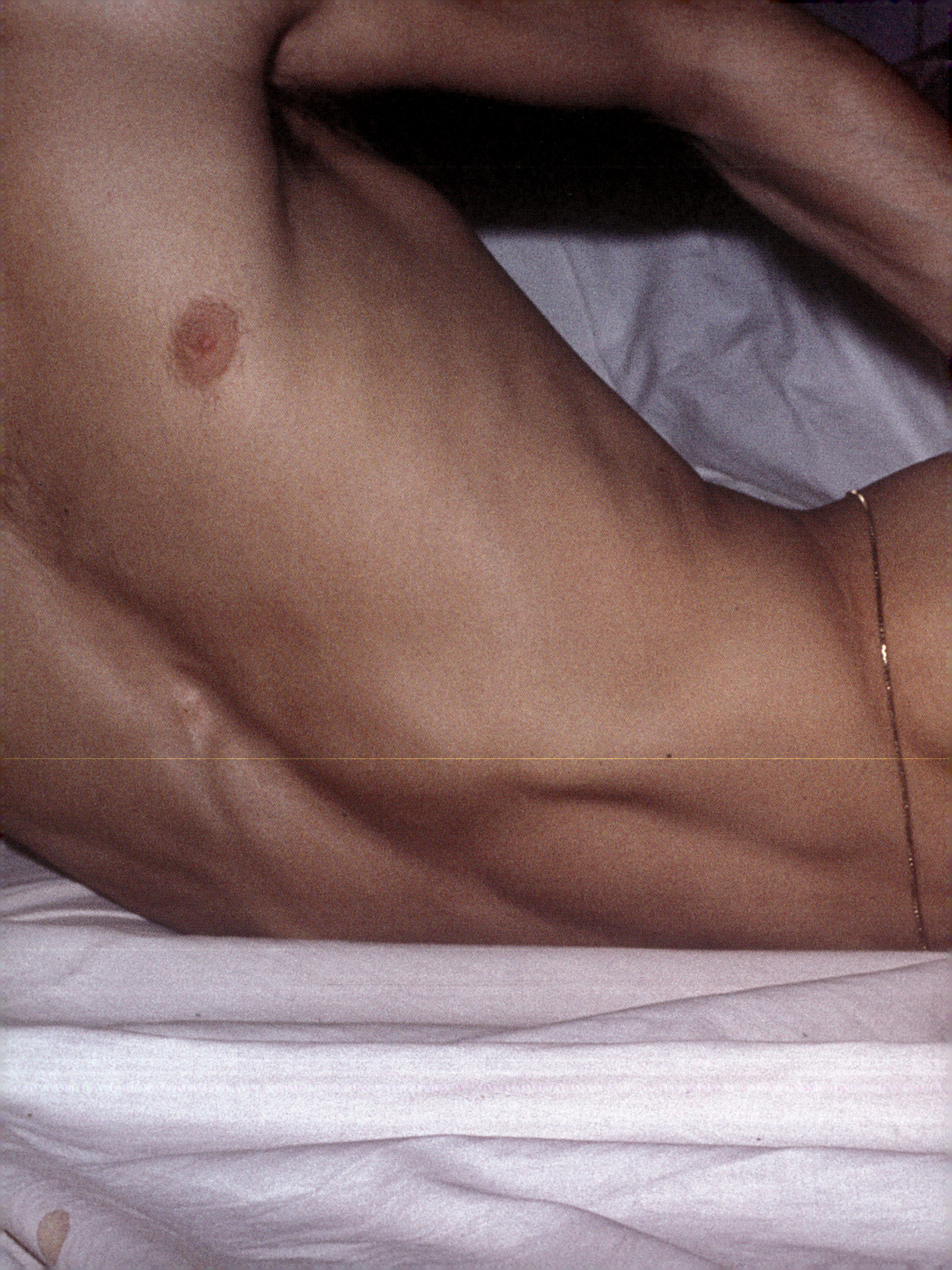

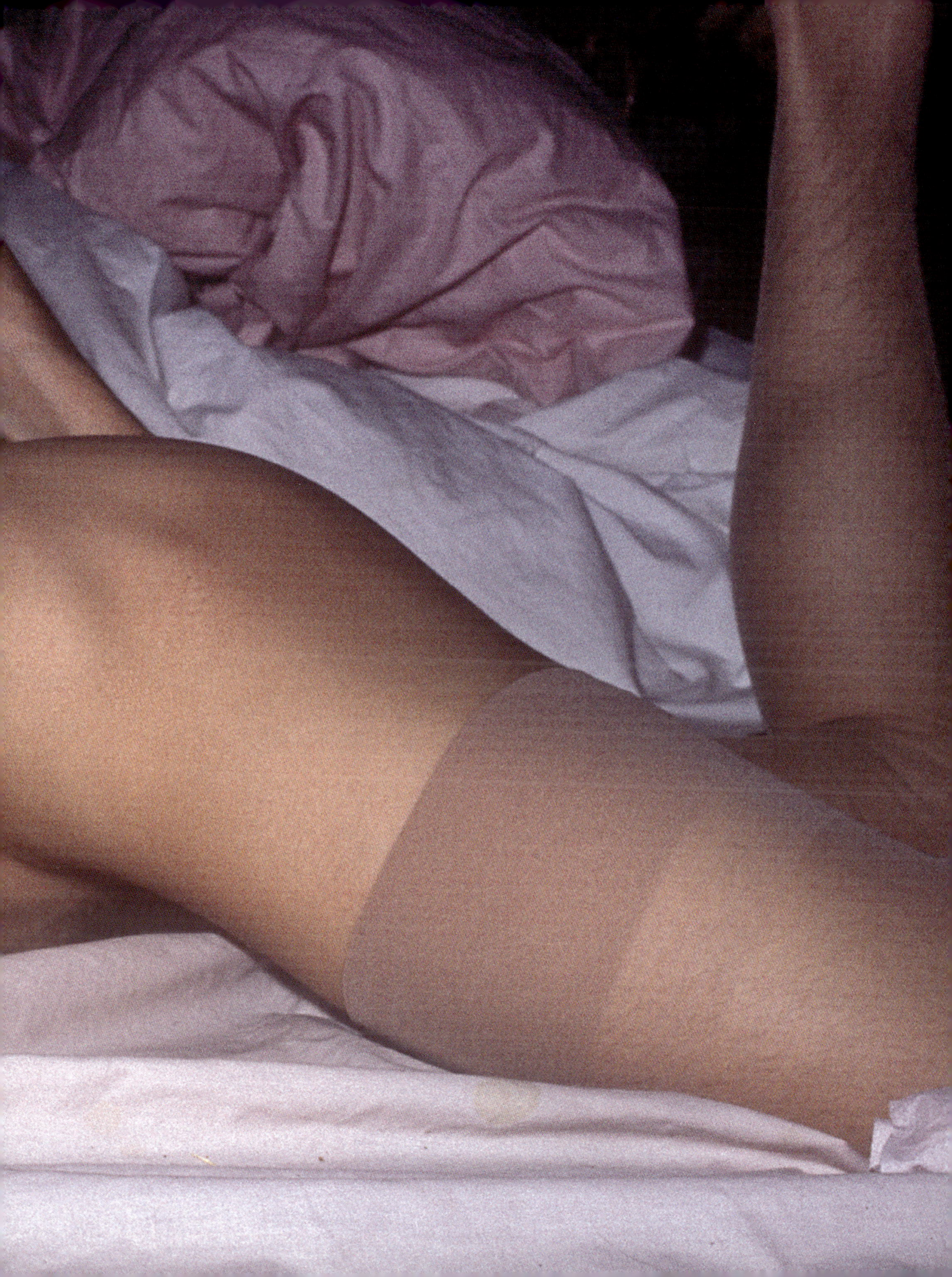

Jimmy desana

120 – 25

Jes Fan

126 – 27

Chitra Ganesh

128 – 29

Martine Gutierrez

130 – 35

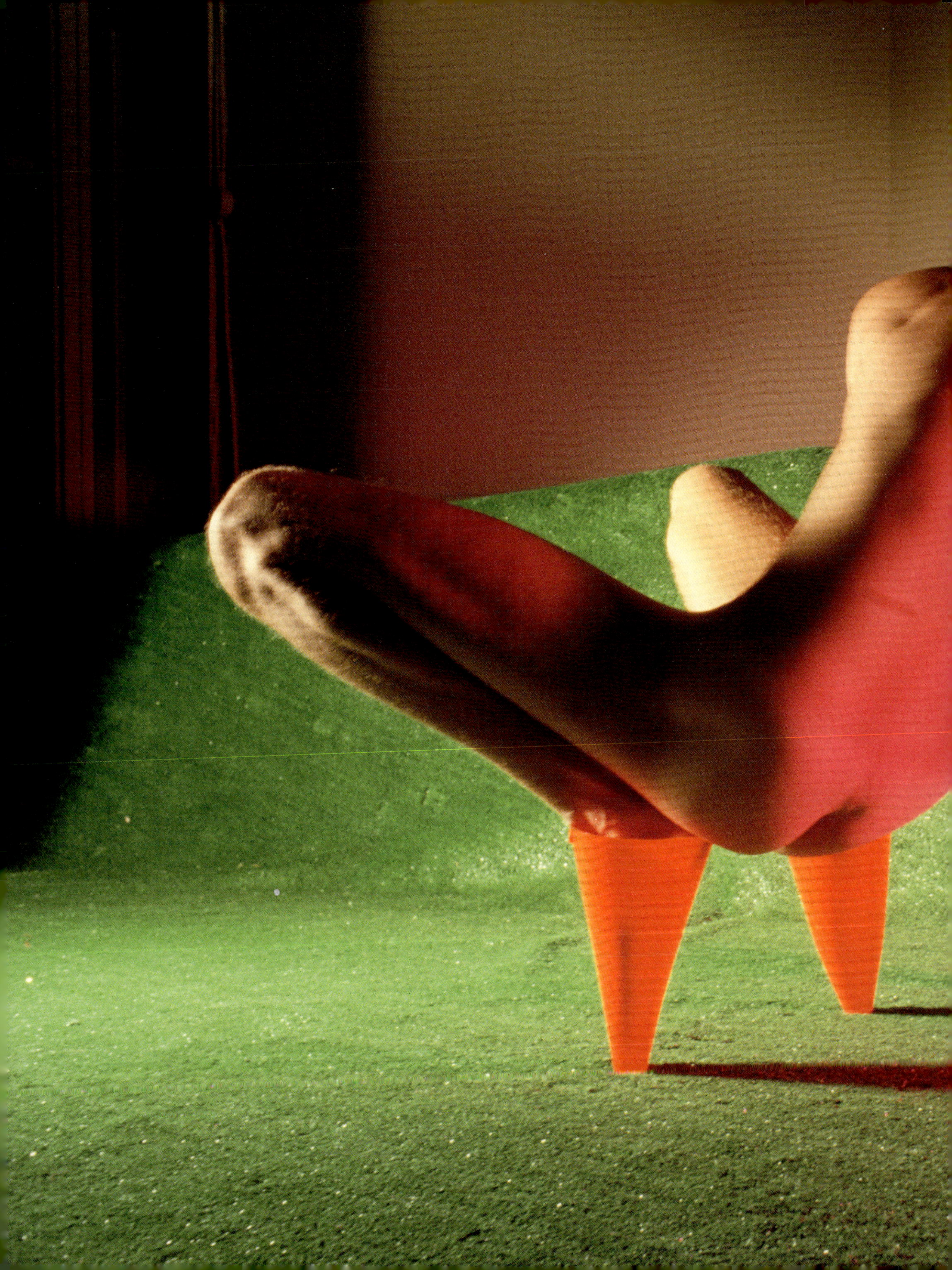

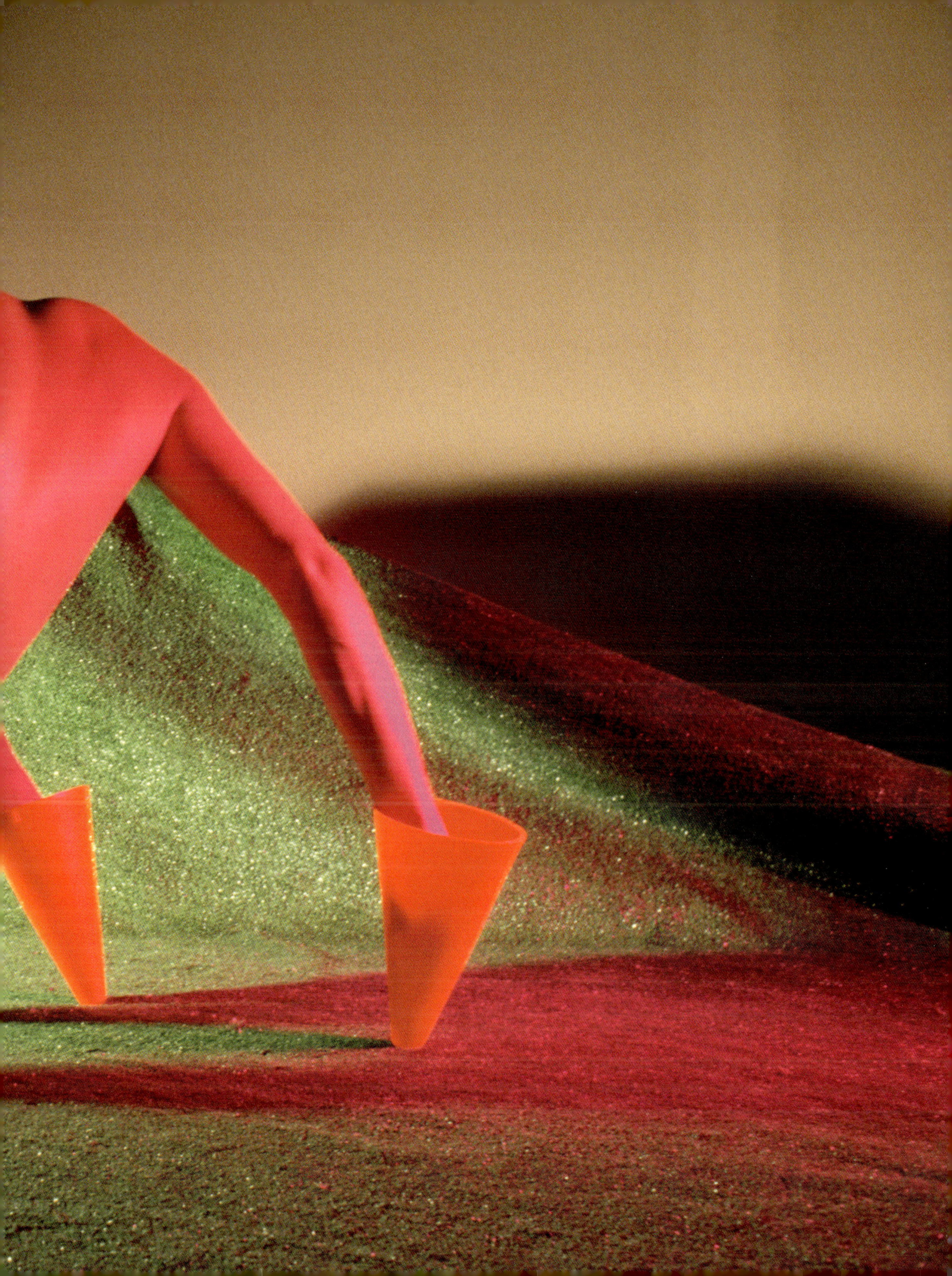

JIMMY DESANA

Sink, 1979

Previous

Marker Cones (No Head), 1982

Overleaf

Four Legs with Shoes,
undated

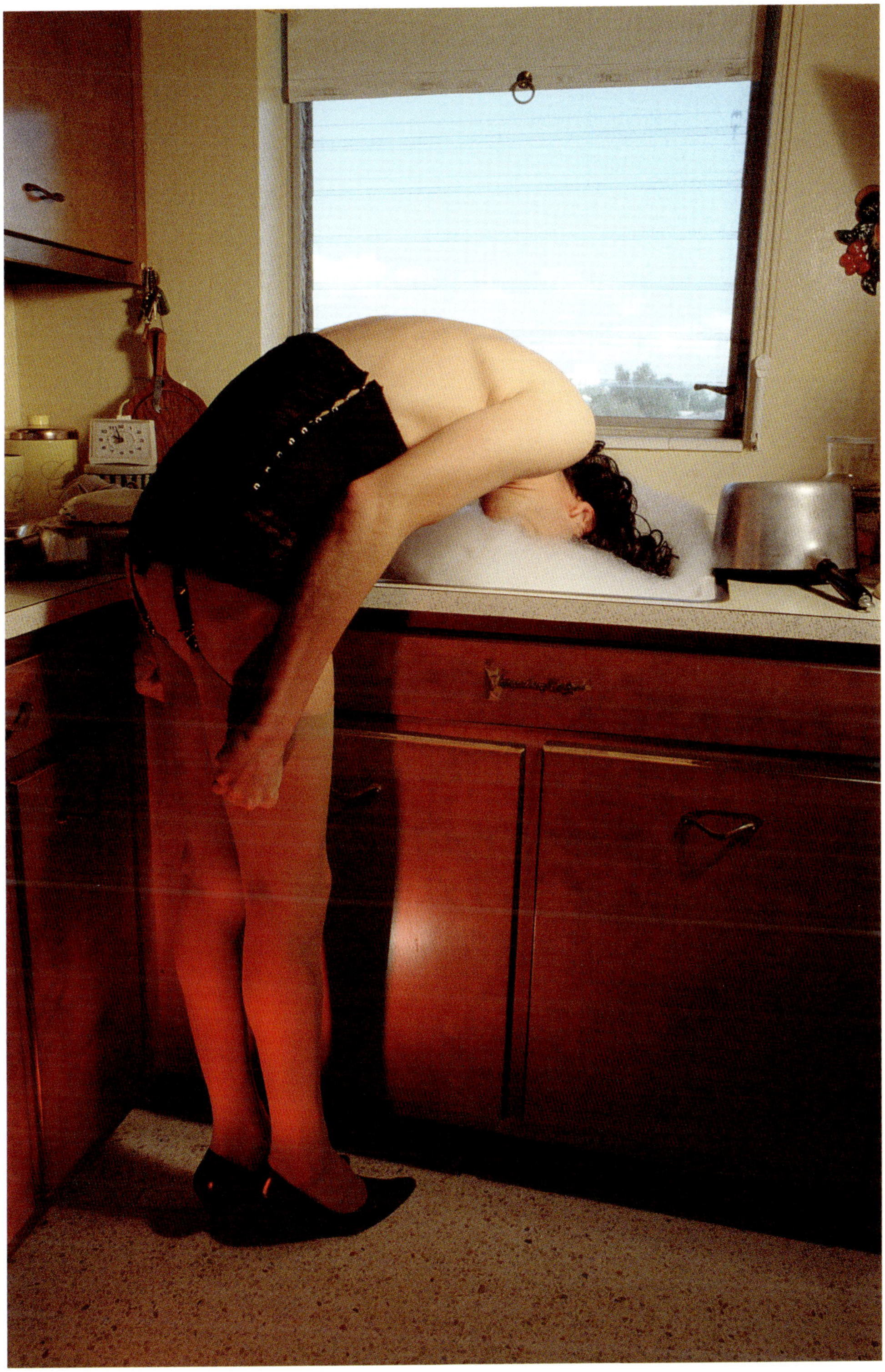

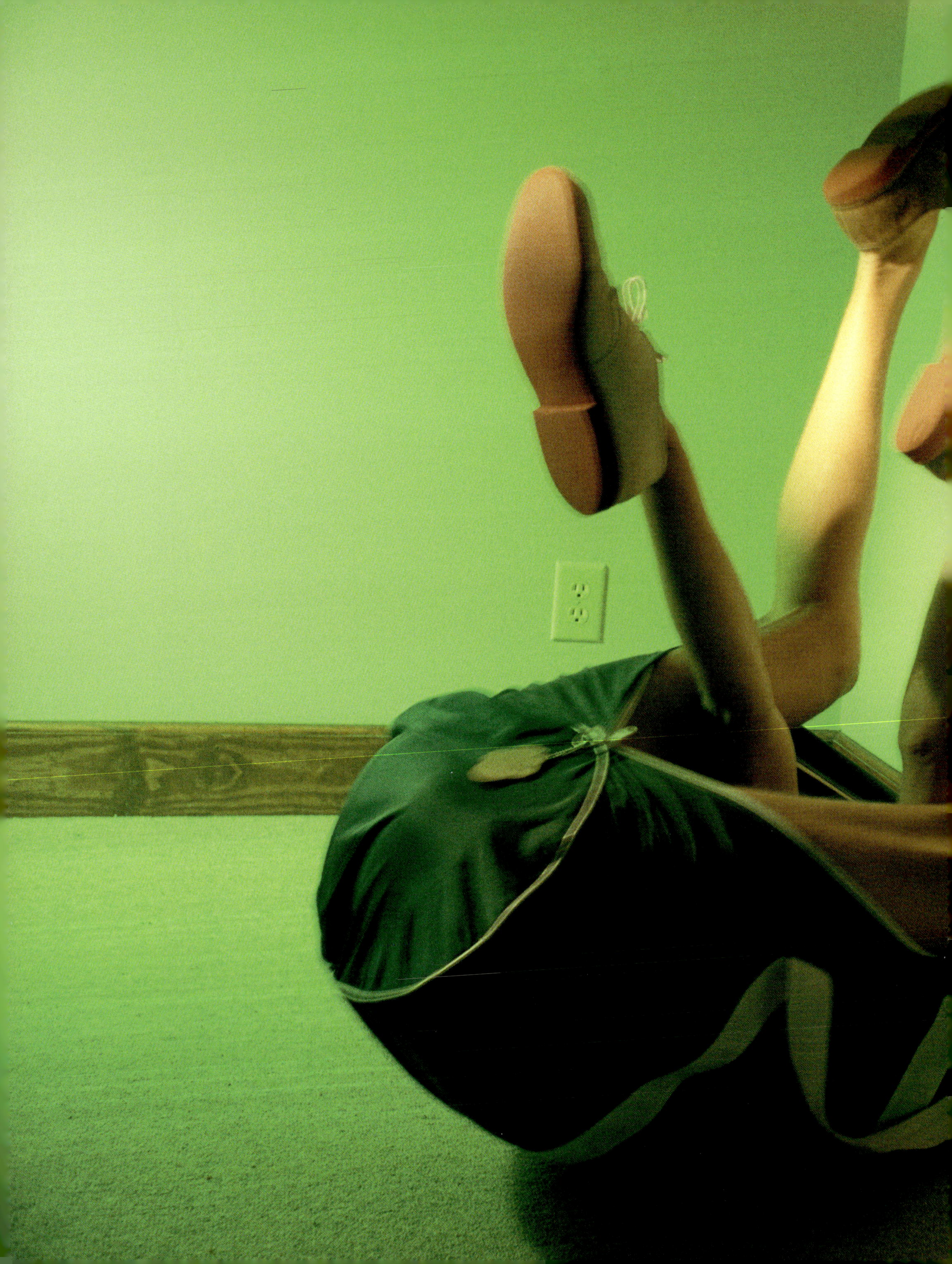

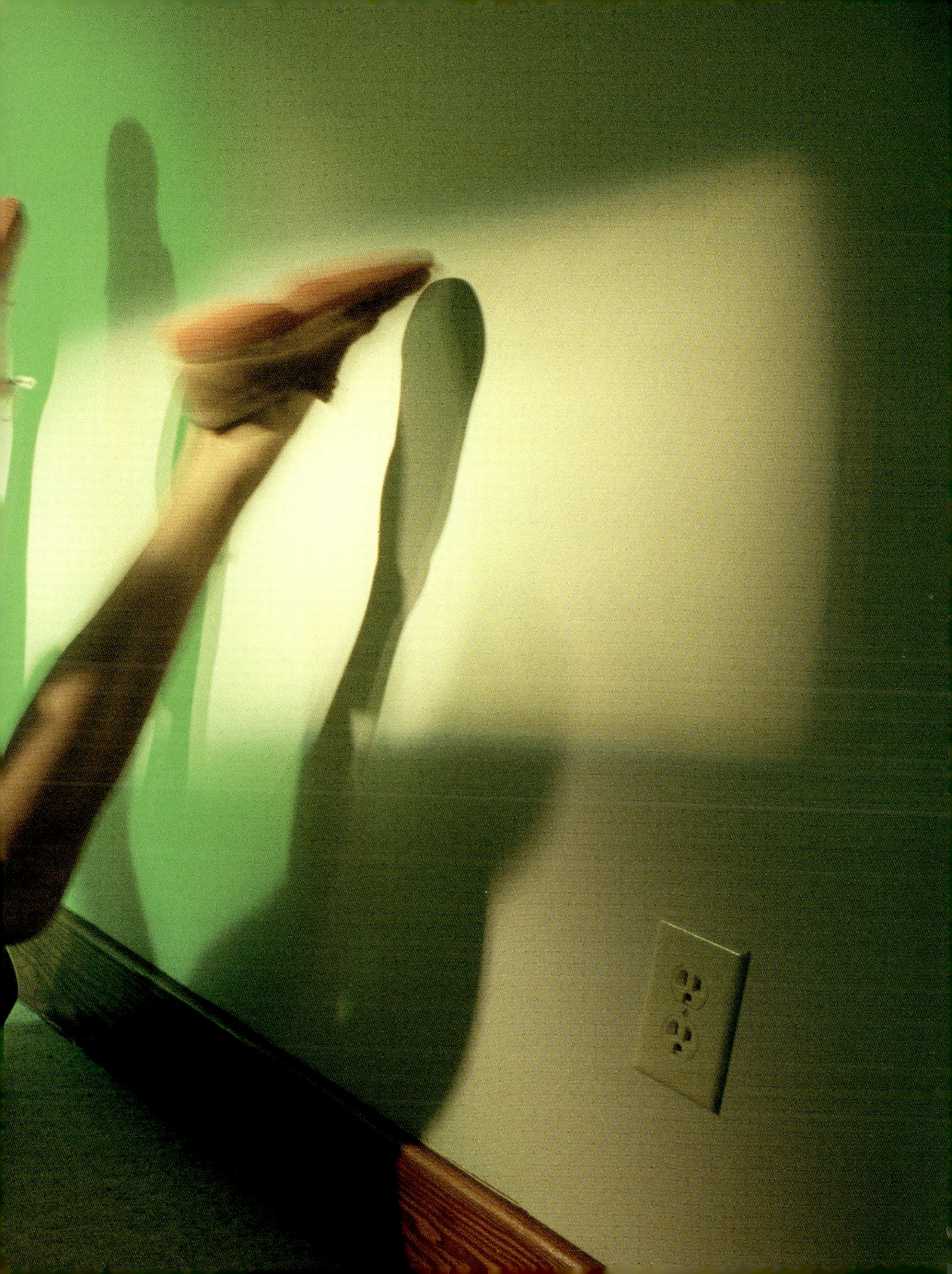

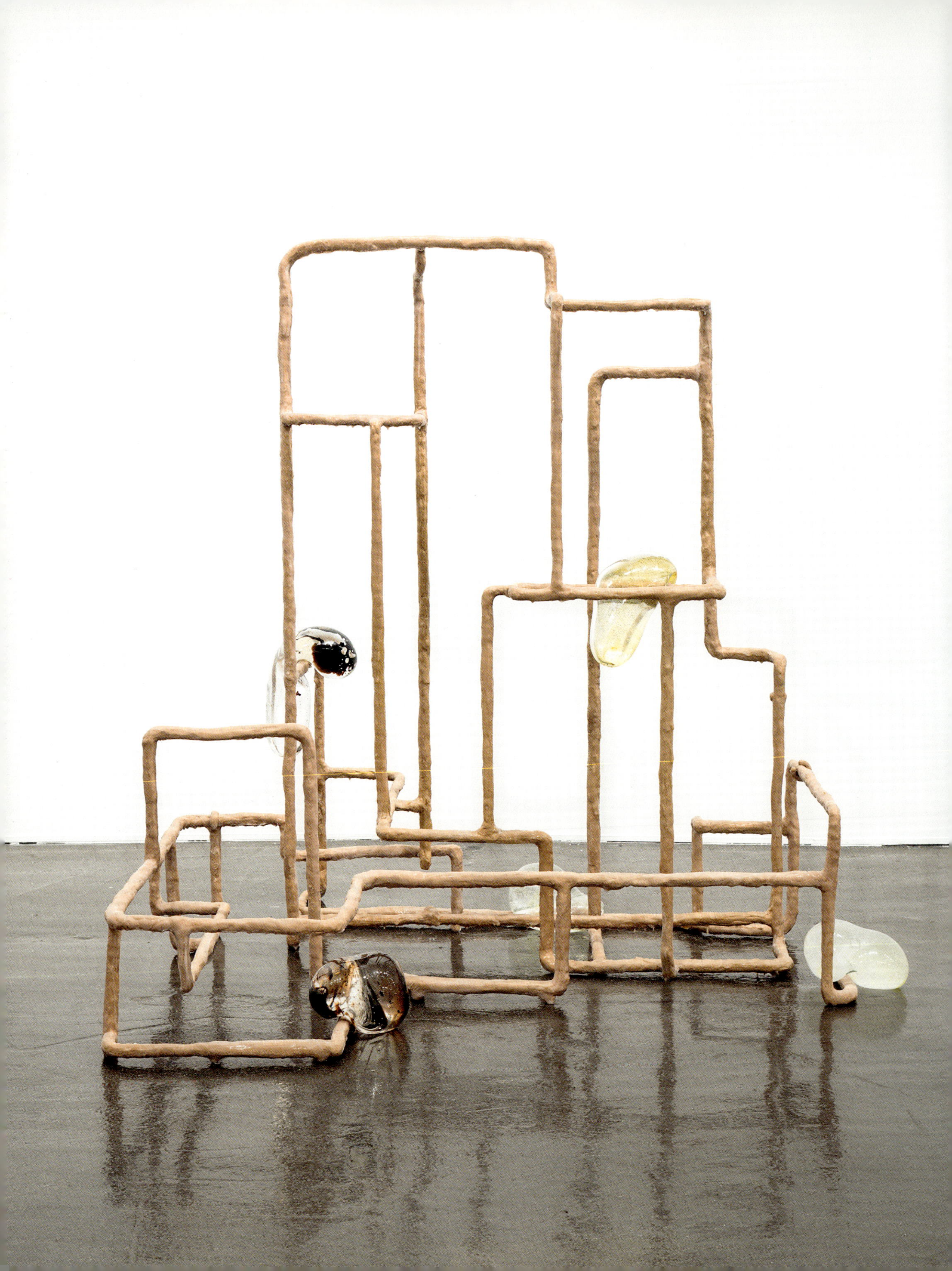

JES FAN

Systems II, 2018

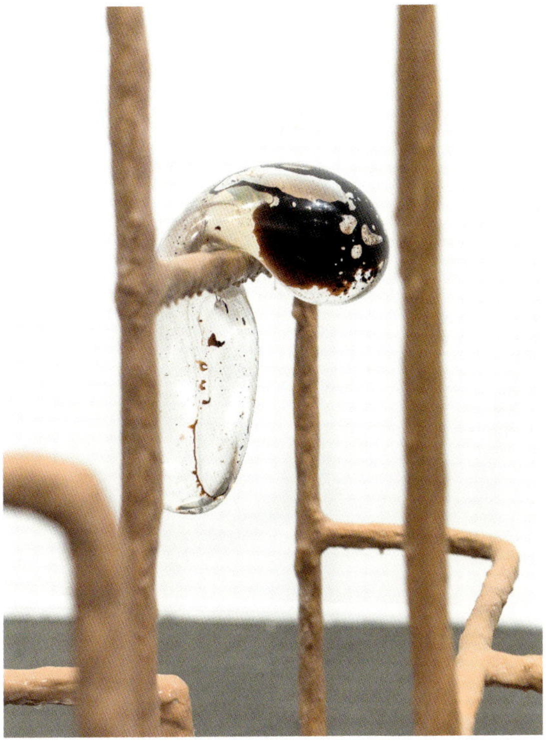

Jes Fan uses primarily sculpture and installation to speculatively re-configure racial and transgender identity. For the installation *Systems I* (2018), Fan injects their ethereal glass sculptures with silicone, followed by melanin pigments, laboriously harvested in scientific laboratories. The resulting plump globules – stained with abstract patterns created by melanin's black pigmentation – are displayed on a steel, jungle-gym-like structure. They are, paradoxically, concrete abstractions of a body. In *Systems II* and *Systems III* (2018), Fan repeats their experimental glassmaking process with hormones. In this series, glass becomes a receptacle for both the essential markers and conceptual metamorphoses of identity. As Fan explains, their practice is a study in material essentialism, albeit to the point of absurdity. In Fan's thoughtful works, identity, when boiled down to its core, is not easily consumed or classifiable.

CHITRA GANESH

Shimmering Pulse, 2009

Rose of My Rose, 2007

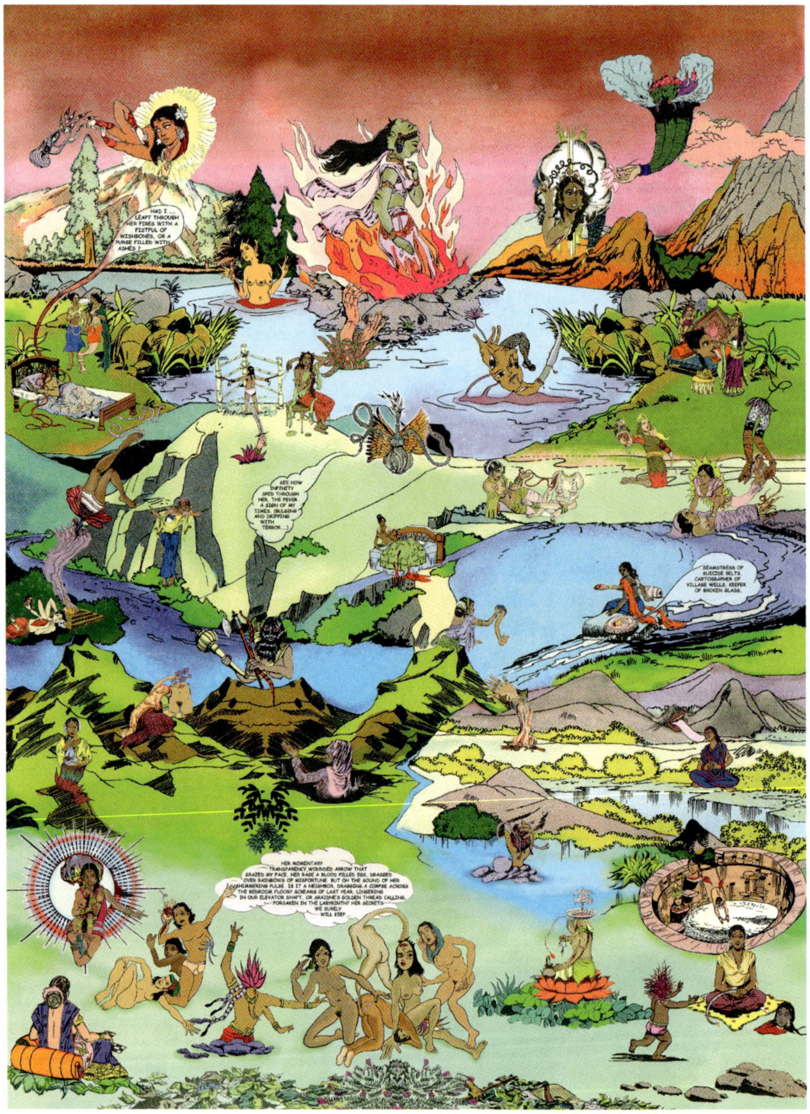

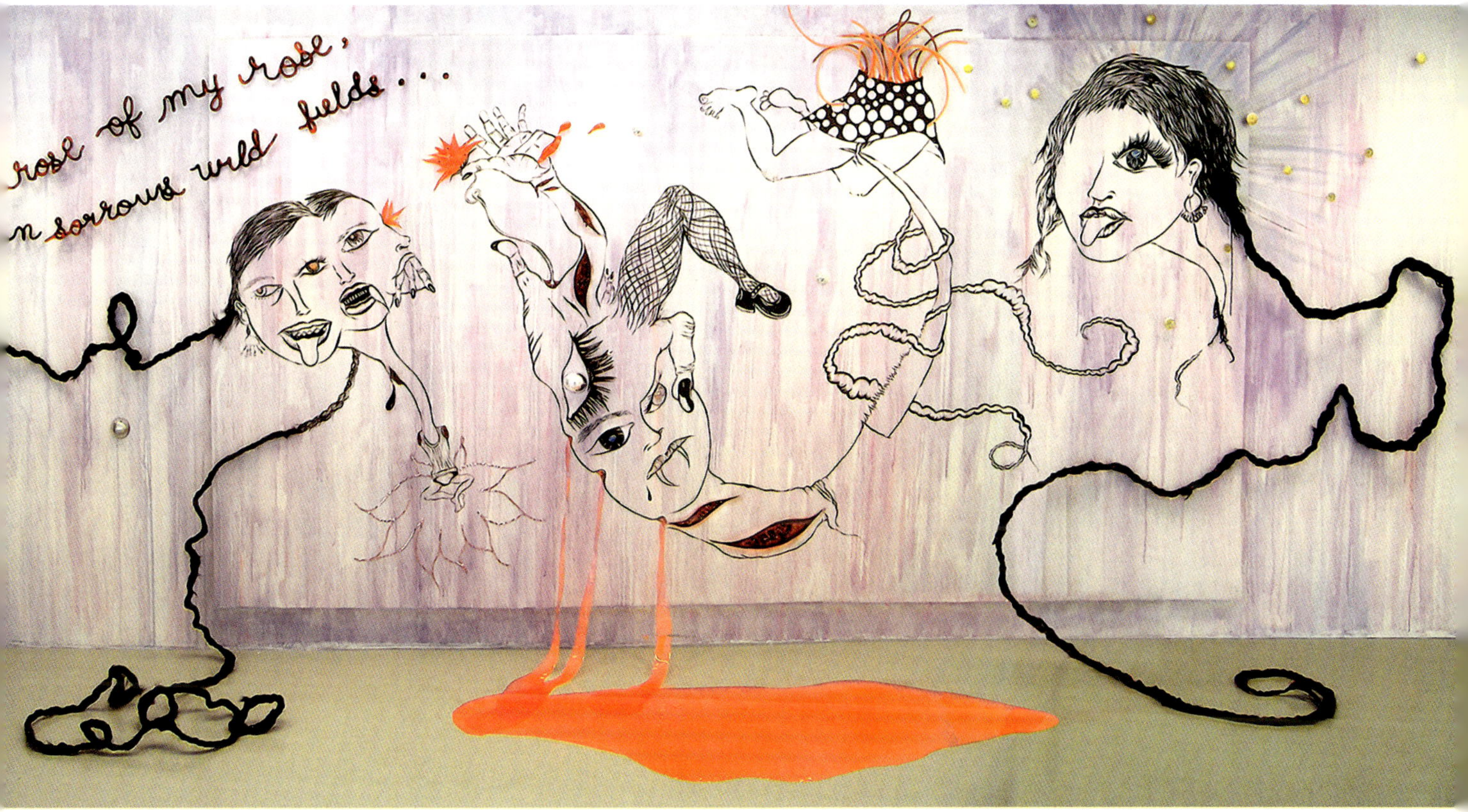
rose of my rose,
n sorrows wild fields . . .

MARTINE GUTIERREZ

Demons, Chin 'Demon of Lust,'
p93 from Indigenous Woman, 2018

For her photographic series *Masking* and *Demons*, Martine Gutierrez acts as model, stylist and photographer. The images were made as part of her one-off publication *Indigenous Woman* (2018), every aspect of which – from the advertisements to the fashion spreads and written editorials – was conceived, crafted and produced by Gutierrez. The artist describes the project as 'a critique and a simultaneous investigation' of her identity, and her claim over a complex set of 'labels, stereotypes and iconographies'. In the *Masking* series – which speaks both to 'the practice of self-care' and 'the masks we wear' – Gutierrez deliberately personifies identity as something 'alien or unfamiliar', while in the *Demons* series she assumes the guise of Aztec, Mayan and Yoruba deities in order to examine the role that they served within their own cultures, as well as the way they have been interpreted and portrayed by the West.

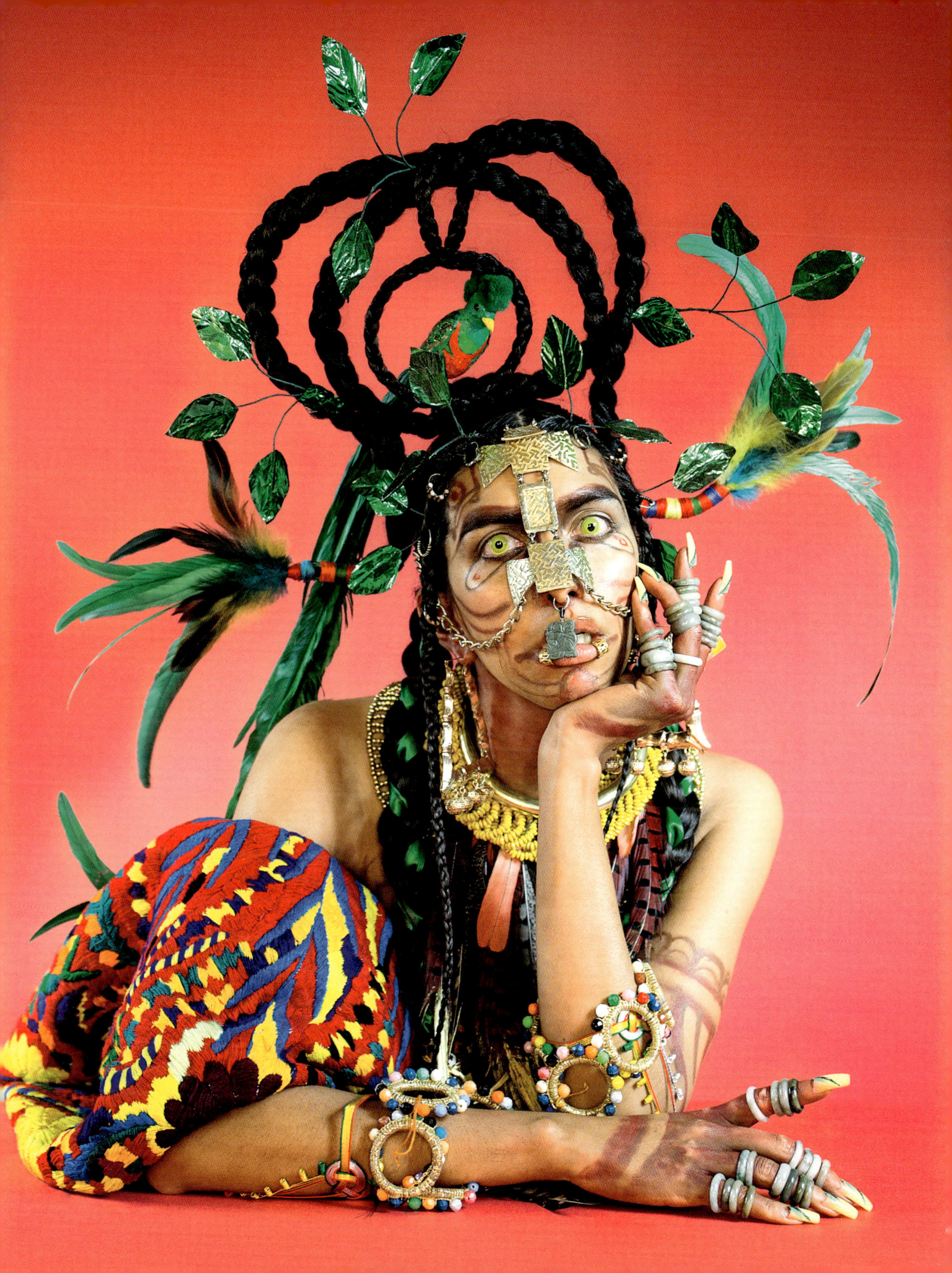

MARTINE GUTIERREZ

Masking, 24k Gold Mask,
p46 from Indigenous Woman, 2018

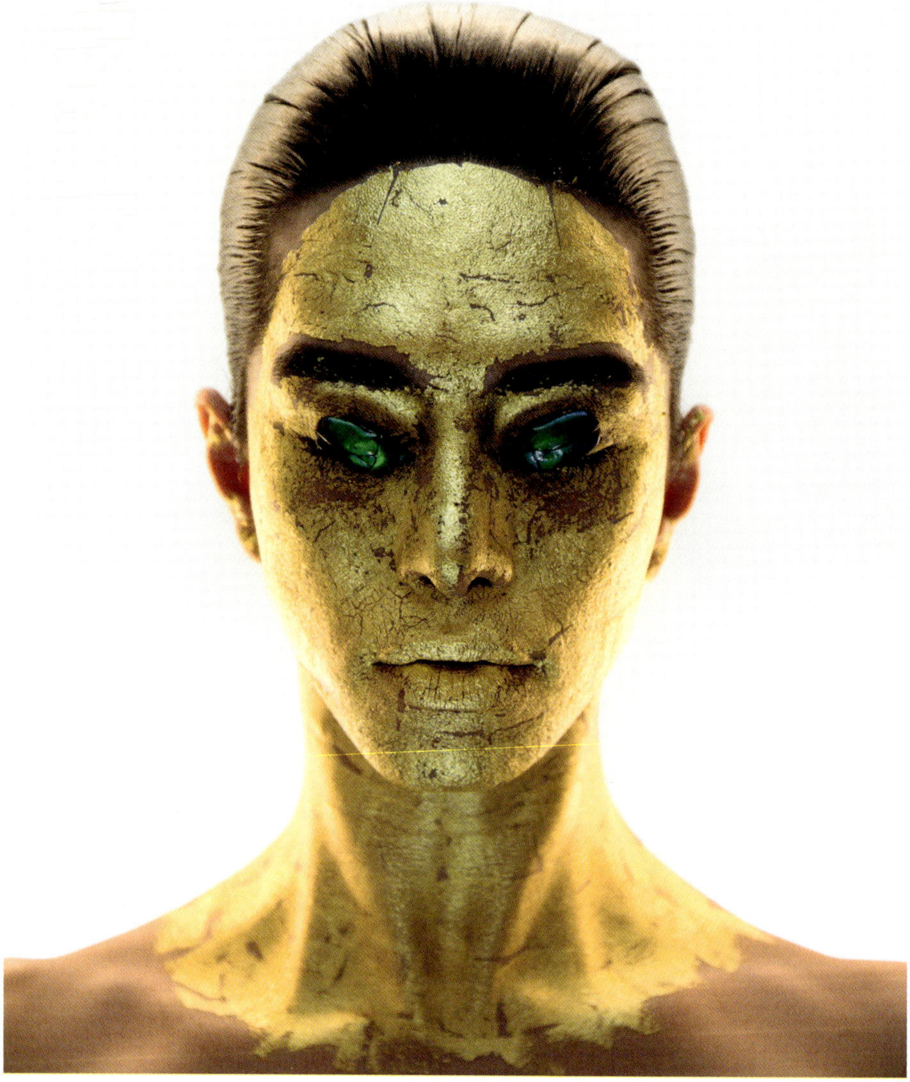

MARTINE GUTIERREZ

Masking, Snail Mask,
p55 from Indigenous Woman, 2018

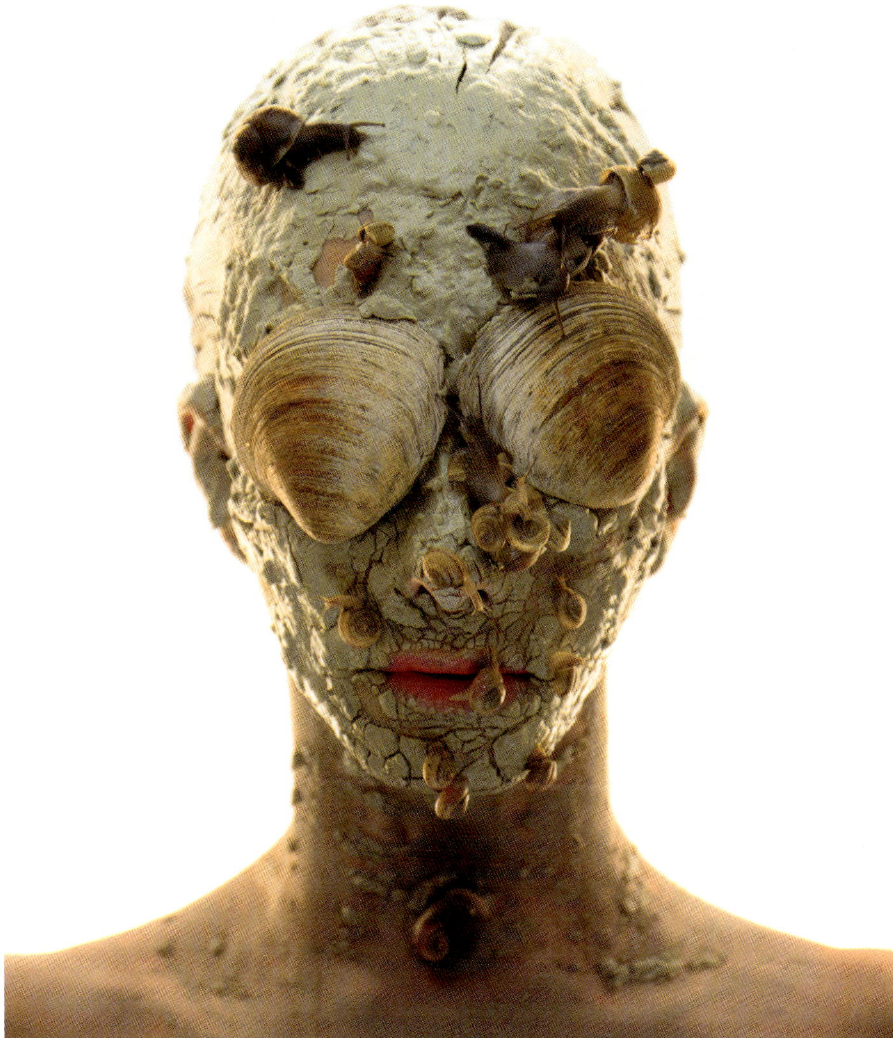

MARTINE GUTIERREZ

Masking, Green-Grape Mask,
p51 from Indigenous Woman, 2018

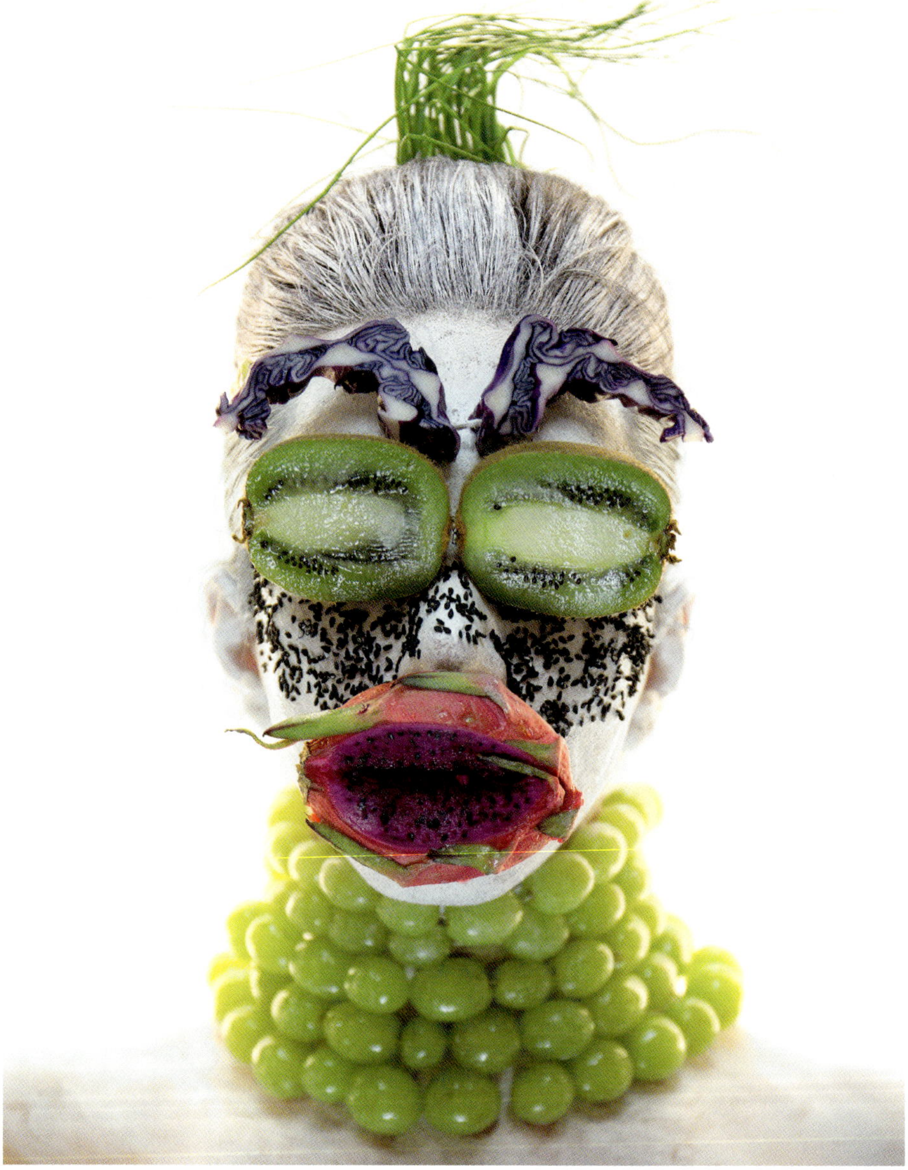

MARTINE GUTIERREZ

Masking, Fish Mask,
p48 from Indigenous Woman, 2018

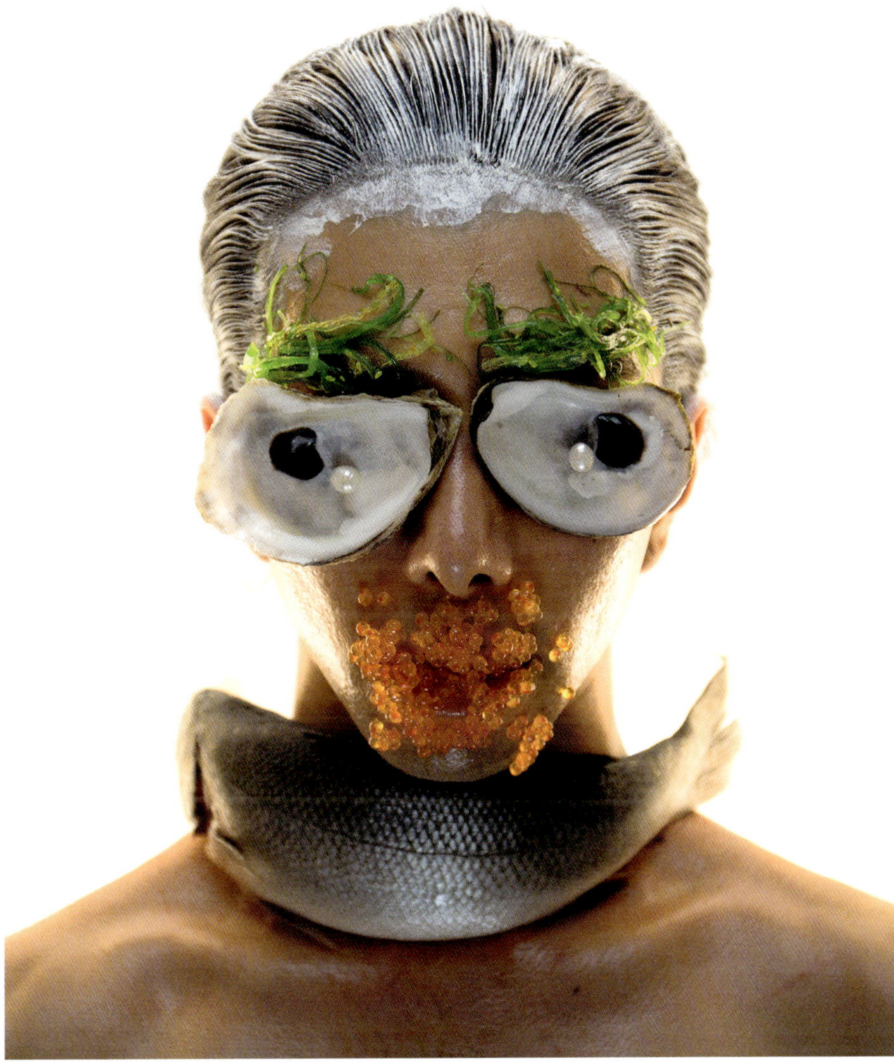

NICHOLAS HLOBO

138 – 41

PETER HUJAR

142 – 51

JULIANA HUXTABLE

152 – 55

JOAN JETT BLAKK

156 – 57

Nicholas Hlobo crafts his sculptures from found objects and materials that include leather, ribbons and rubber from discarded inner tyres. Selecting his materials for the associations they carry, as well as their formal properties, he purposefully brings together what he has described as 'the sex and industrialisation' of rubber with the 'femininity and labour' of his intricately stitched, brightly coloured ribbons. Hlobo's wall-based works and sculptures are at once personal and political. Concerned with the history of South Africa, as well as the way that colonialism continues to inform contemporary life, they also draw on and explore his own identity as a gay Xhosa man. By giving the works Xhosa titles, a language that the artist describes as rich in poetry and metaphor, Hlobo deliberately side-steps English, the language of public life in South Africa, and helps to 'chip away at its dominance, little by little'.

NICHOLAS HLOBO

Jong' emva rhamncwa ndini, 2017

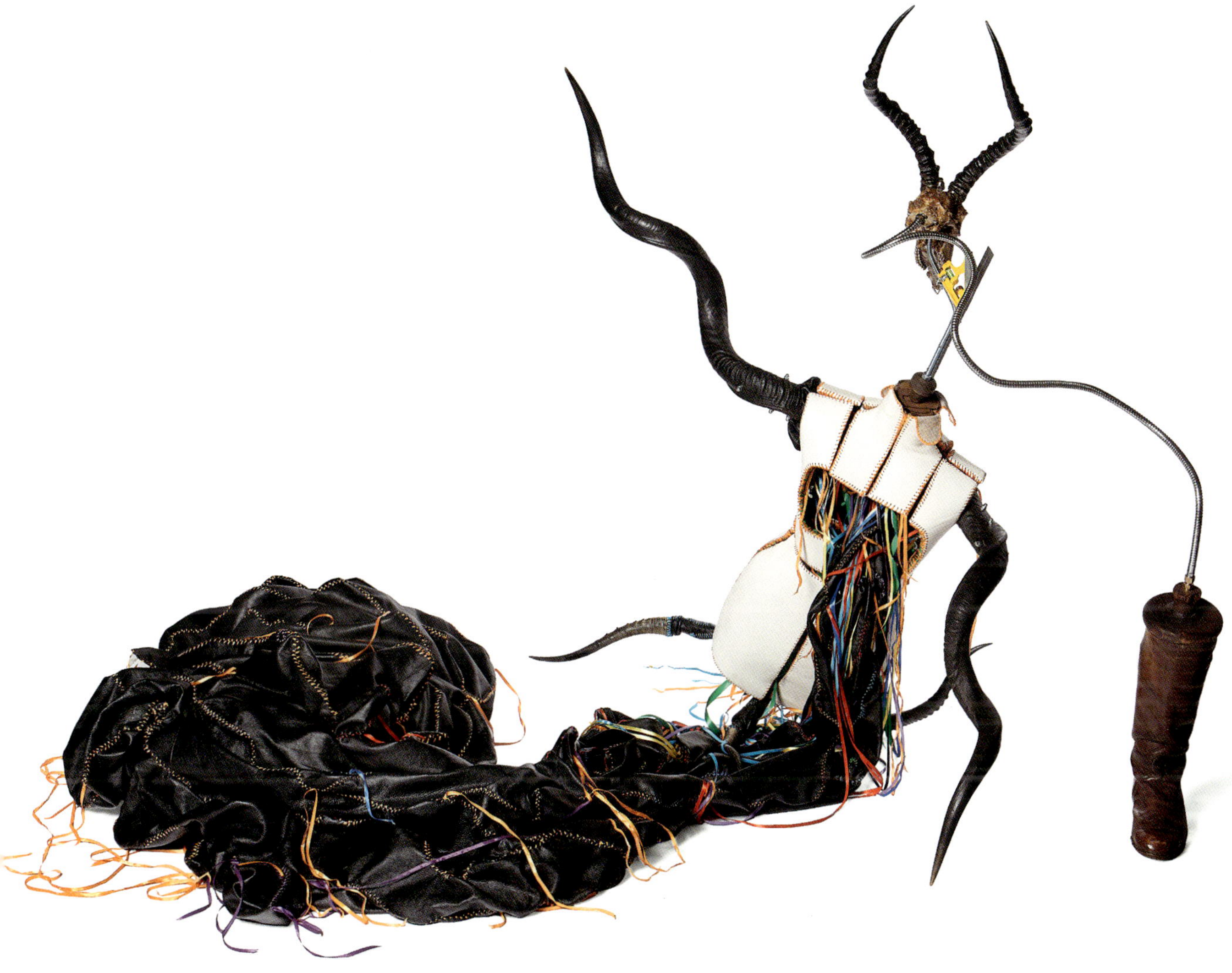

NICHOLAS HLOBO

Babelana Ngentloko, 2017

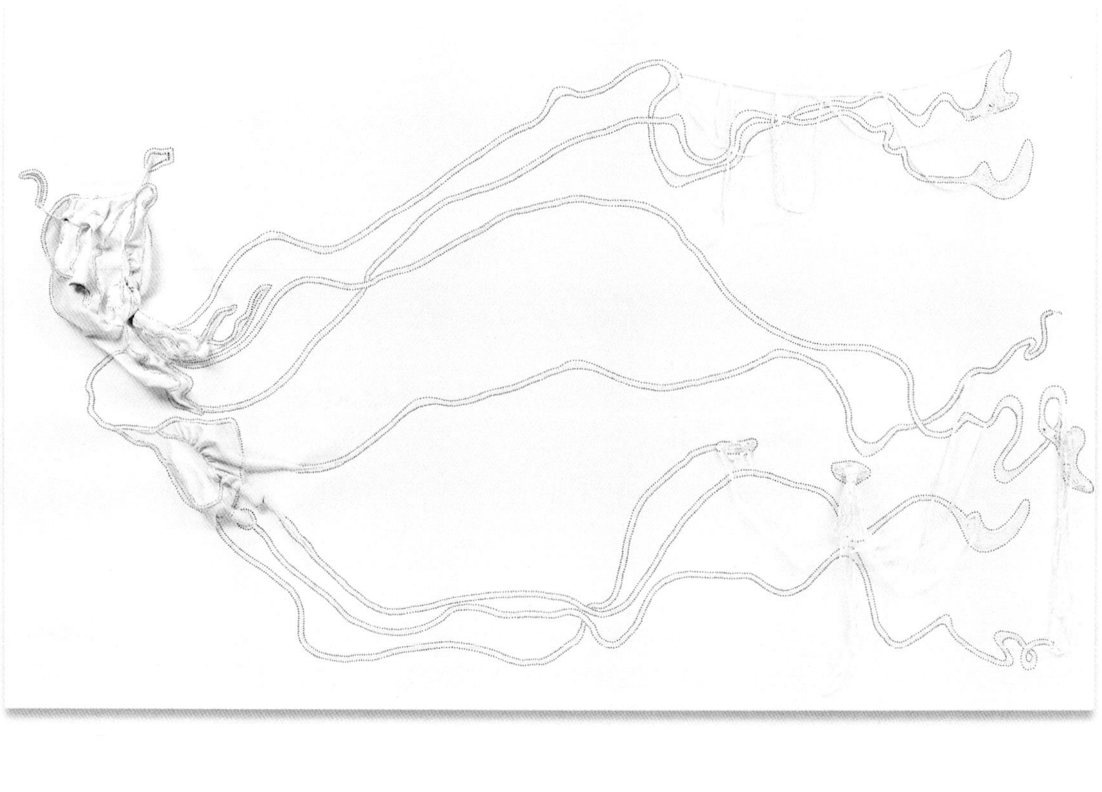

NICHOLAS HLOBO

Unduluko, 2017

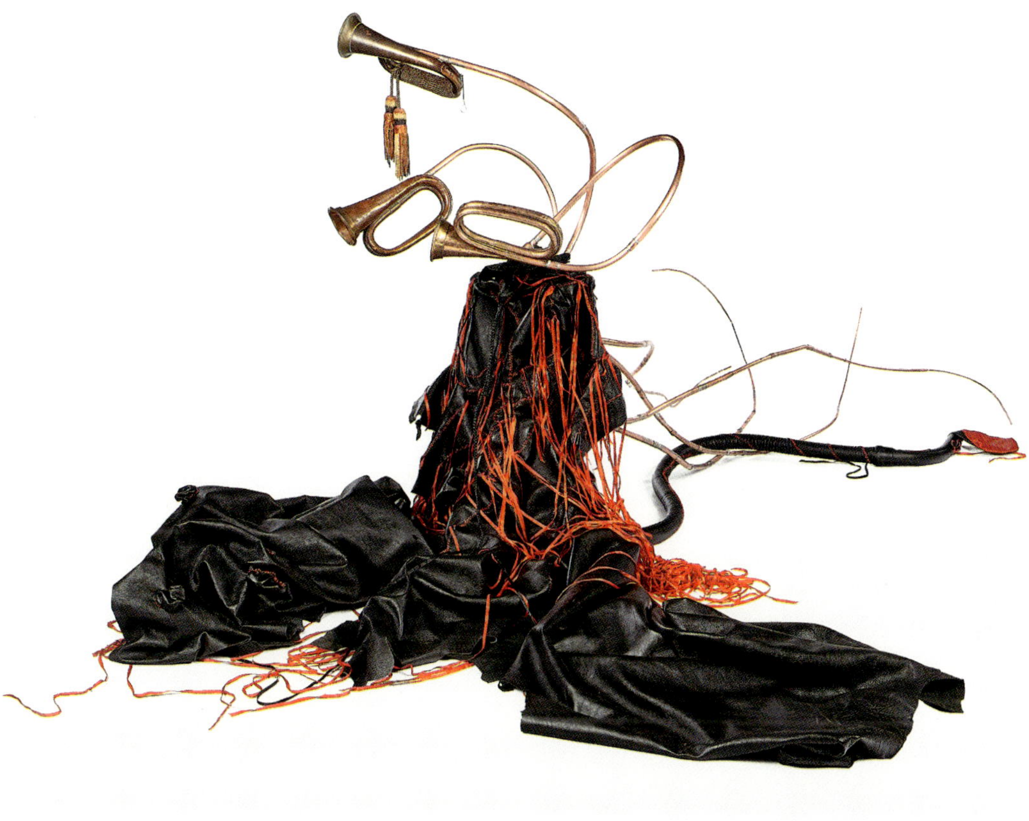

PETER HUJAR

Hudson River (IV), 1975

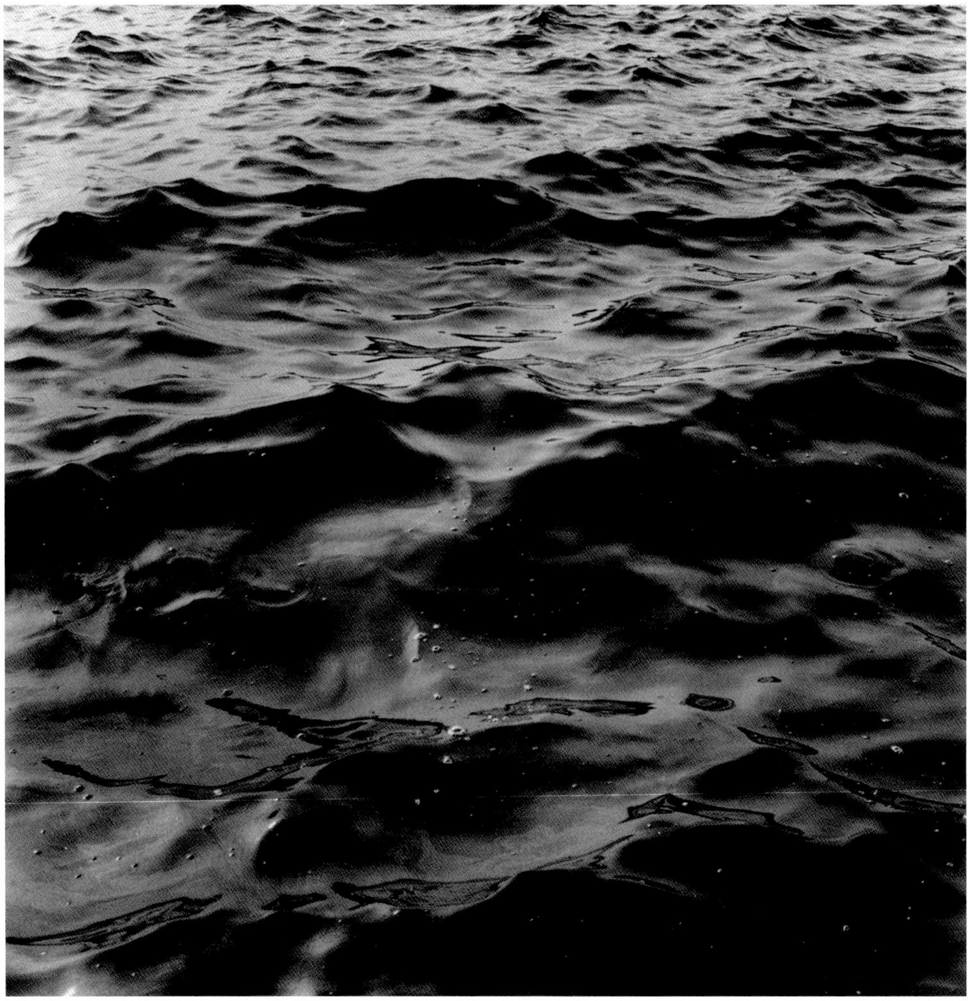

PETER HUJAR

Greer Lankton's Legs, 1983

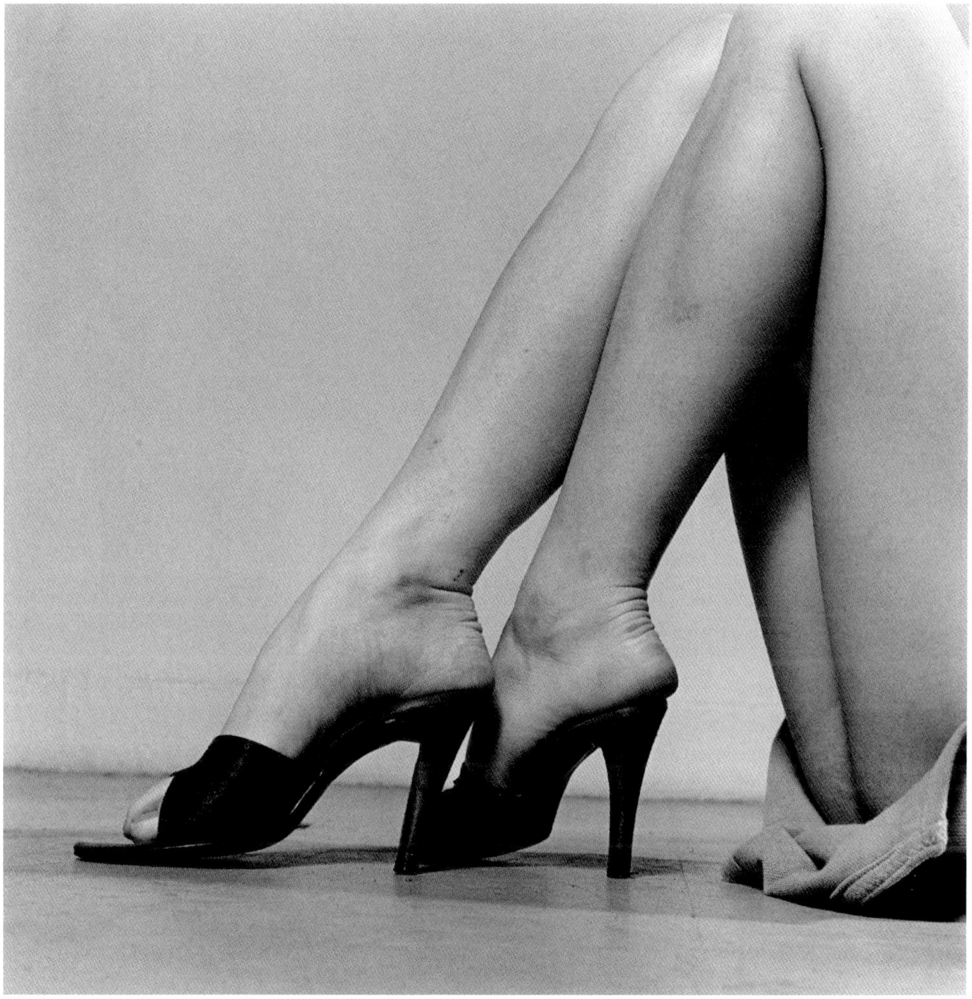

PETER HUJAR

John Heys in
Lana Turner's Gown (I), 1979

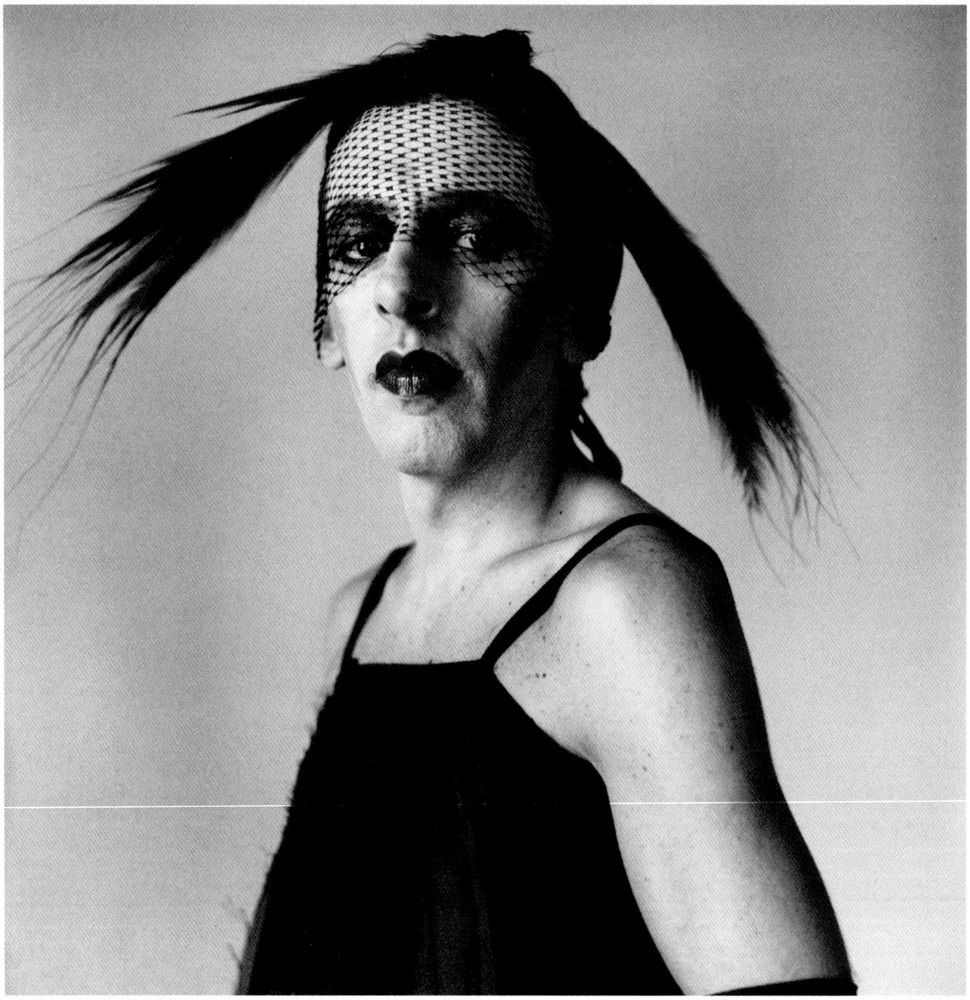

PETER HUJAR

John Heys in
Lana Turner's Gown (II), 1979

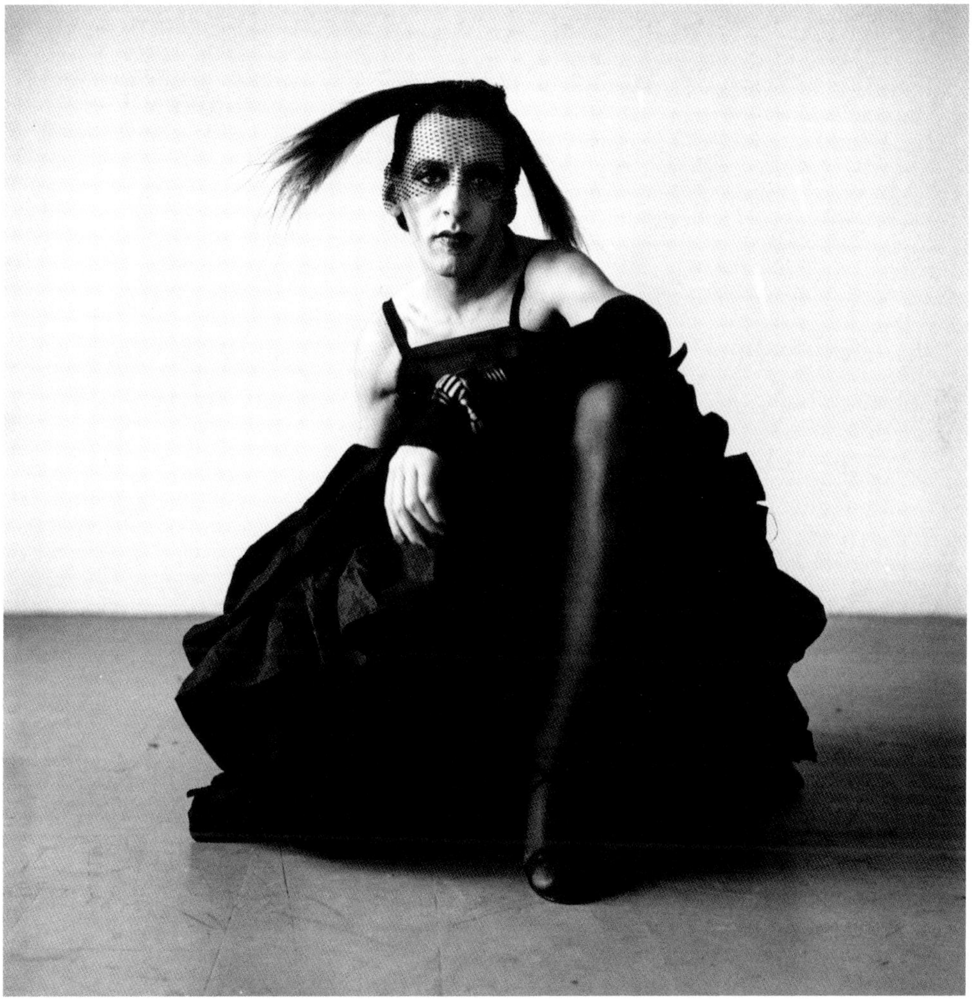

Peter Hujar was part of a group of artists, writers and performers who lived and worked in downtown New York during the 1970s and 1980s. Hujar's intimate black-and-white photography includes portraits of friends and acquaintances, among them drag performers Ethyl Eichelberger, Divine and The Cockettes. The artist also regularly photographed New York City – its streets and public spaces, the abandoned buildings along the Hudson River waterfront, and the river itself. One of his best-known photographs, *Candy Darling on Her Deathbed* (1973), is a portrait of the American transgender actress Candy Darling six months before she died of lymphoma. Speaking of his photographs, Hujar said 'My work comes out of my life', and of his sitters, 'I like people who dare'.

PETER HUJAR

Candy Darling
on Her Deathbed, 1973

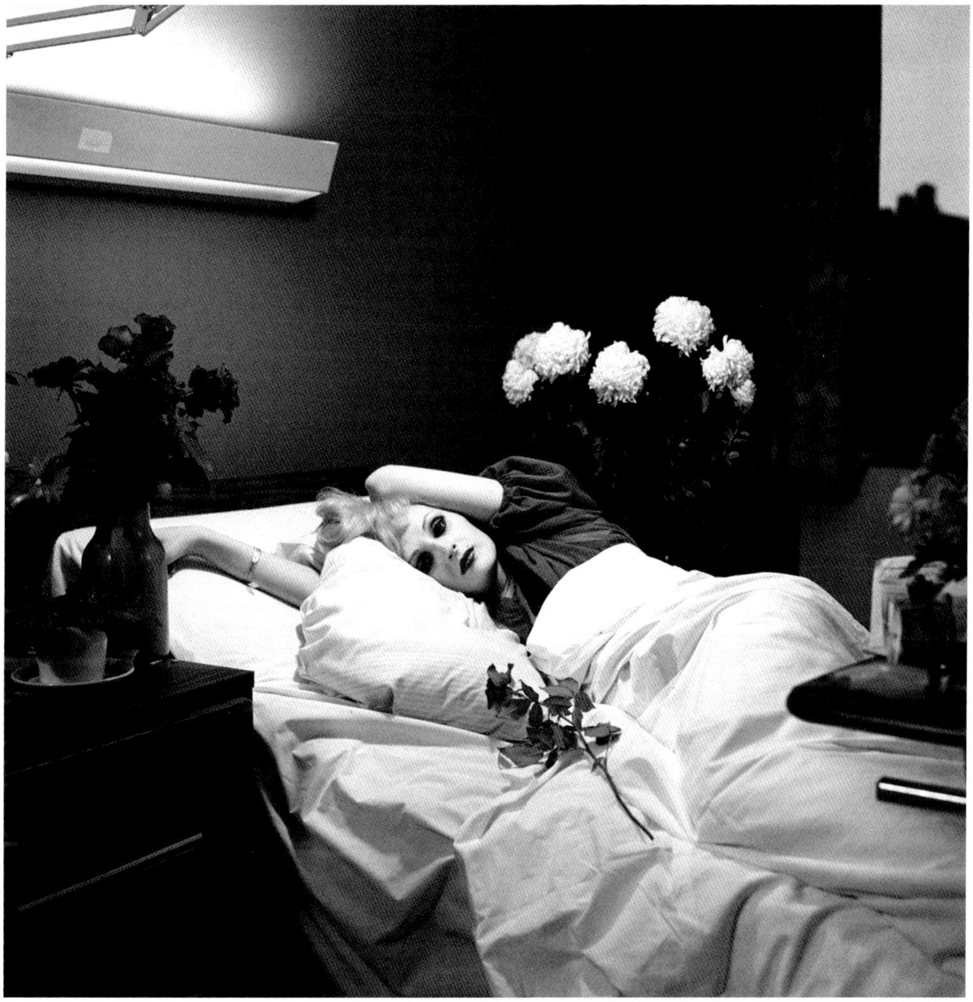

PETER HUJAR

John Heys with Orange Breasts, 1983

Two Cockettes (Reggie Dunnigan and Goldie Glitters), 1971

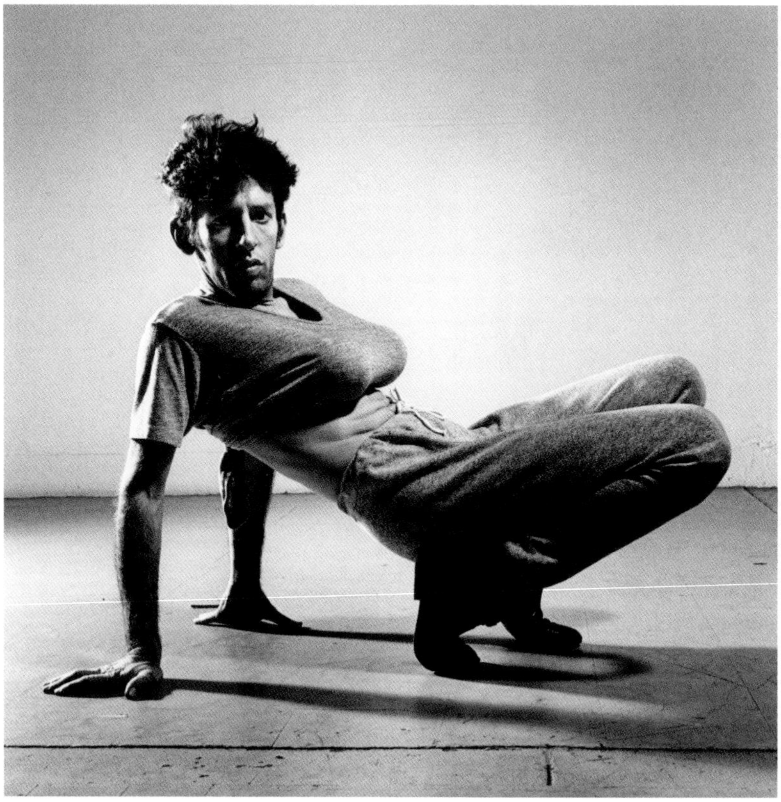

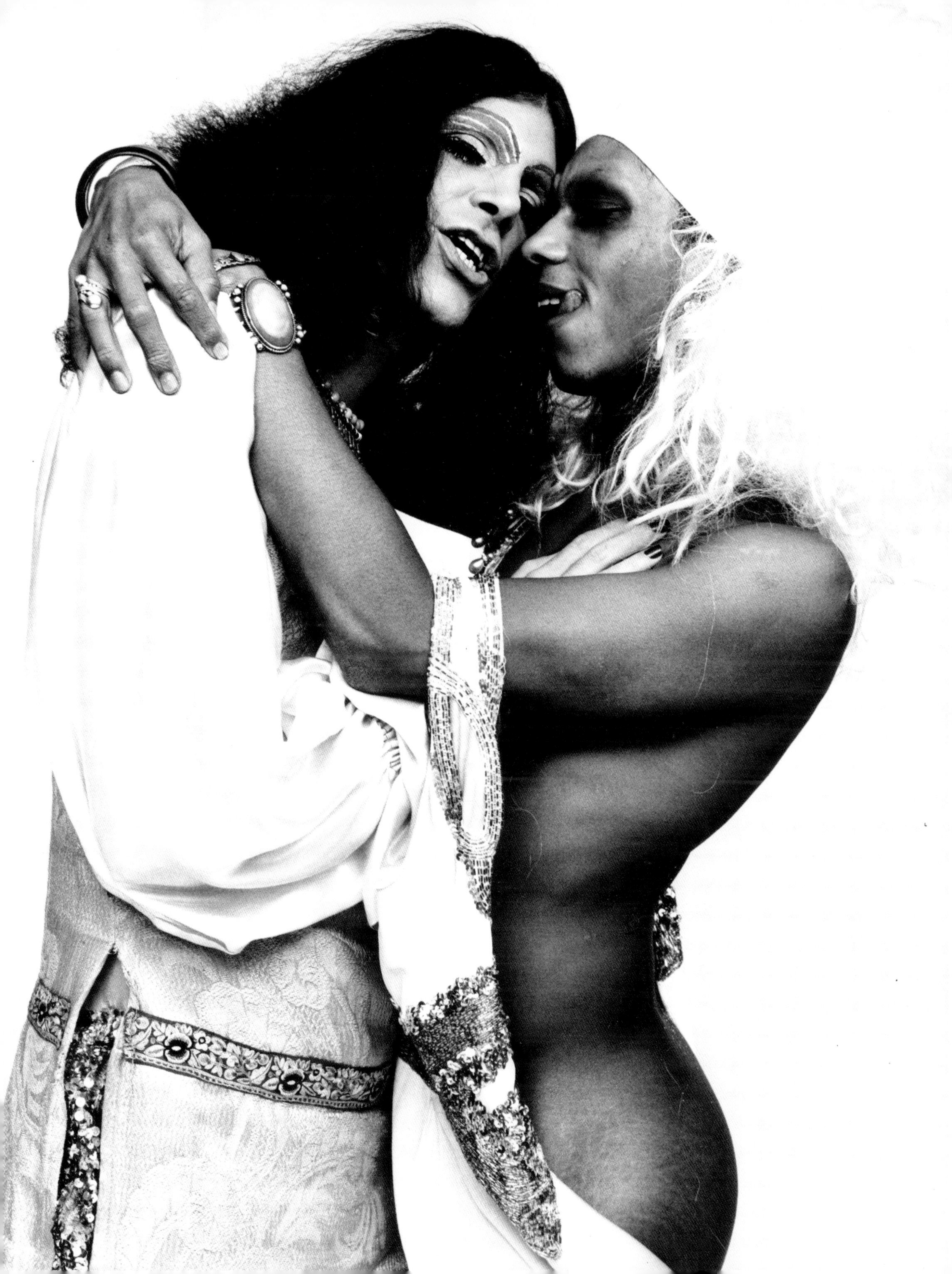

PETER HUJAR

Reclining Nude on Couch, 1978

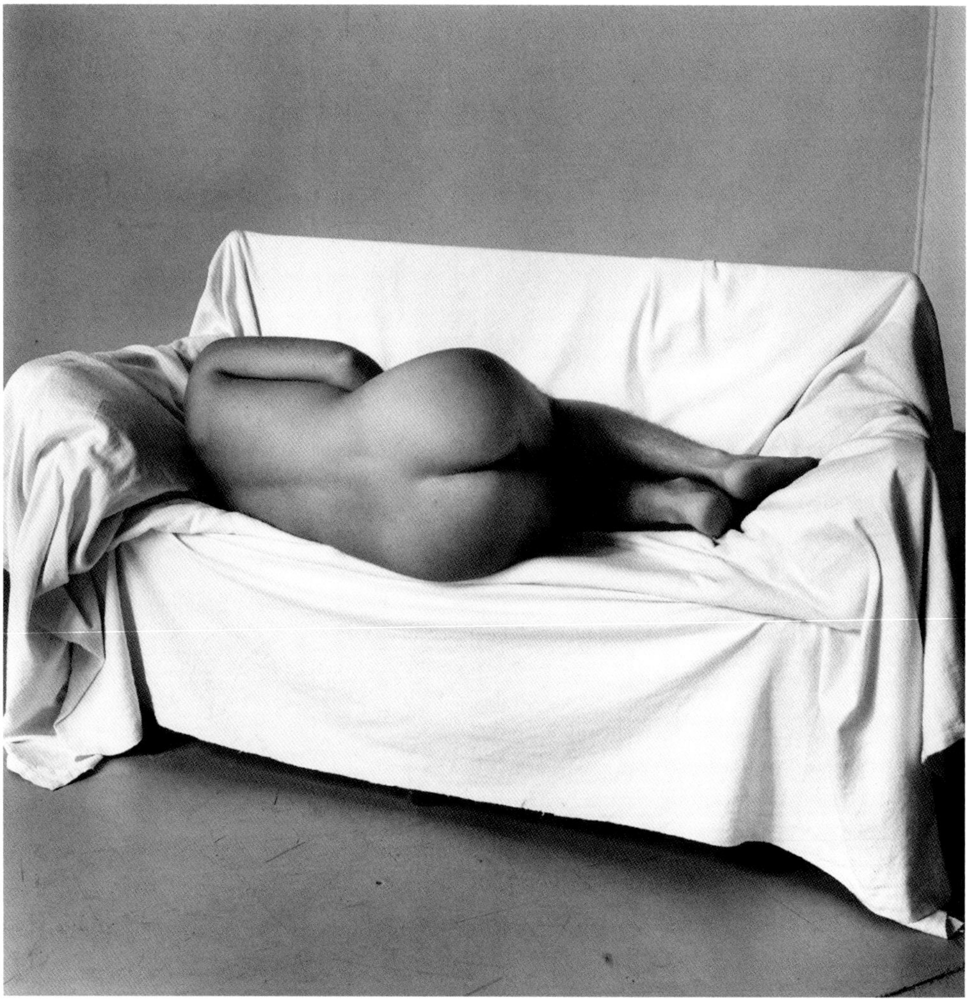

PETER HUJAR

Ethyl Eichelberger as Nefertiti (III), 1979

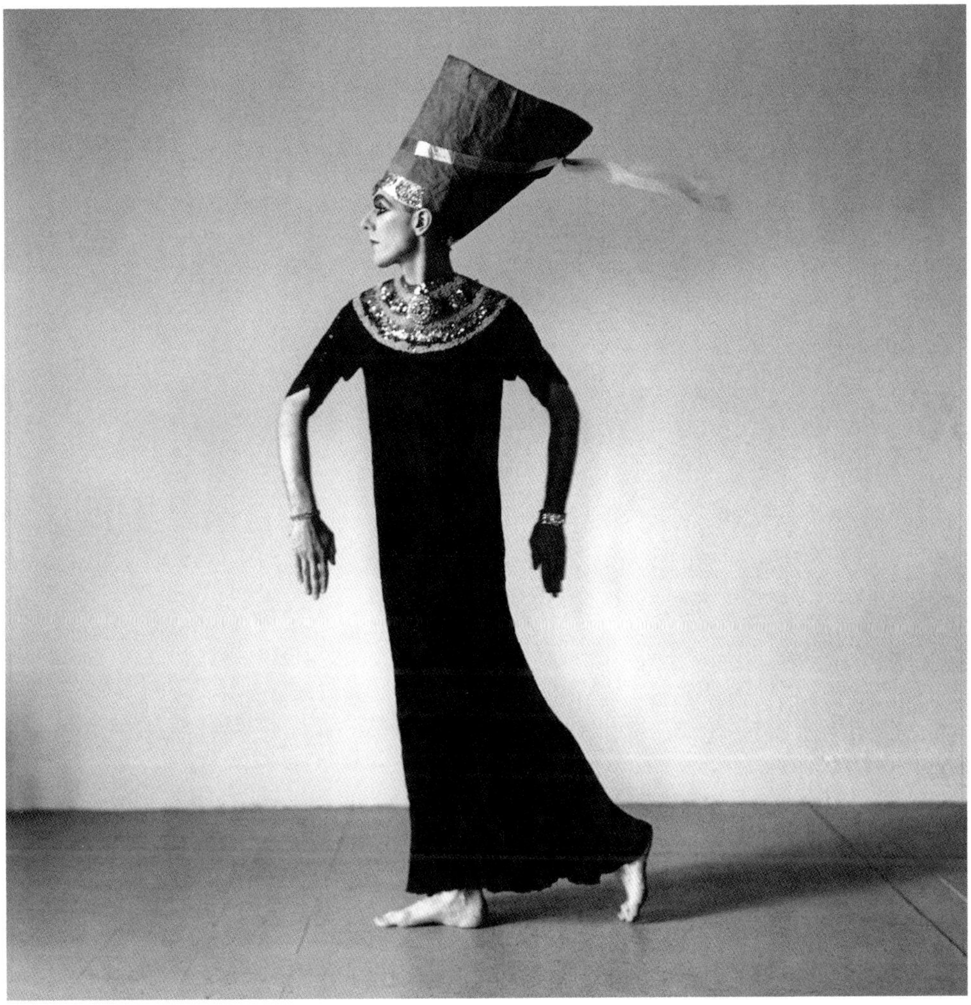

JULIANA HUXTABLE

Untitled in the Rage
(Nibiru Cataclysm), 2015

The title of this 'self-imagining' by Juliana Huxtable refers to a prediction, circulated online in the early 2000s, that Nibiru, a planet from ancient Sumerian mythology, was shortly to collide with Earth, introducing humans to its race of extraterrestrial inhabitants. Huxtable, who was born intersex and exploded into the public consciousness as a writer and image maker through the internet and social media, has described her awareness of being 'sort of... fantastical'. She is concerned with the way in which marginalised groups are, 'forced to be their own saints', a challenge of representation that she addresses through her self-fashioning images. Skin painted copper-green and hair lurid yellow, Huxtable places her own body at the centre of this mythologising scene, inscribing an iconic image of black trans identity into visual culture.

Overleaf

Untitled (Psychosocial Stuntin'), 2015

Untitled (Lil' Marvel), 2015

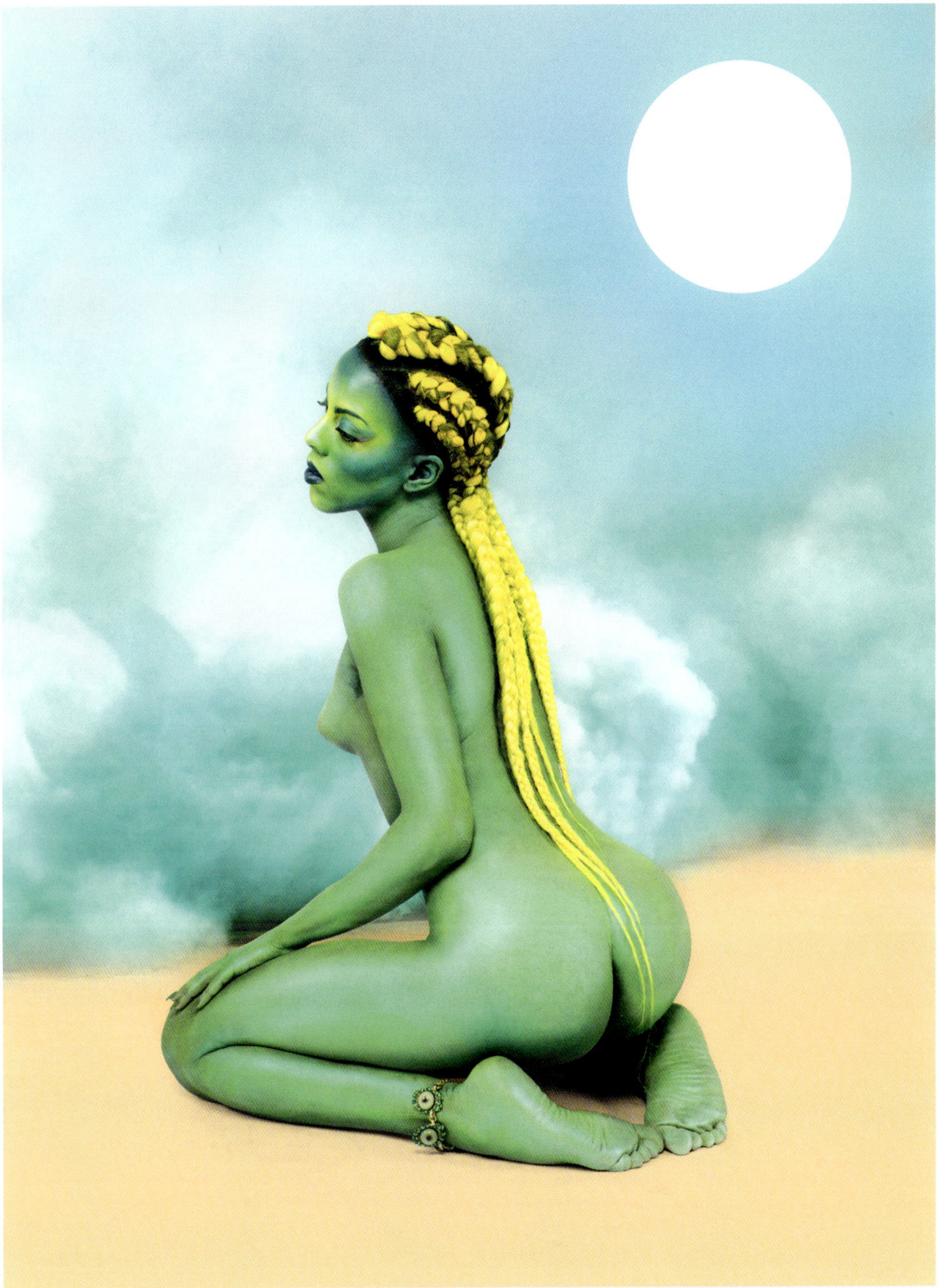

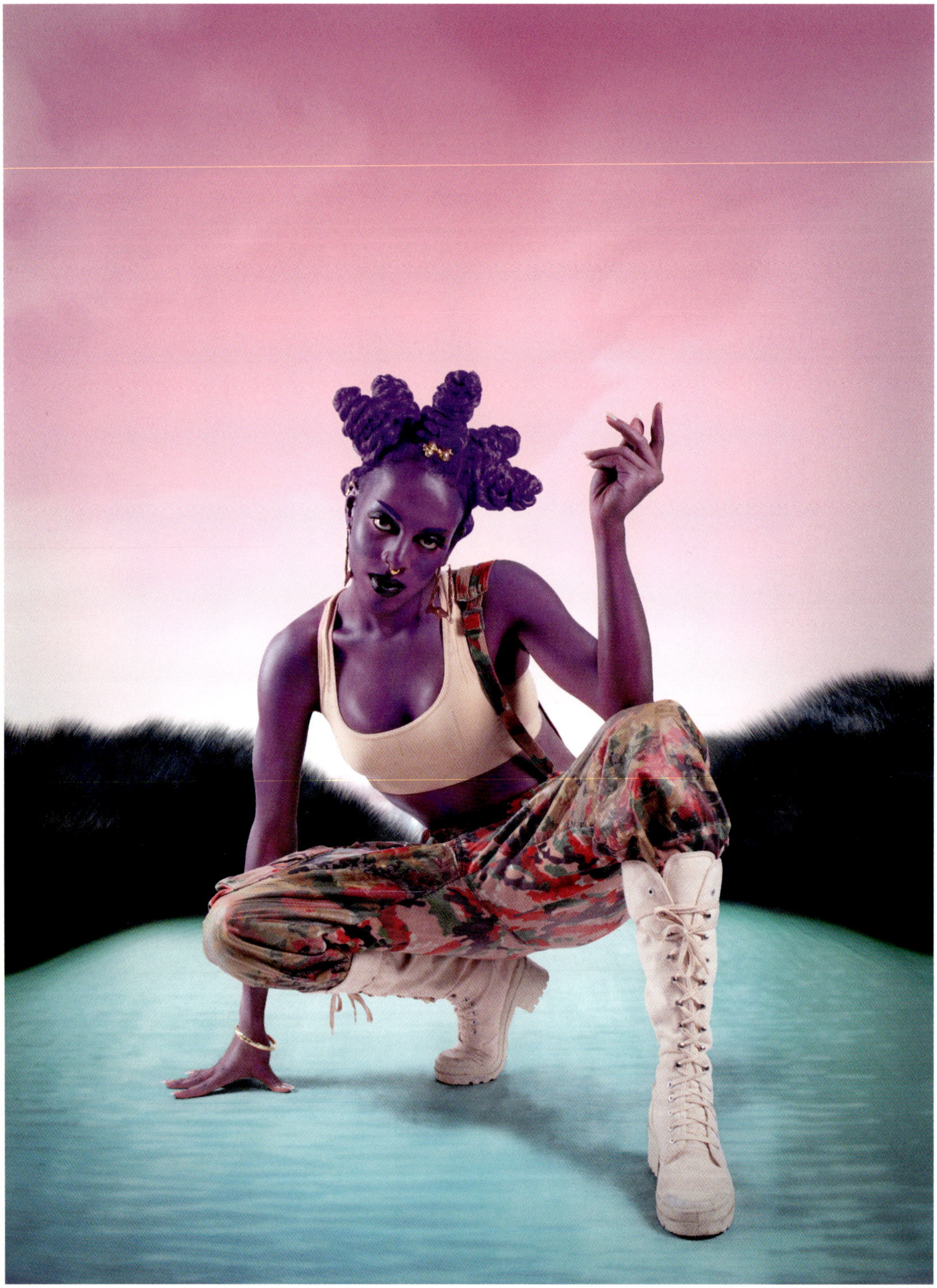

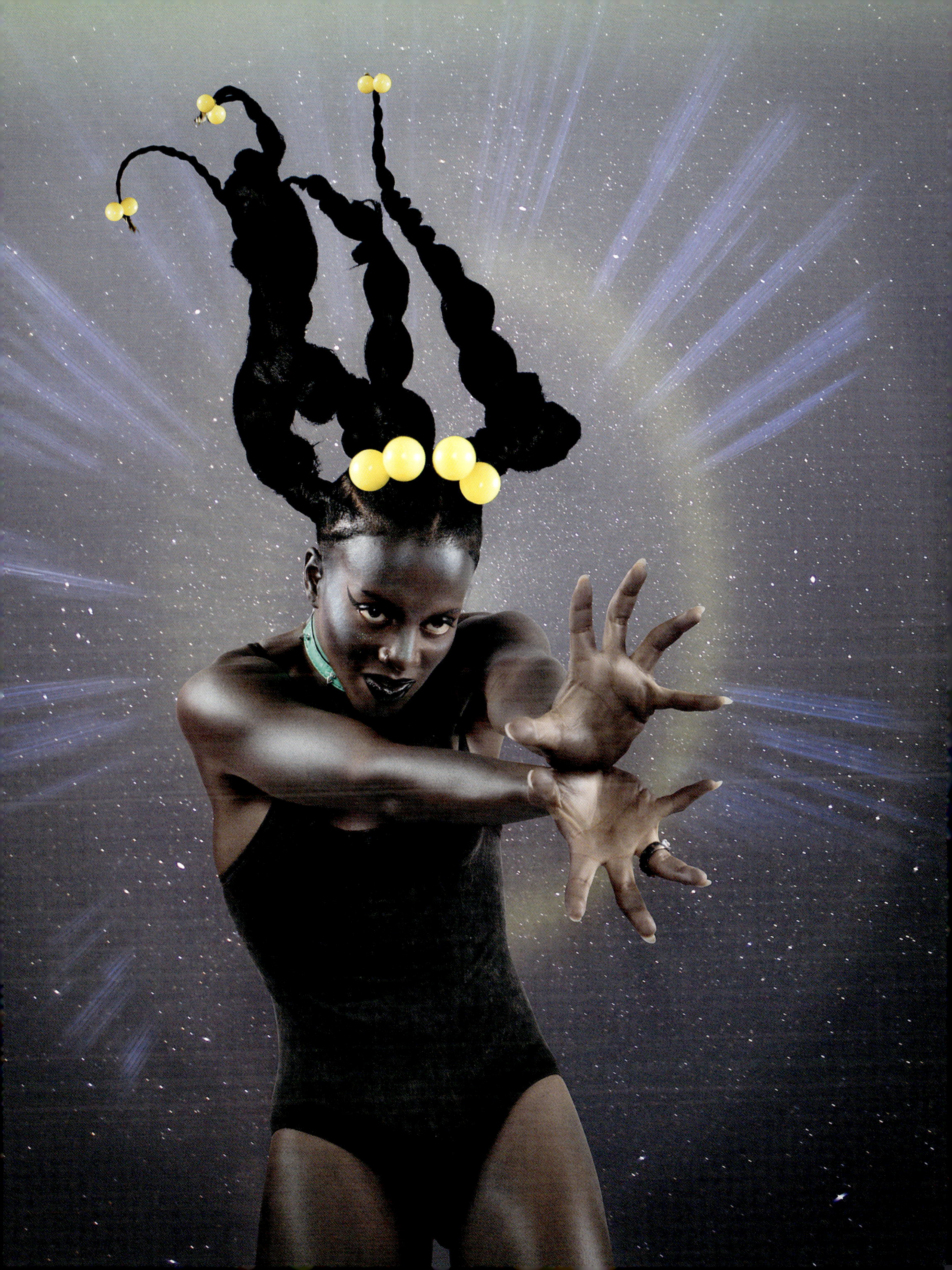

JOAN JETT BLAKK

Joan Jett Blakk for President, 1992

Joan Jett Blakk is the alter ego of drag performer Terence Smith. In 1992, Blakk – who describes herself as 'a combination of Divine, David Bowie in his early days and Grace Jones' – became the first drag queen to run for president. Running for the Queer Nation Party – an LGBTQ activist organisation founded in 1990 – under the slogan 'Lick Bush in '92', Blakk set out to 'make America beautiful again', while drawing attention to LGBTQ issues. This poster for Blakk's presidential campaign resembles an iconic photograph of Huey P. Newton, co-founder of the Black Panther Party, and makes use of a phrase that entered the civil rights movement in a speech delivered by Malcolm X, in 1965. Speaking at the time of her presidential campaign in 1992, Blakk said: 'We're taught from the time we're children that anyone can be president. We had a bad actor, why not a good drag queen?'

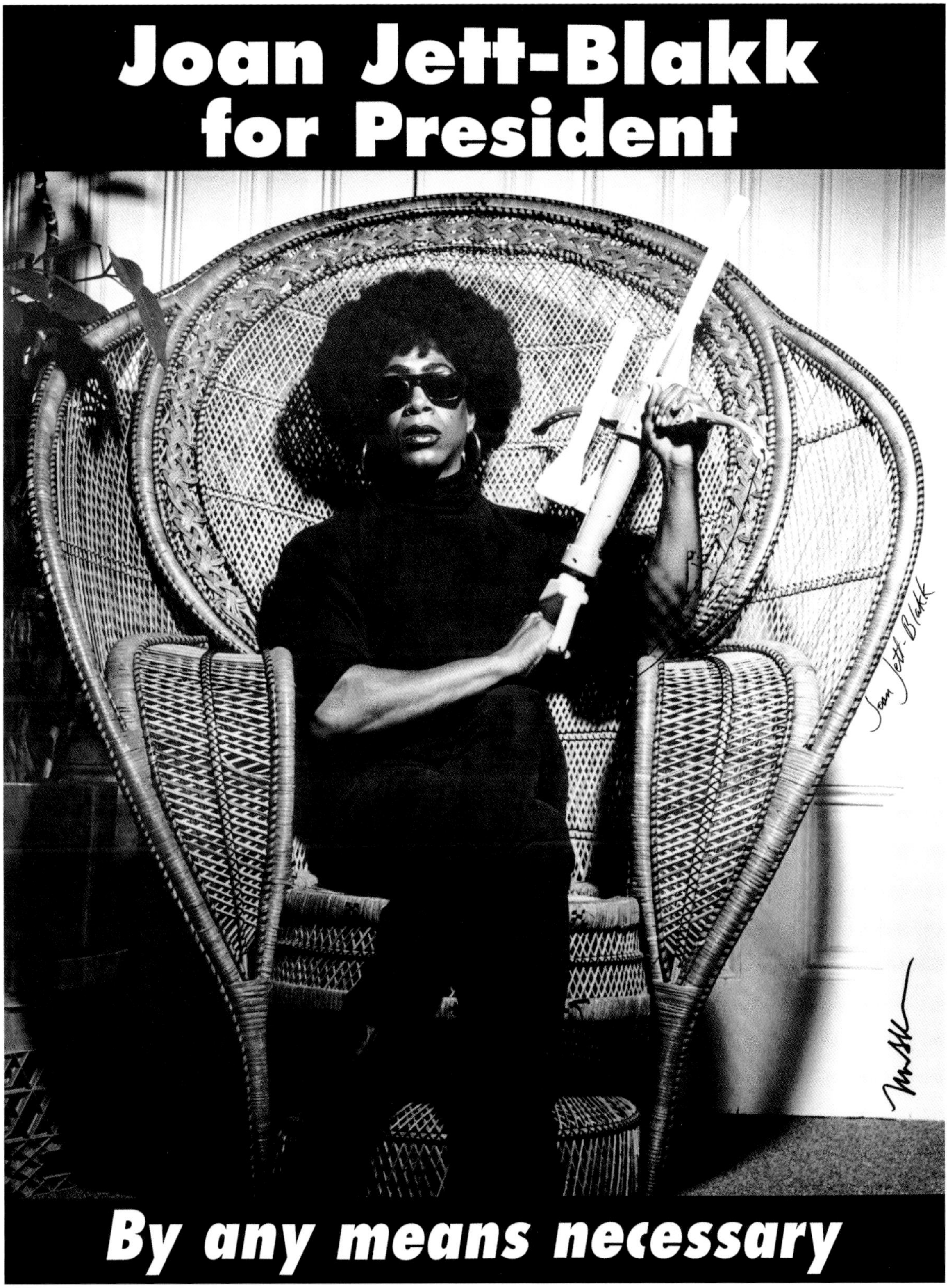
Joan Jett-Blakk
for President
Joan Jett-Blakk
By any means necessary

ZOE LEONARD

160 – 61

Ad Minoliti

162 – 63

Pierre Molinier

164 – 69

ZOE LEONARD

Pin-up #1 (Jennifer Miller does Marilyn Monroe), 1995/1997

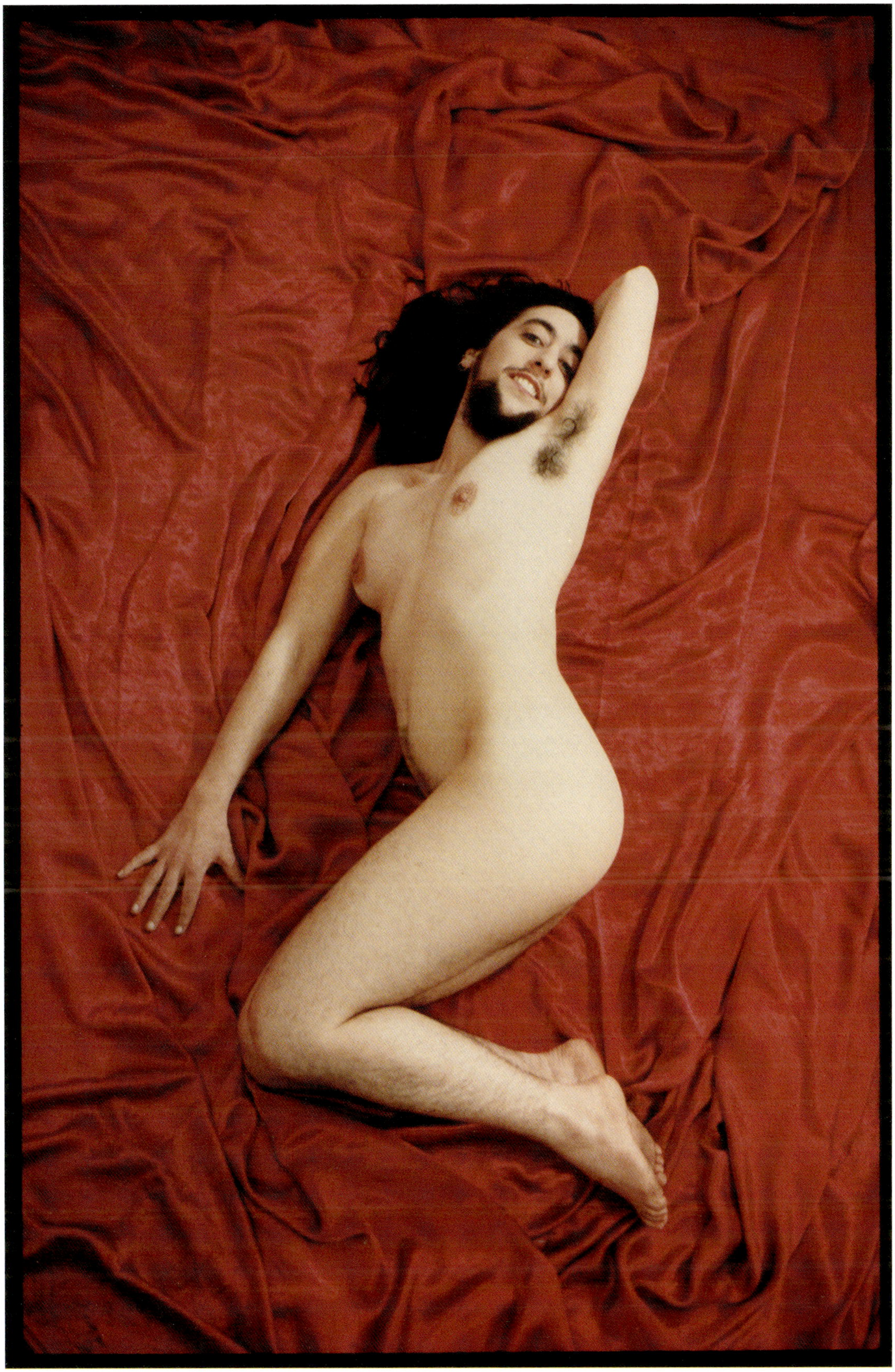

AD MINOLITI

The Feminist School of Painting, 2018

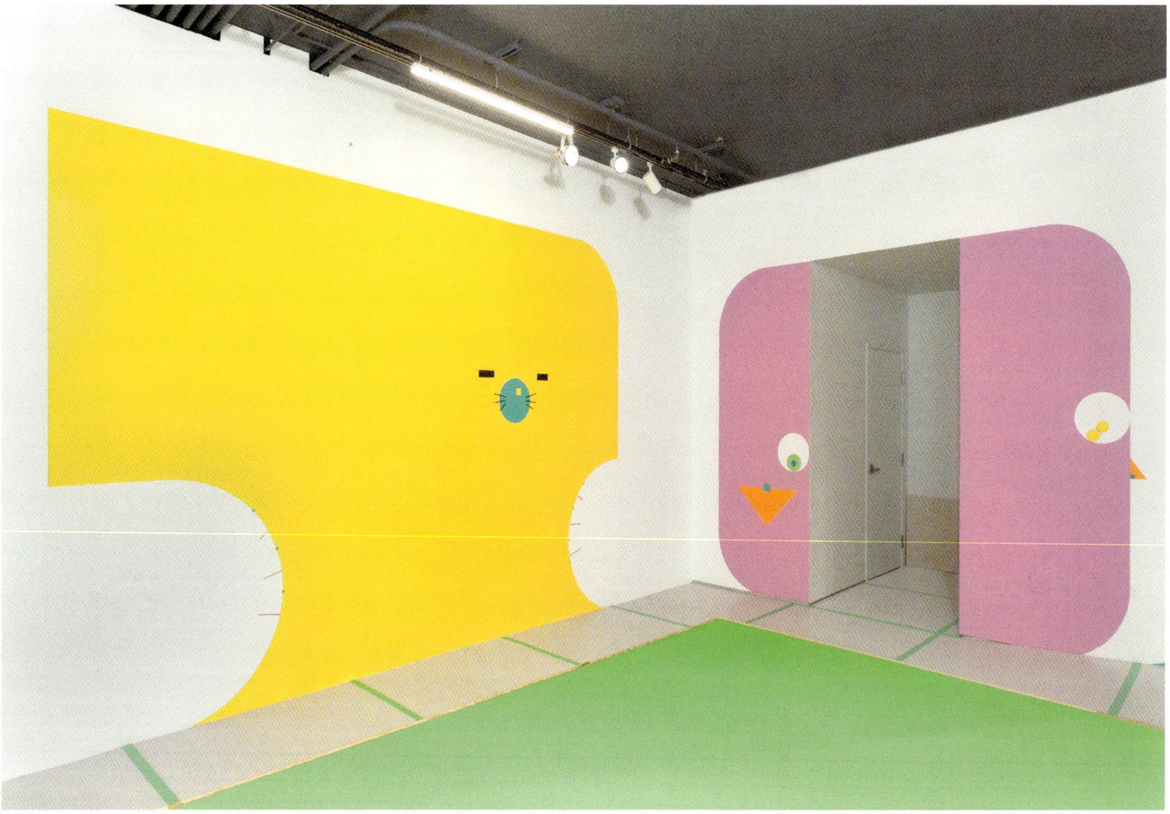

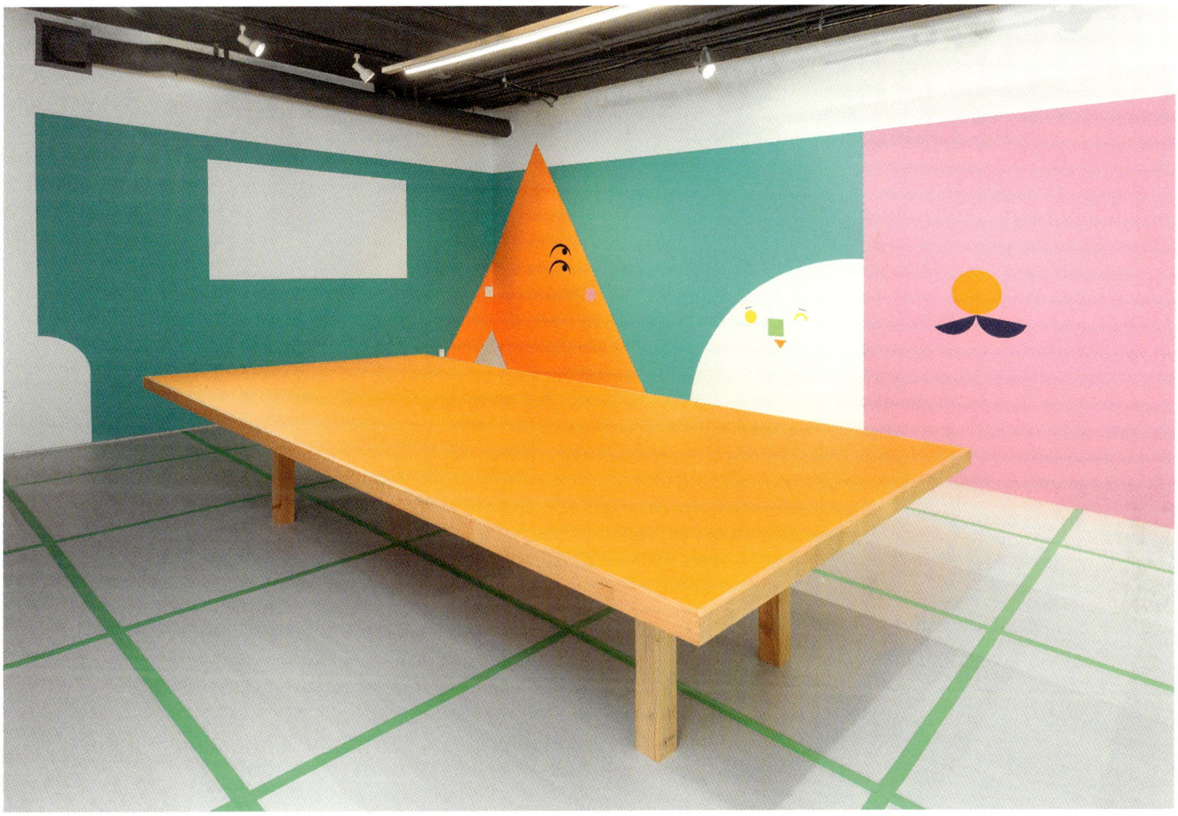

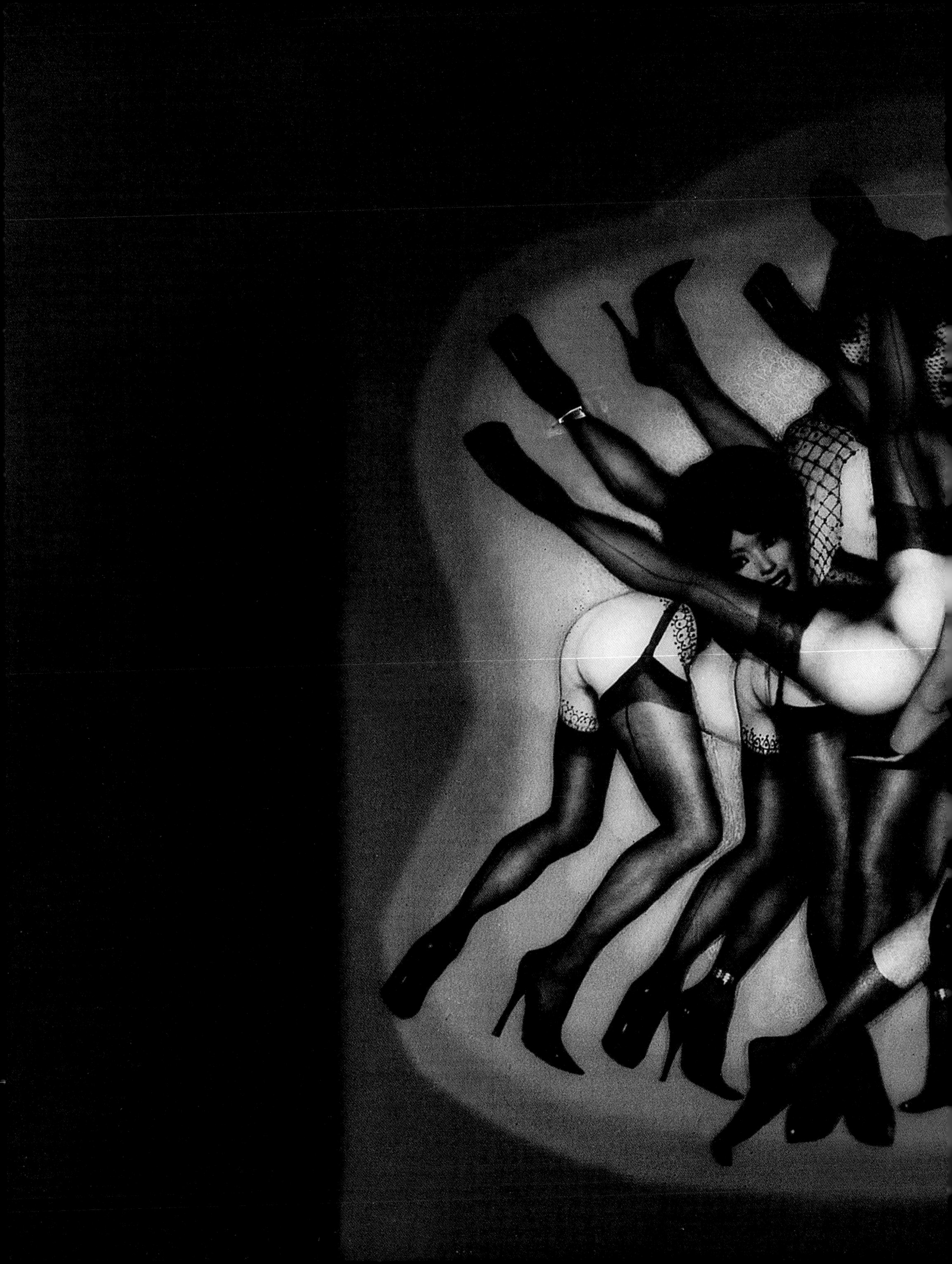

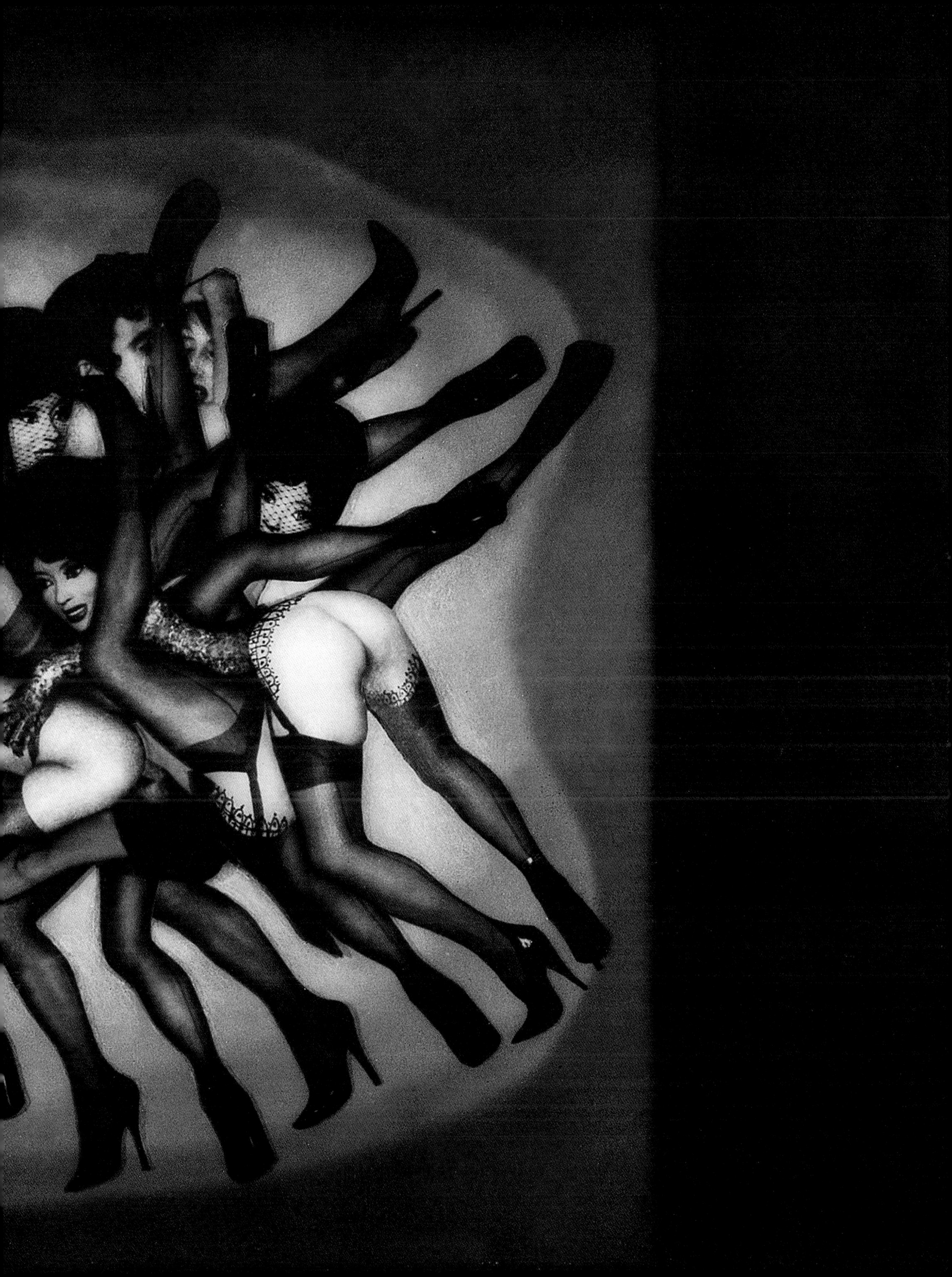

PIERRE MOLINIER

Luciano Castelli, 1974

Previous

Grande Mêlée - Photomontage, 1968

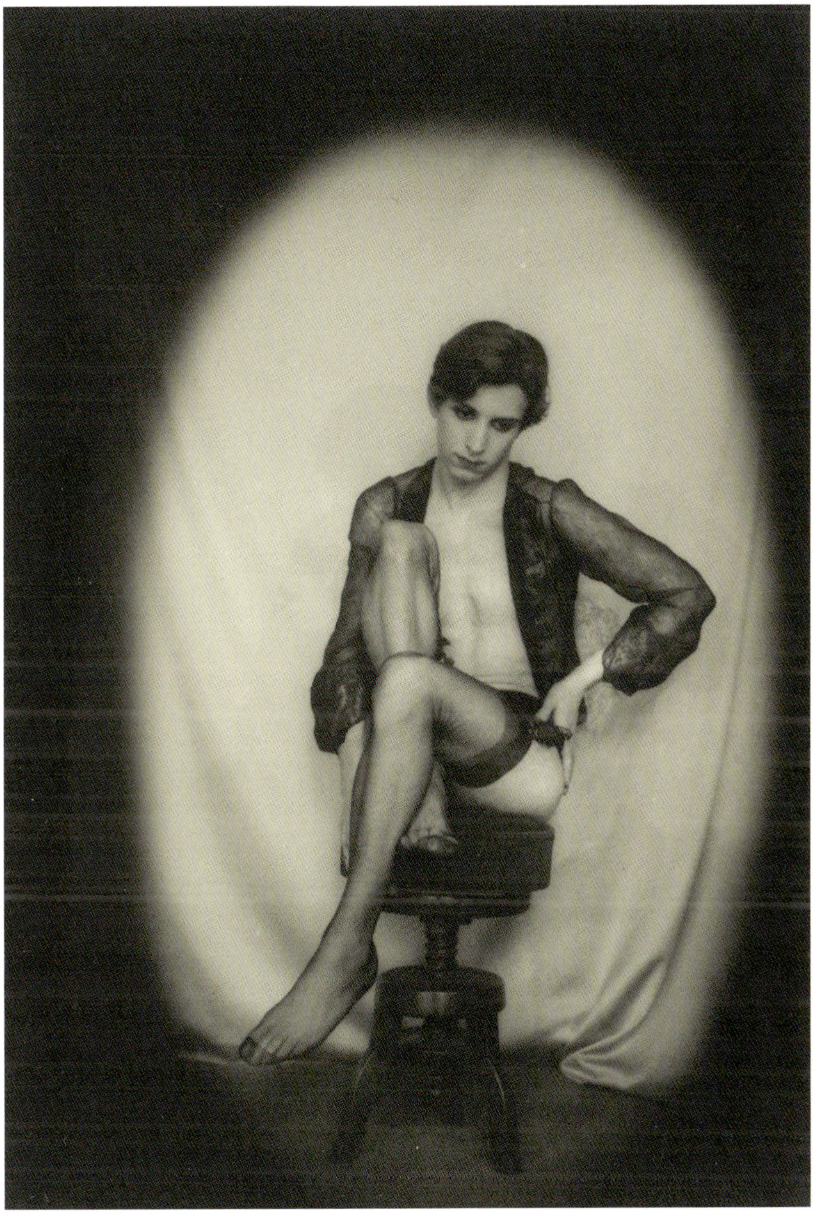

PIERRE MOLINIER

"Pantomine Céleste" (Photo-Montage pour "Le Chaman et ses créatures"), undated

Le Chaman, 1970

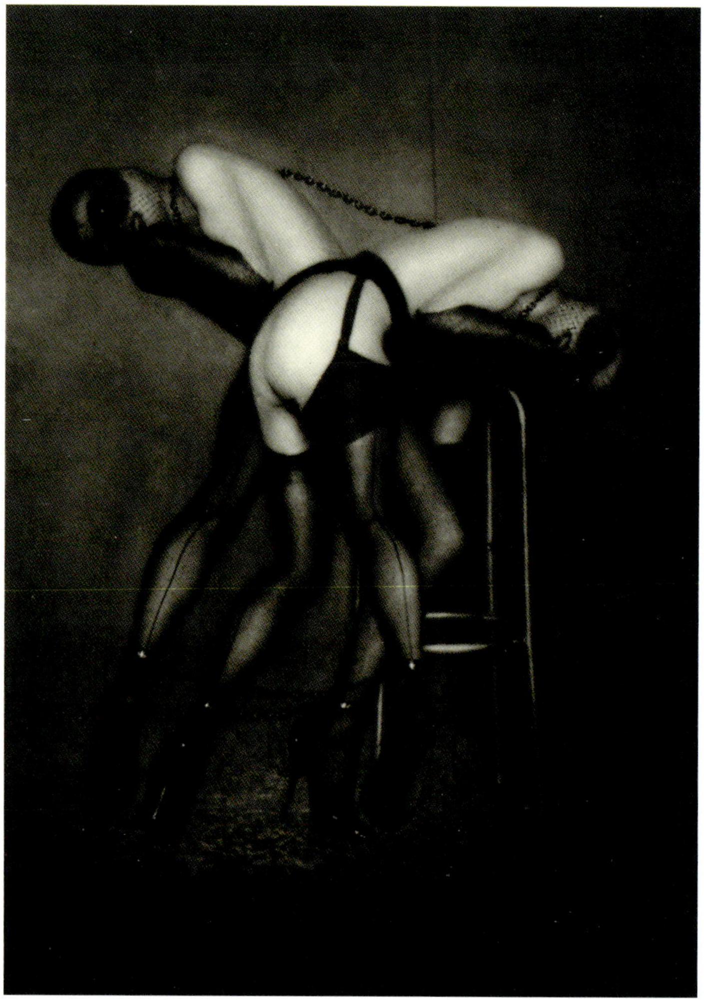

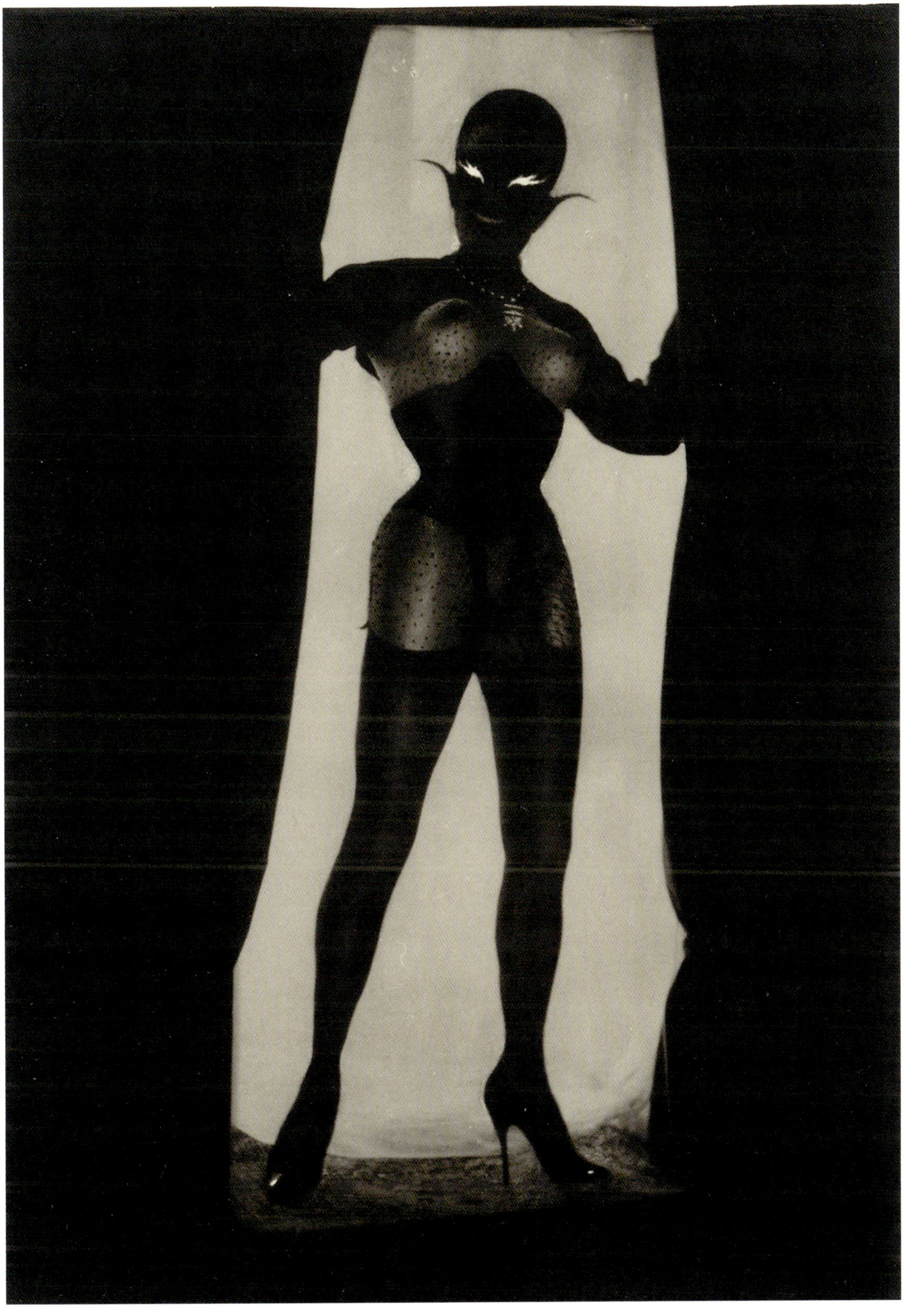

Kent Monkman

172 – 75

Zanele Muholi

176 – 81

Catherine Opie

182 – 89

KENT MONKMAN

Stag Hunting
(After Theodor de Bry), 2018

Kent Monkman reinvents European history painting as a means of upending conventional narratives around history, race and representation. Monkman splices his Cree and queer identities to create Miss Chief Eagle Testickle, an alter ego identifiable by her stilettos who embodies the 'two-spirit', or third gender accepted in many First Nation cultures of North America. This scene, based on a sixteenth-century Flemish engraving, depicts Miss Chief and others disguised beneath furs to stalk a group of unsuspecting stags. The image conjures multiple associations, referencing the trade in furs central to the historic Cree economy whilst also pointing to queer strategies of masquerade and performance used to upset stable notions of gender.

Overleaf

The Three Bachelors, 2018

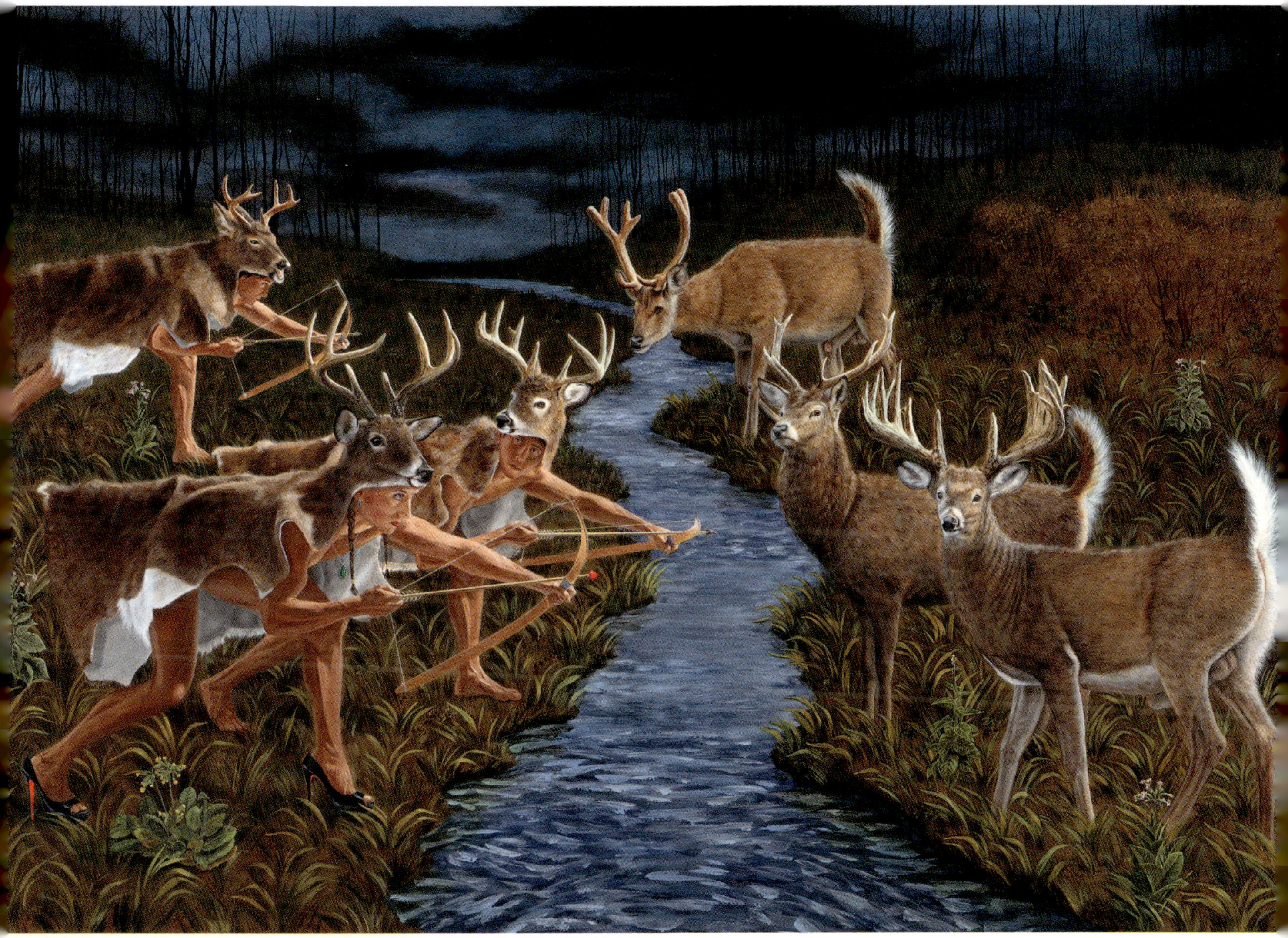

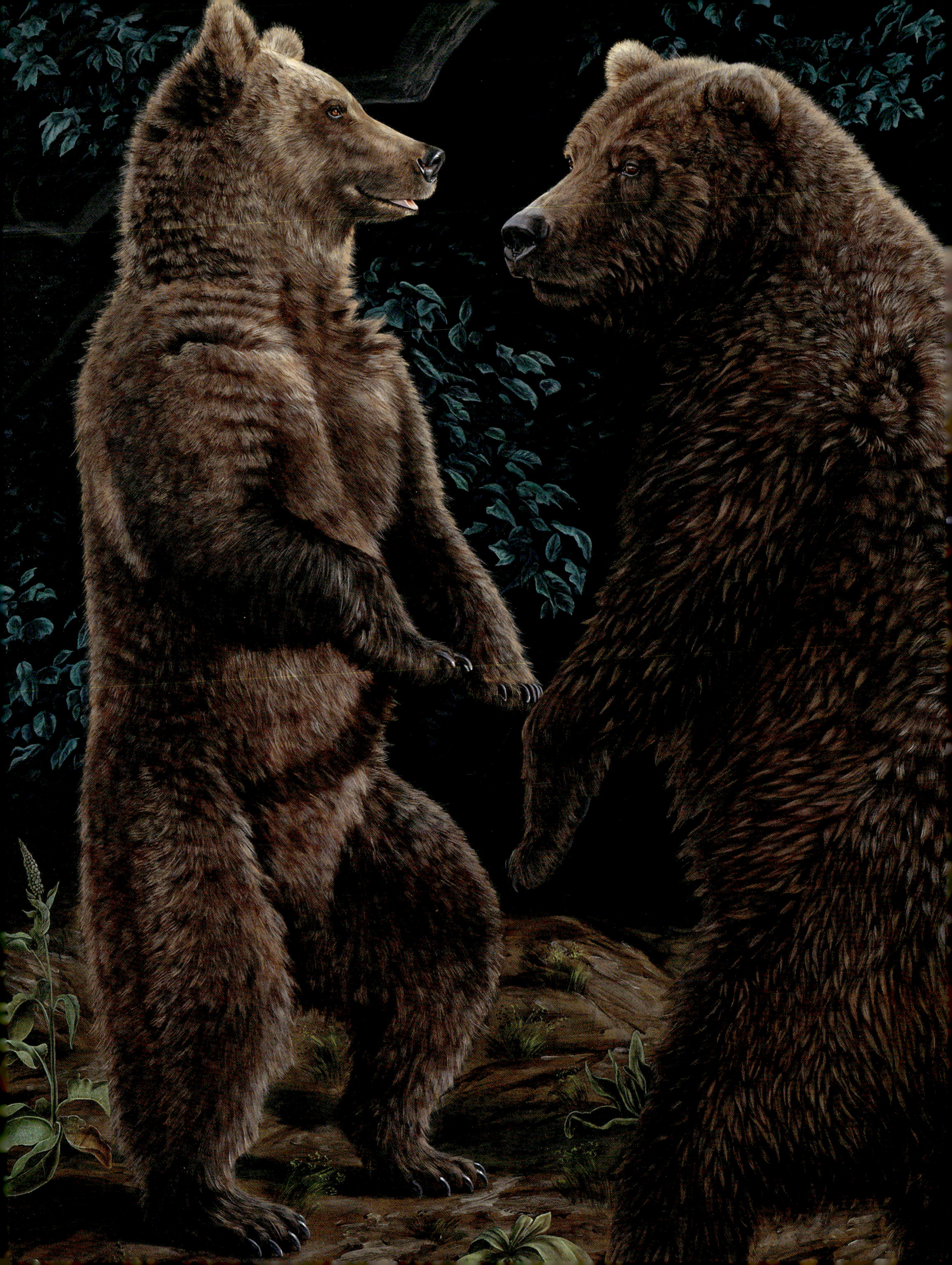

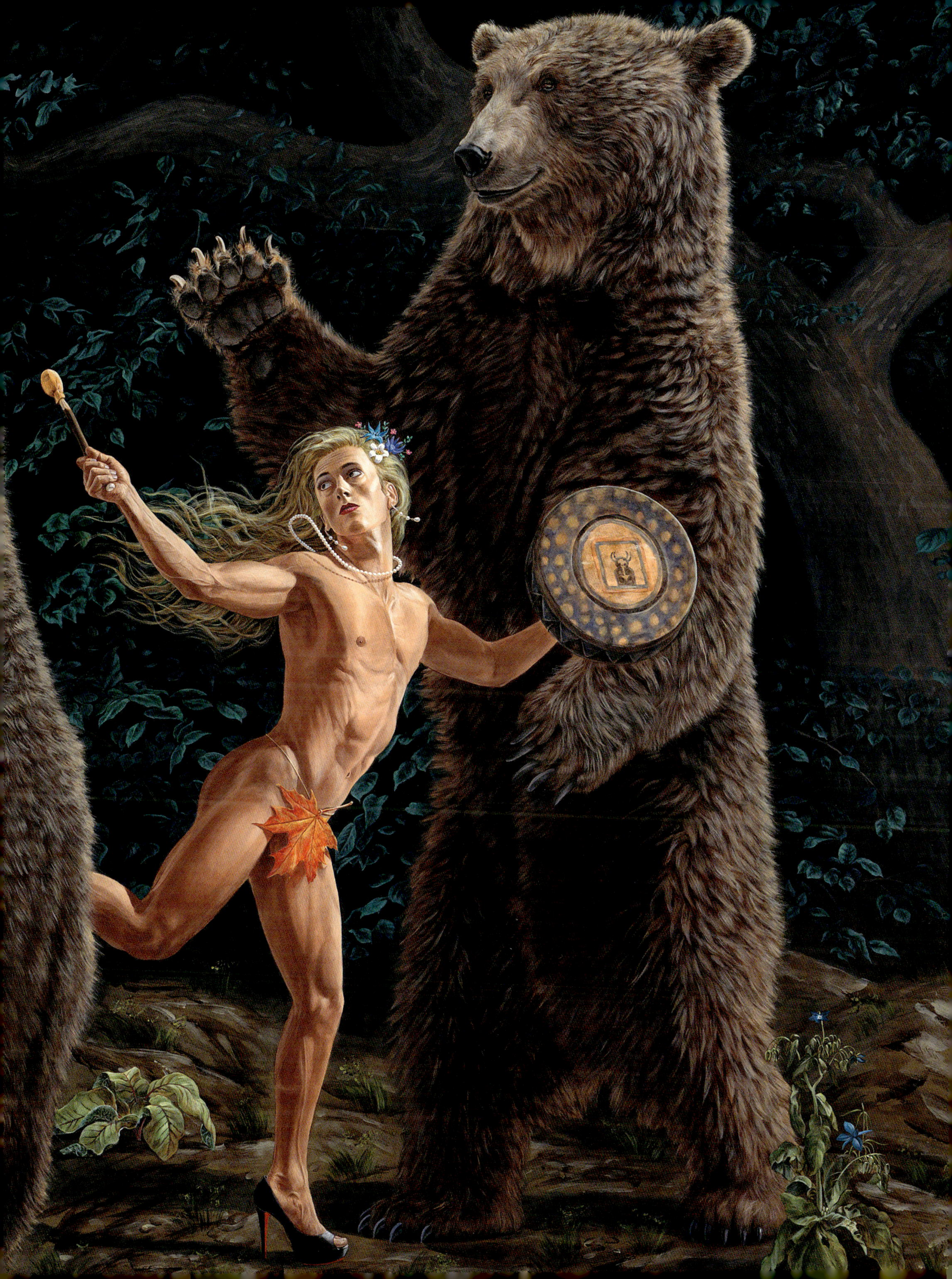

ZANELE MUHOLI

Phila I, Parktown, 2016
(*Somnyama Ngonyama: Hail the Dark Lioness* series)

For visual activist Zanele Muholi, photography is 'a space for people to be visible, respected and recognised.' In 2006, Muholi began documenting members of the black lesbian community in South Africa. A later series, *Crime Scene* (2012), draws attention to the brutal violence that is routinely inflicted on the same community. In *Somnyama Ngonyama: Hail the Dark Lioness* (2012–present), the artist turns the camera on themself. This ongoing series of self-portraits sees the artist use everyday, domestic materials – including rubber gloves, clothes pegs and scouring pads – to craft elaborate costumes or backdrops that hold deep psychological importance. Muholi has deliberately altered the contrast of these black-and-white images in order to enhance the dark tones. Speaking of this series, Muholi has said: 'I'm reclaiming my blackness, which I feel is continuously performed by the privileged other'.

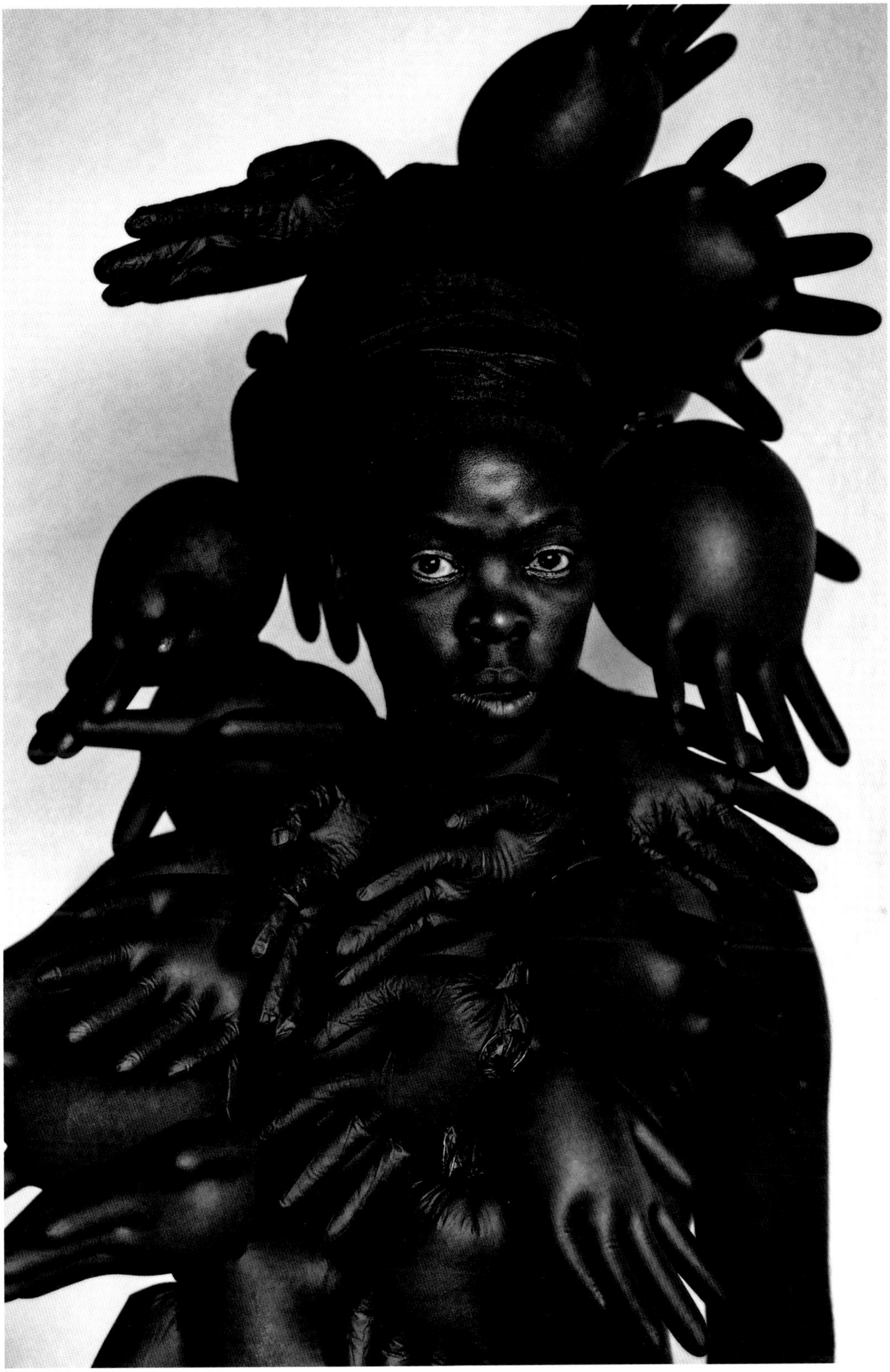

ZANELE MUHOLI

Untitled, 2006

Isiko I, 2006

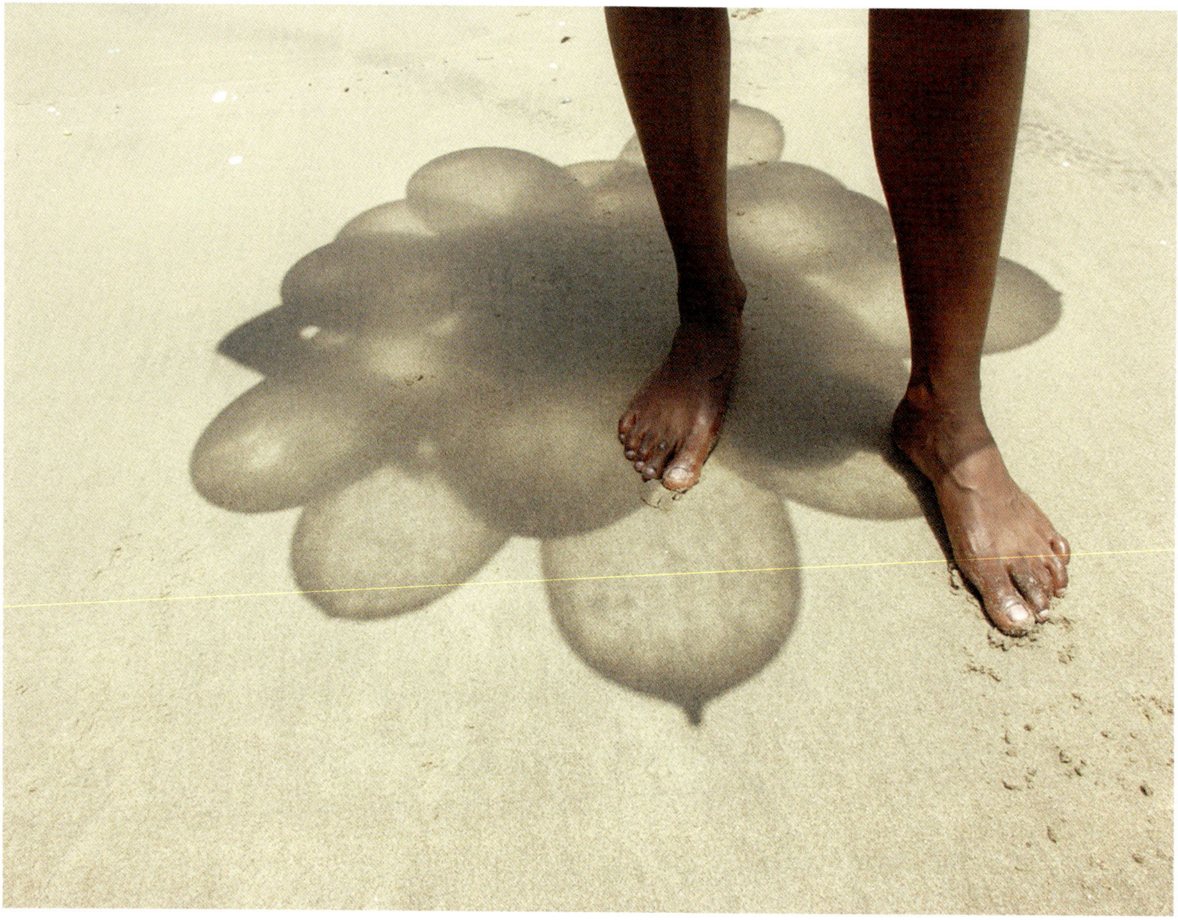

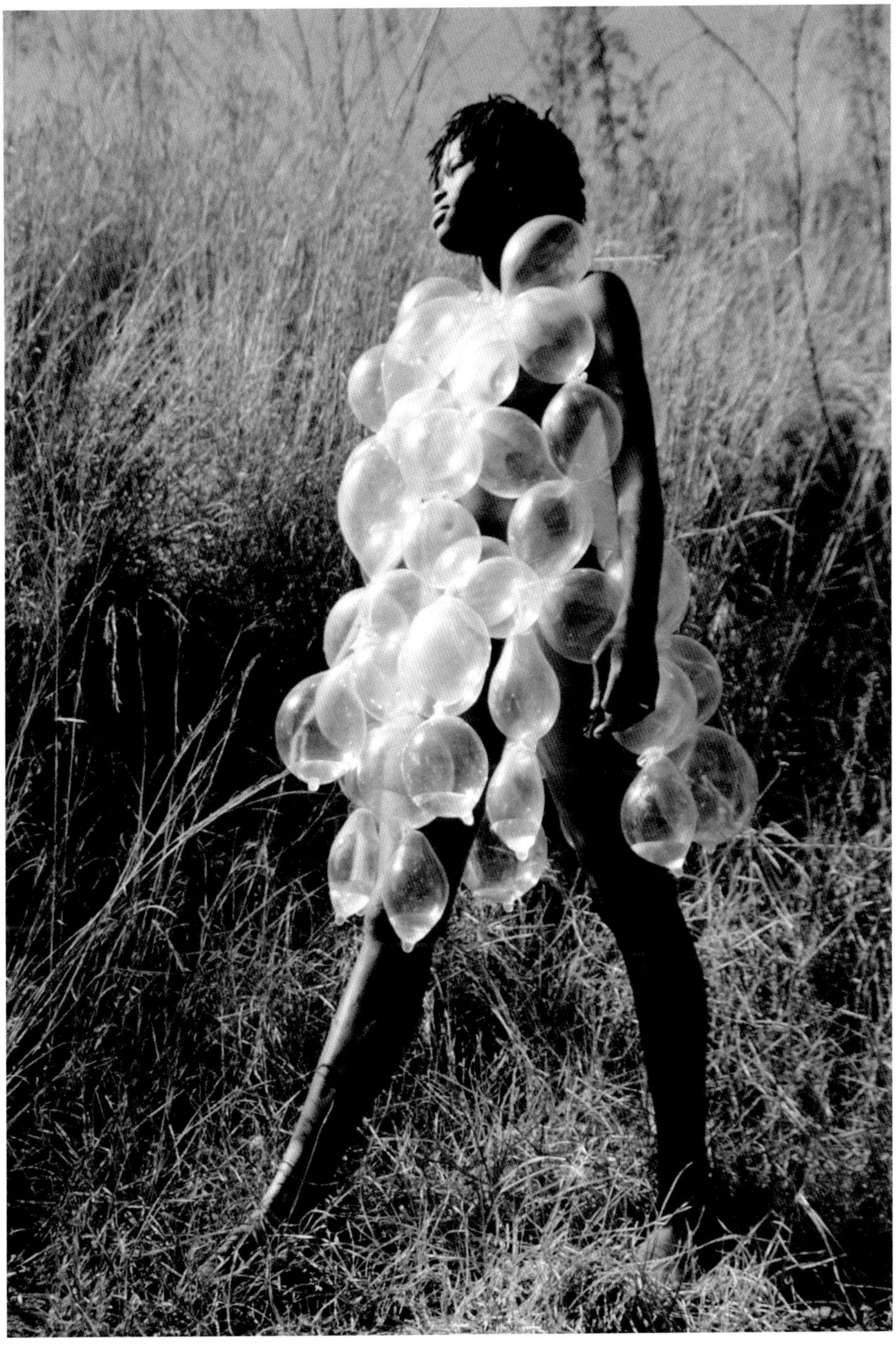

ZANELE MUHOLI

Crime Scene #1, 2012

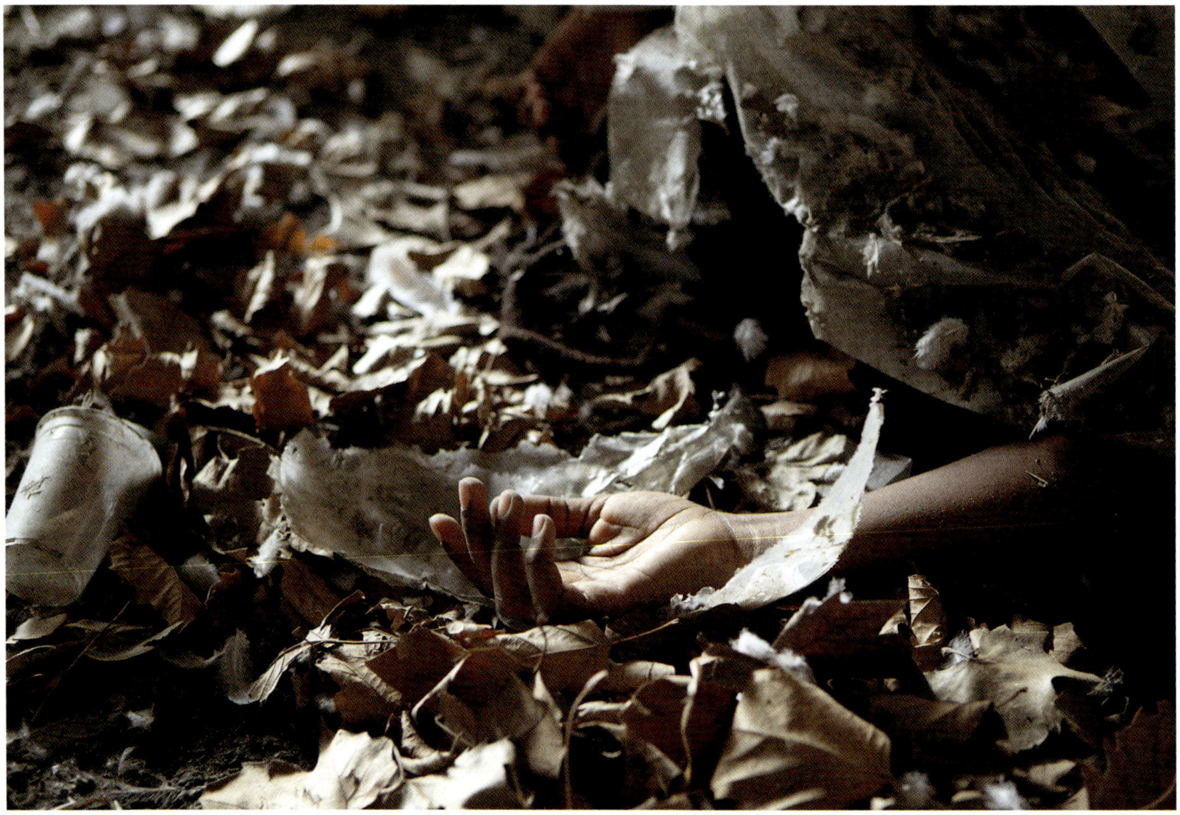

ZANELE MUHOLI

Crime Scene #3, 2012

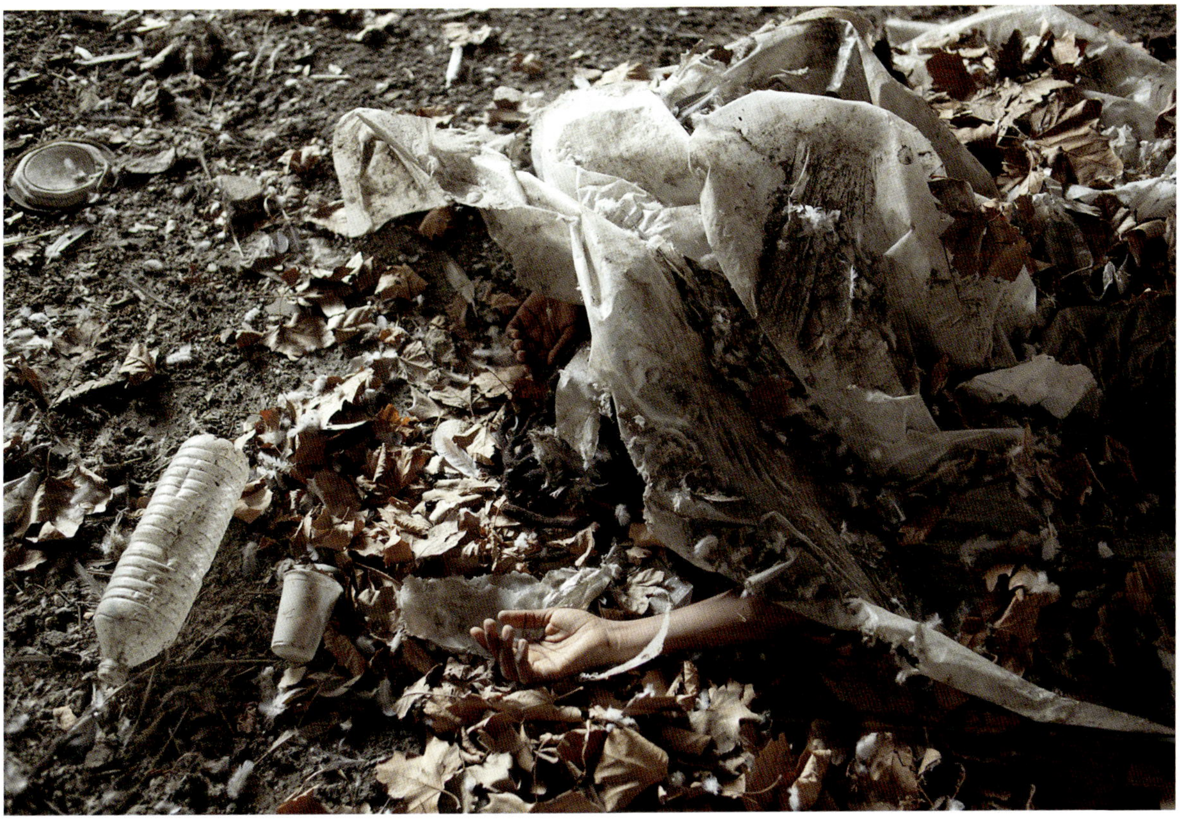

In the early 1990s, Catherine Opie photographed members of San Francisco's gay, lesbian and sadomasochistic communities that she herself was part of. Each sitter in the series is isolated against a brightly coloured backdrop. Speaking of this formal strategy, which was informed by the paintings of Hans Holbein, Opie says: 'the coloured backdrop allows your eye to go through the photograph in a different way than if it was, say, a person sitting in their house. It's about separating the subject from their world, but still representing their world through their body'. Opie's practice is rooted in documentary photography. As well as close friends, her subjects have included the built environment, landscapes and large bodies of water. *Sunset 4* (2009) and *Sunrise 4* (2009) are part of a series that the artist made on board a container ship travelling from South Korea to California. Choosing to explore what she has described as 'the biggest cliché in photography', Opie documented the start and close of every day for the duration of the journey.

CATHERINE OPIE

Justin Bond, 1993

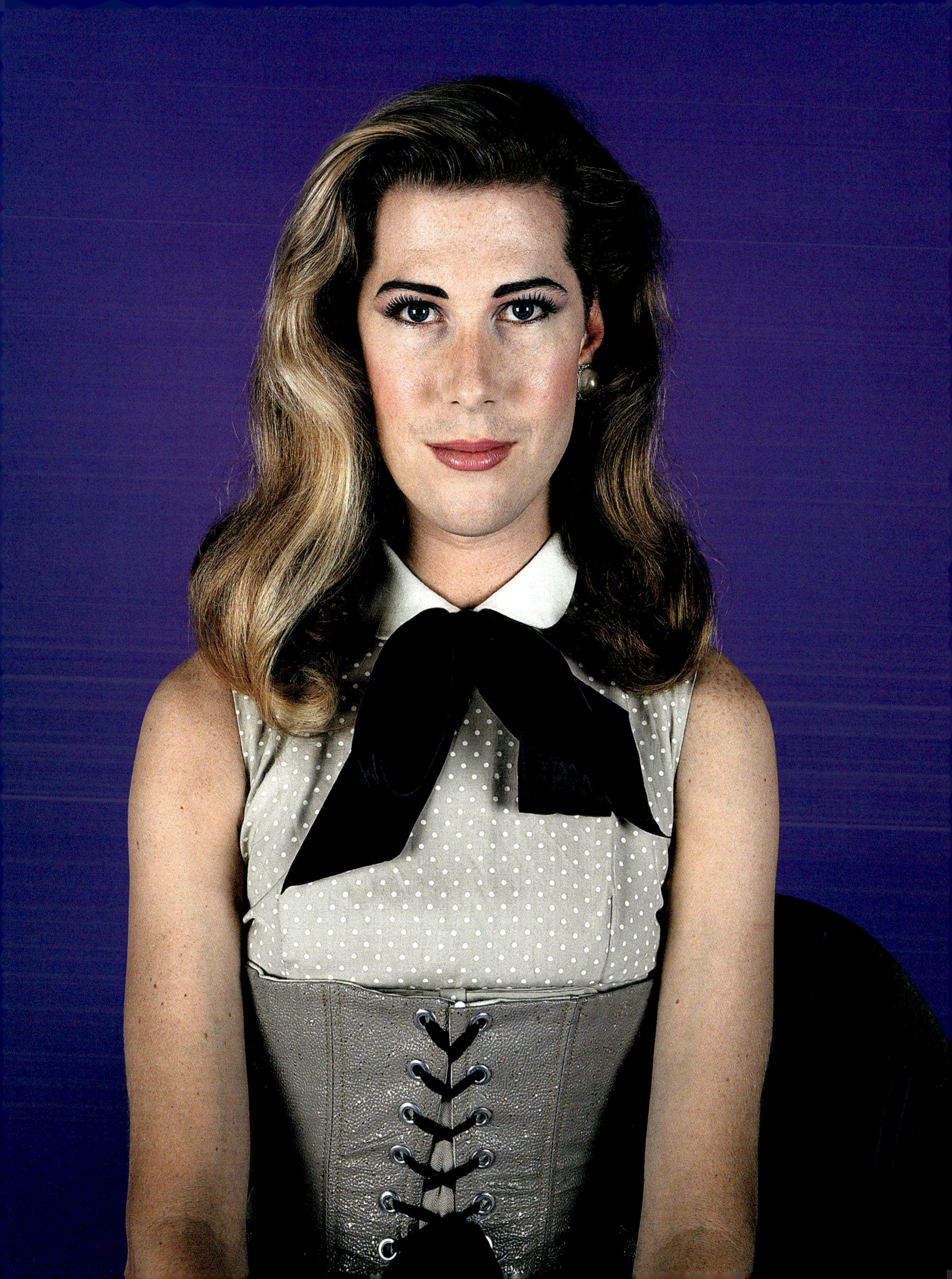

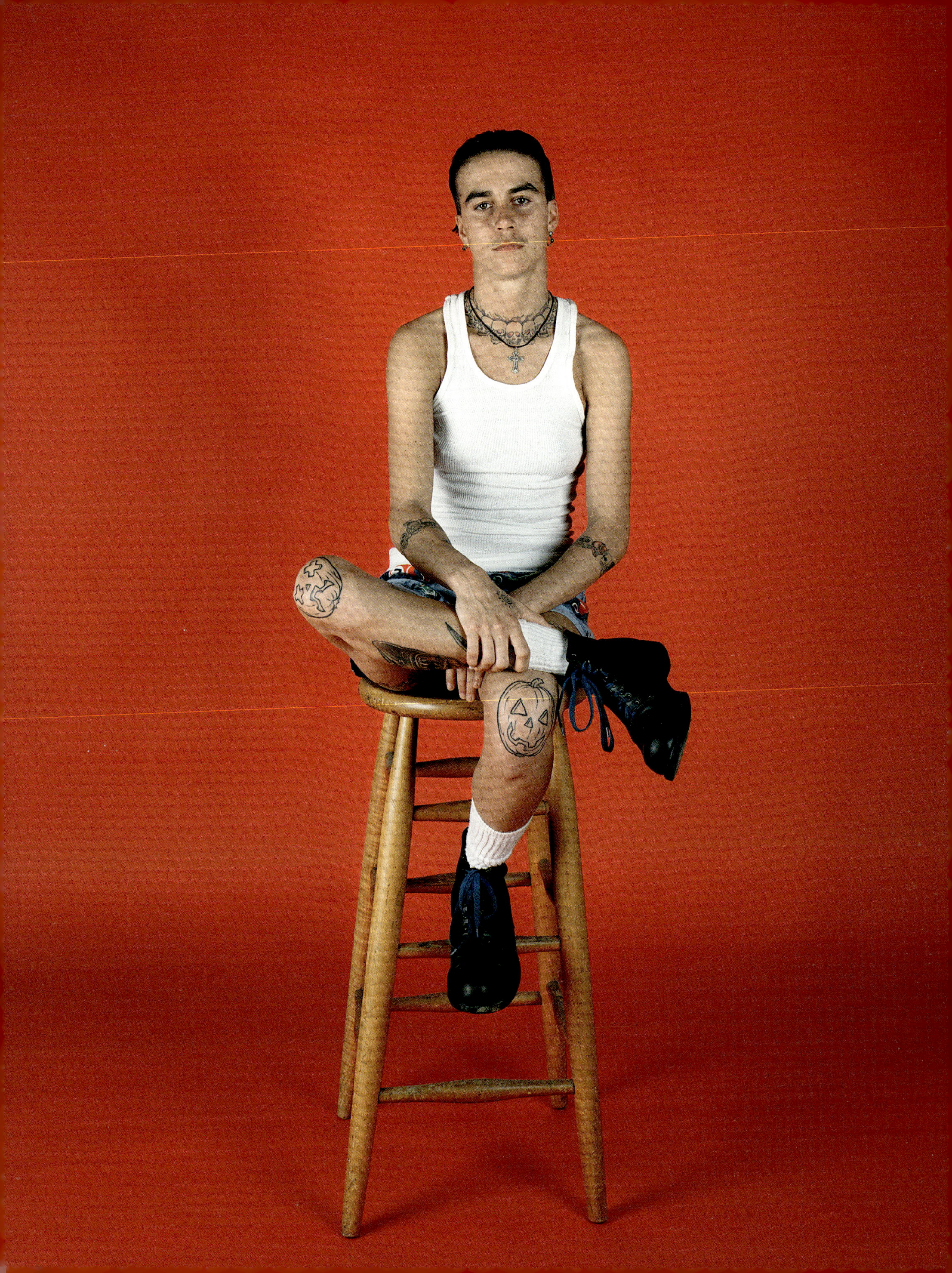

CATHERINE OPIE

Pig Pen, 1993

Mike and Sky, 1993

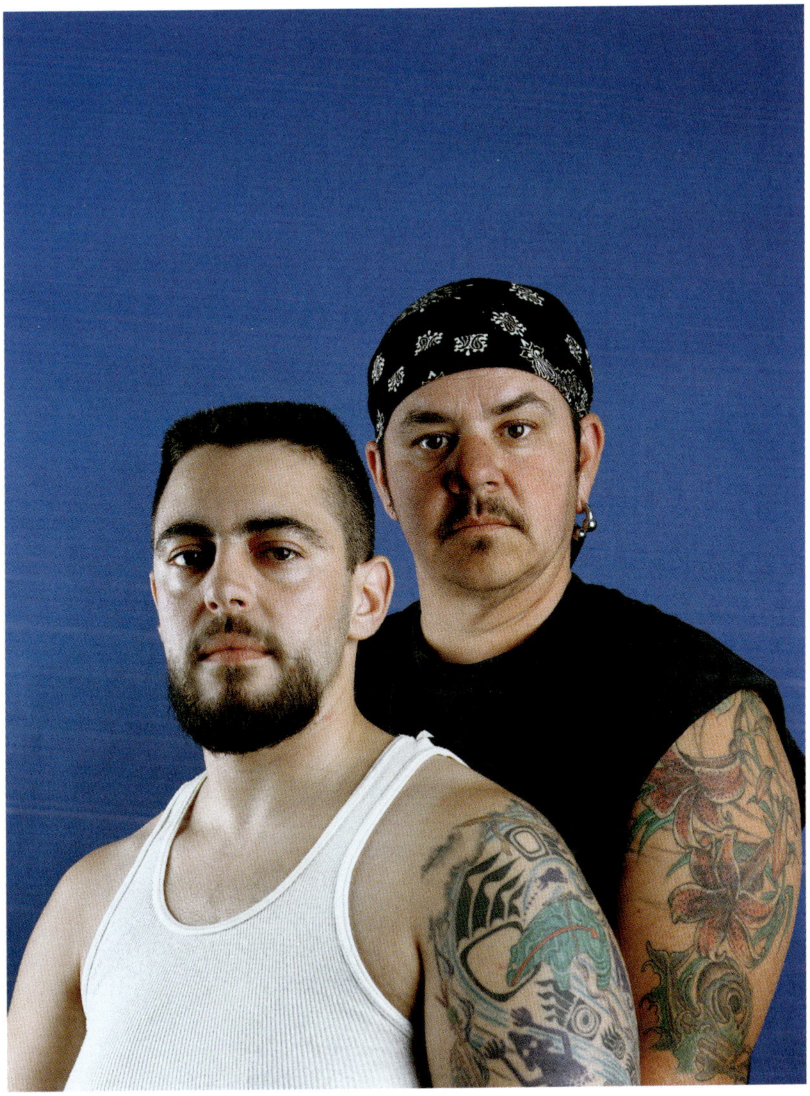

CATHERINE OPIE

Vaginal Davis, 1994

Amy, 1996

Overleaf

Sunrise 4, 2009

Sunset 4, 2009

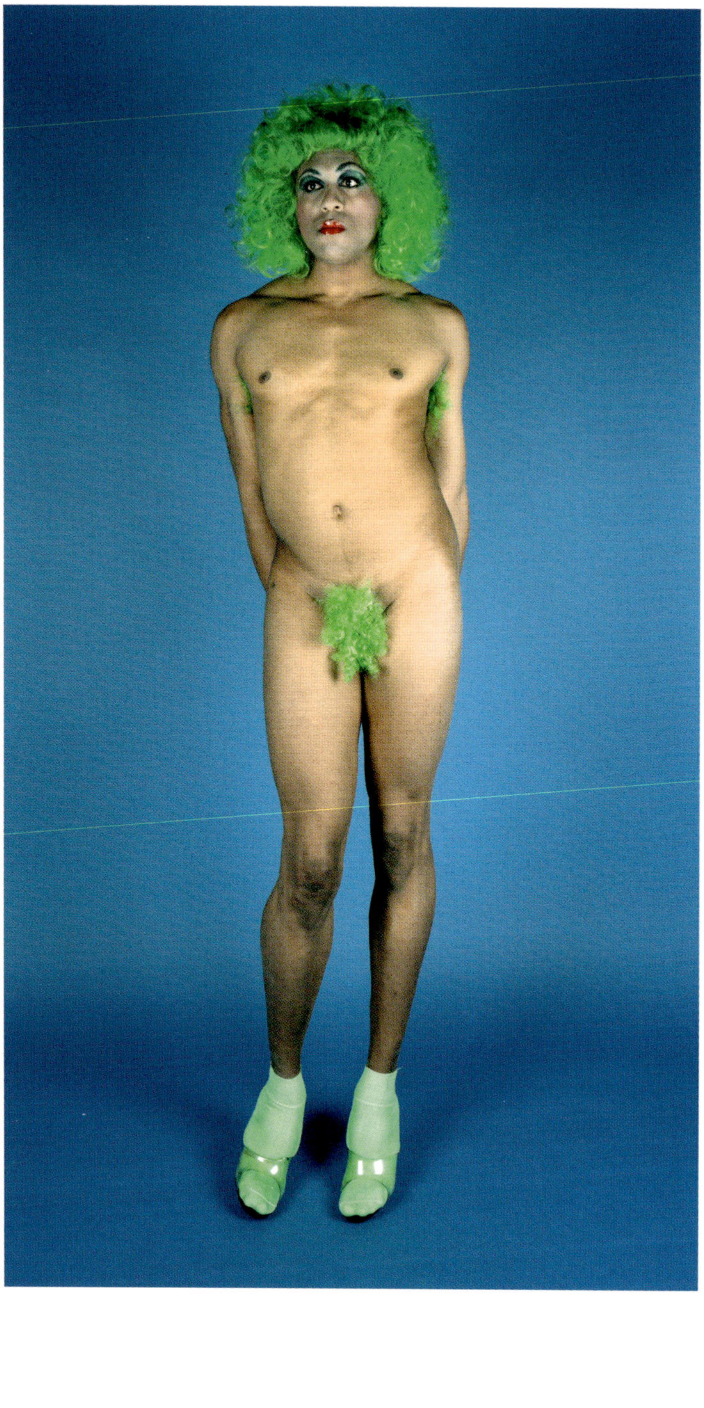

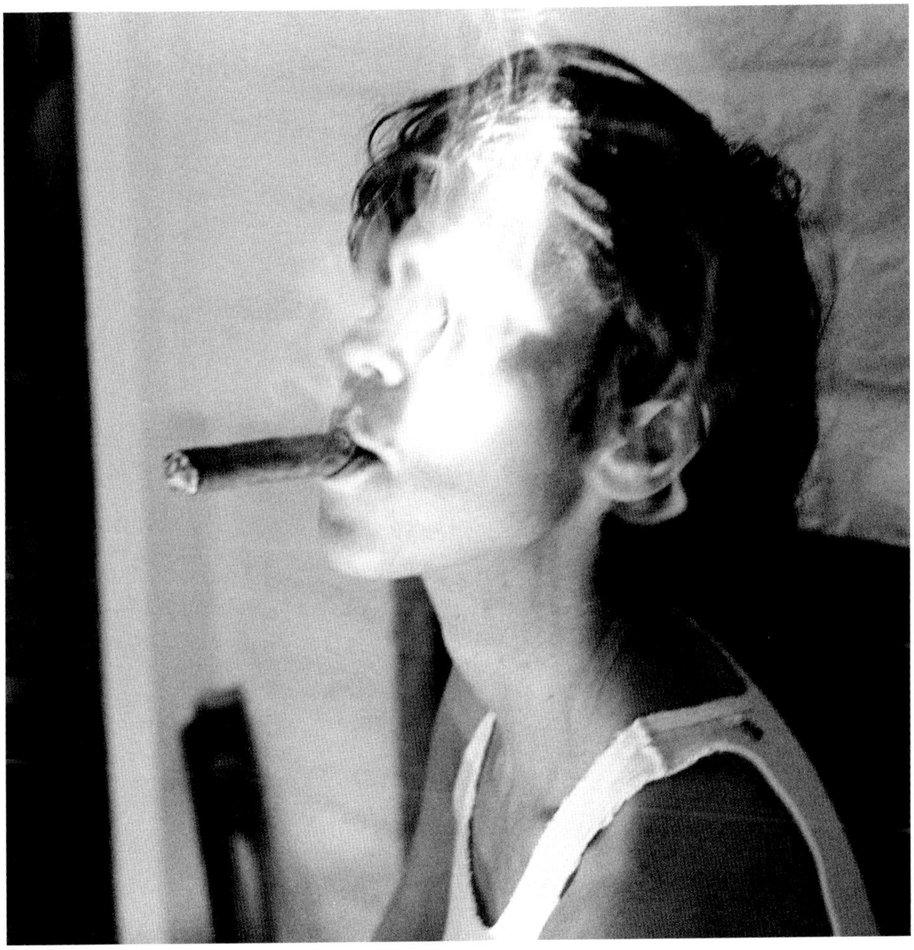

PLANNINGTOROCK

192 – 93

CHRISTINA QUARLES

194 – 97

hannah Quinlan + Rosie Hastings

198 – 201

PLANNINGTOROCK

Portrait Planningtorock, 2011

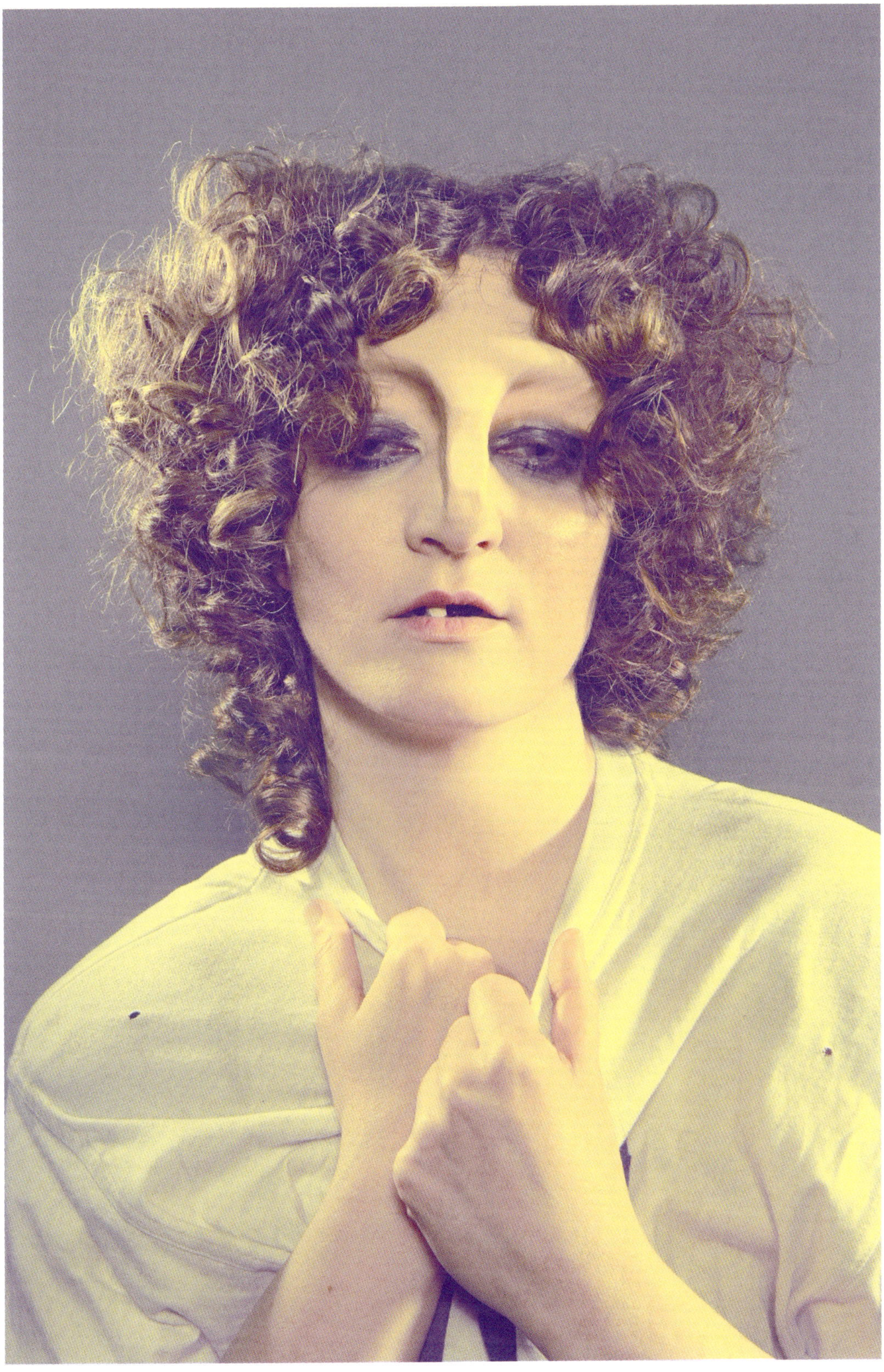

In her paintings and installations, Christina Quarles attempts to communicate the experience of 'living in a body rather than looking at a body'. The many-limbed figures that appear in her work are not portraits of any one individual, but rather – as she puts it – 'portraits of being an individual'. As a 'queer, cis woman who is black but often mistaken as white', Quarles is used to being misread. Partly as a result, she views ambiguity and illegibility as political tools. 'My work is about existing within the limitations of a legible body, and about how our own sense of self exceeds those limitations', she comments. Keen to remind us that a painting is a constructed visual space governed by rules and conventions, Quarles will often create an elaborate *trompe l'oeil* effect only to disrupt it with elements that break out, misbehave and draw attention to the way that the illusion is constructed.

CHRISTINA QUARLES

It's Gunna Be All Right, Cause Baby, There Ain't Nuthin' Left, 2016

Overleaf, detail

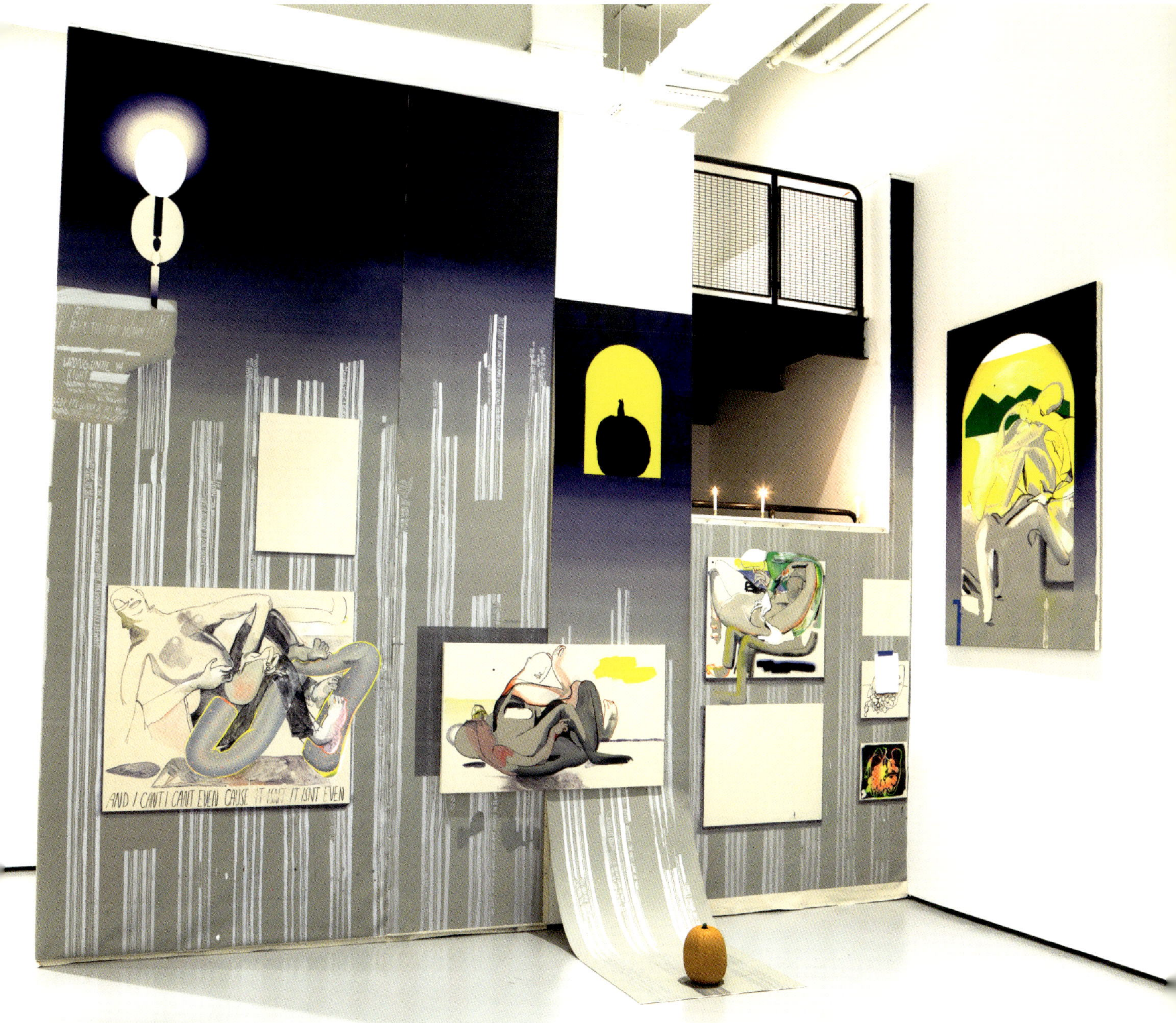
AND I CANT I CANT EVEN CAUSE IT ISNT IT ISNT EVEN

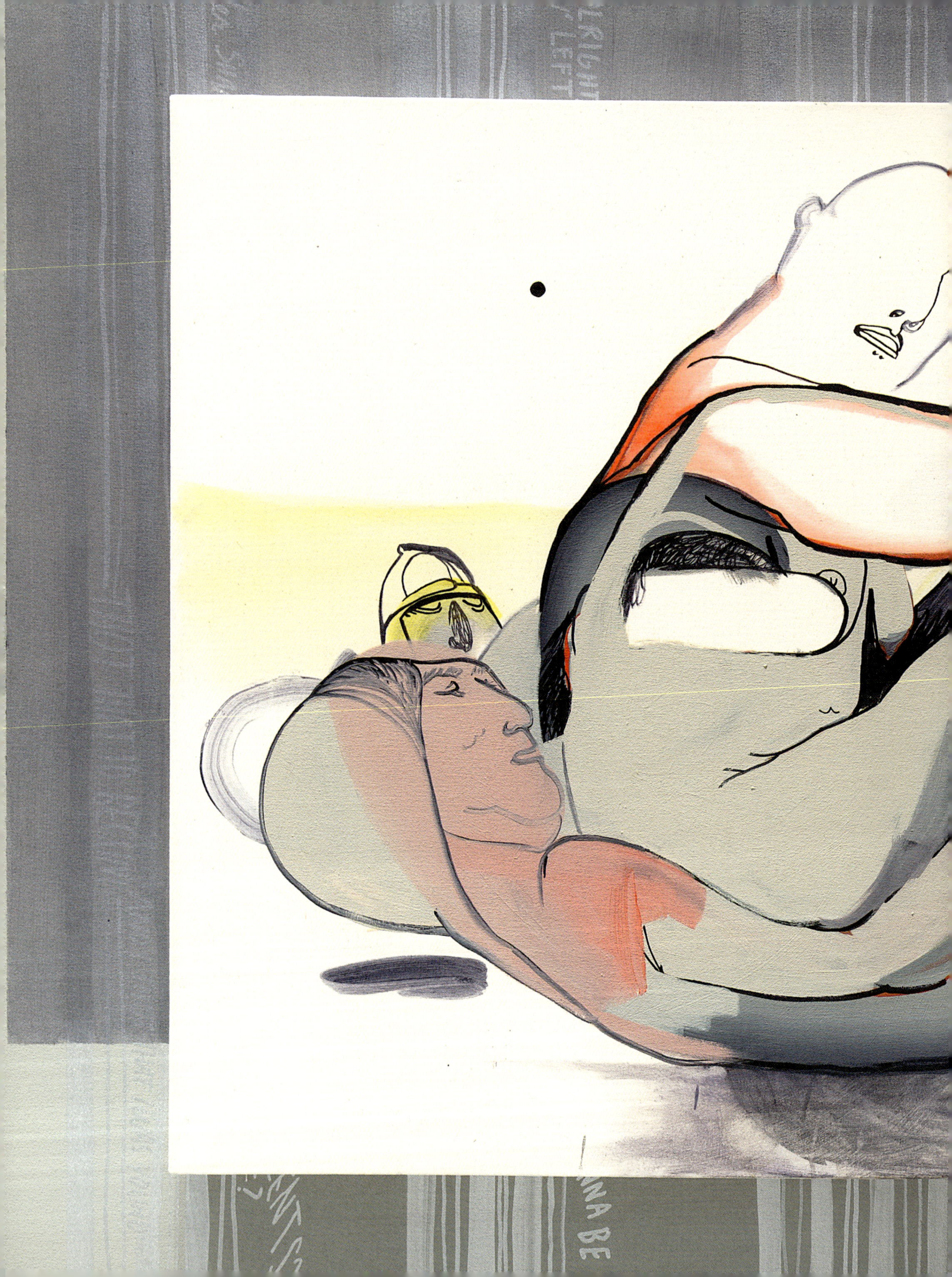

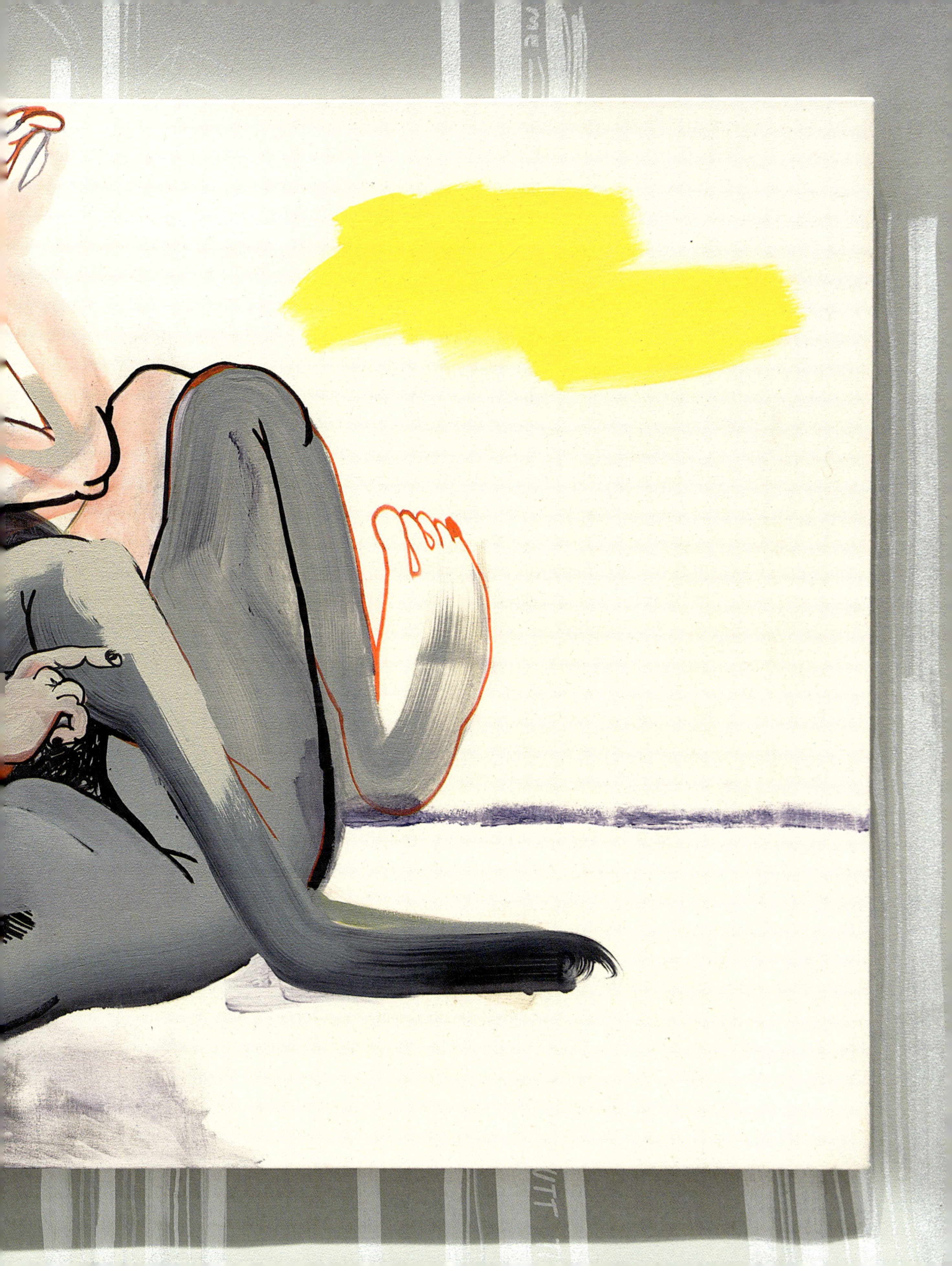

HANNAH QUINLAN
AND ROSIE HASTINGS

Something for the Boys, 2018

Hannah Quinlan and Rosie Hastings's *Something for the Boys* (2018) explores LGBTQI spaces in Blackpool. Filmed in two locations – the cabaret club Funny Girls and the men-only gay sex bar Growlr – it focuses on two very different communities within the city's queer scene. *Something for the Boys* features performances by Miss Betty Legs Diamond and dancer Ted Rogers, material from the city's LGBTQI archive and a soundtrack by Owen Pratt. As with Quinlan and Hastings's earlier video work *UK Gay Bar Directory* (2015–16), the tone of *Something for the Boys* is melancholic, even elegiac. Both explore the politics, histories and aesthetics of queer spaces, a context where questions of class, nationalism, gentrification and patriarchy often collide. Speaking of their recent work, Quinlan and Hastings comment, 'We were considering the closure of queer spaces, but also more broadly the loss of public space and the dismantling of state infrastructure, which are the results of more than a decade of austerity.'

Overleaf

The Dudes, 2017

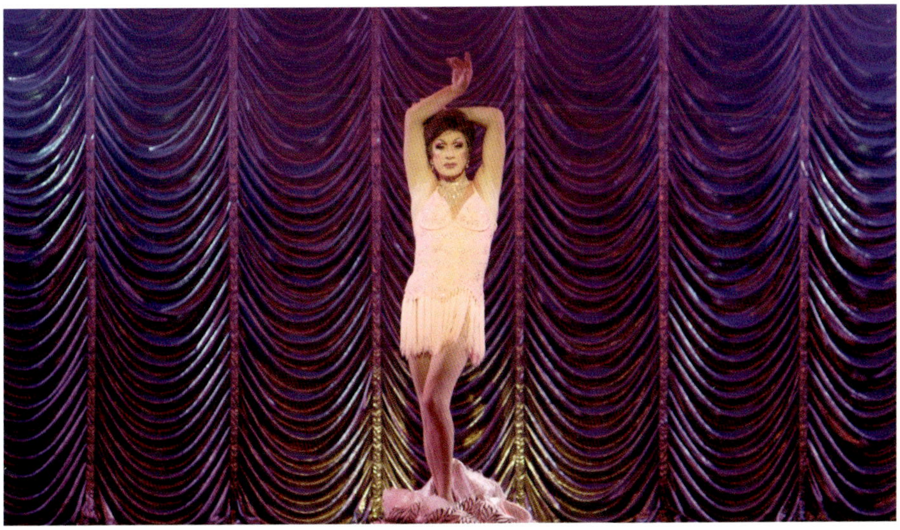

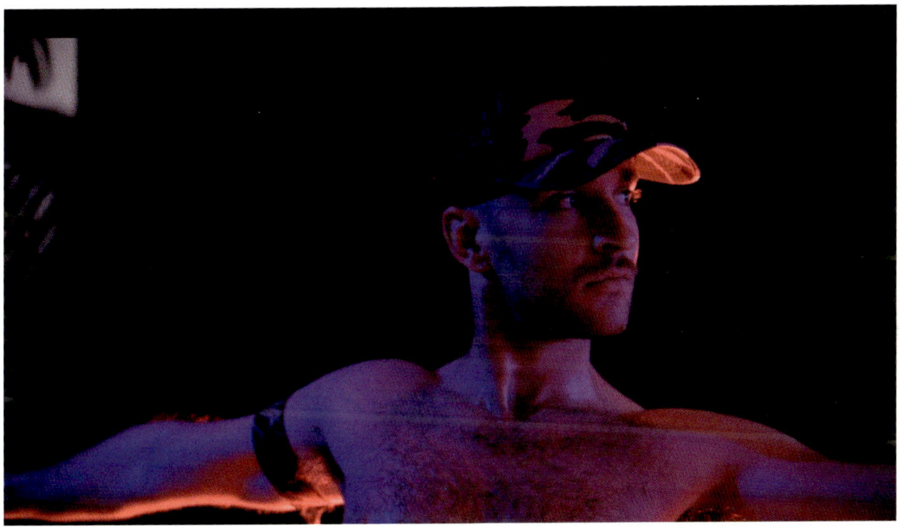

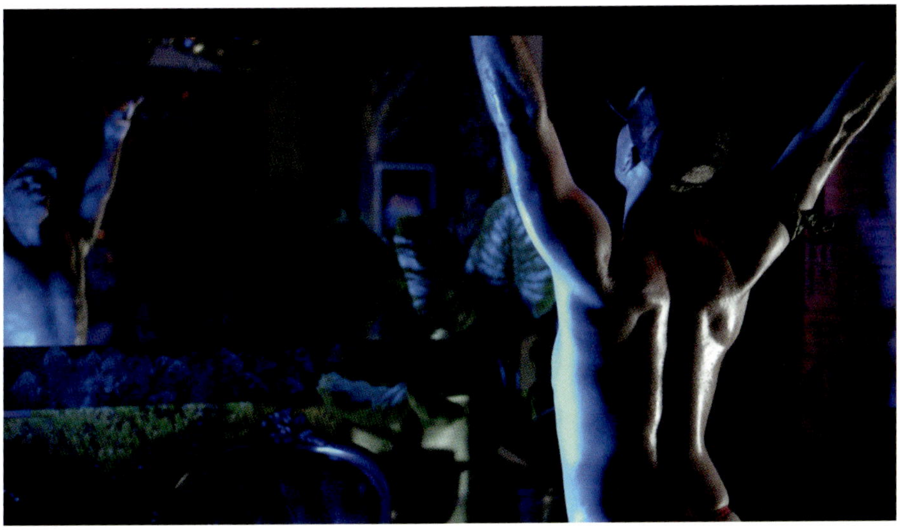

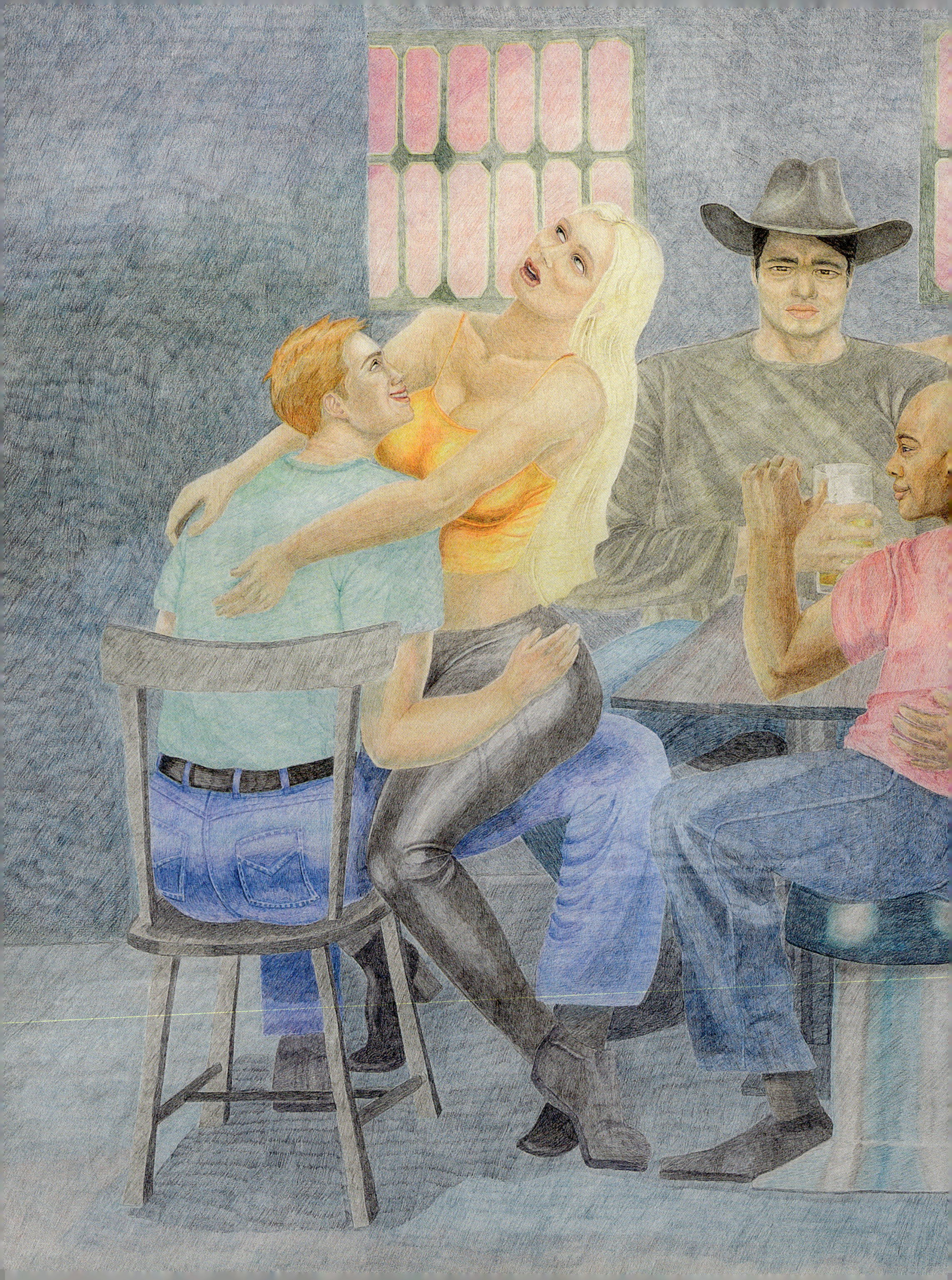

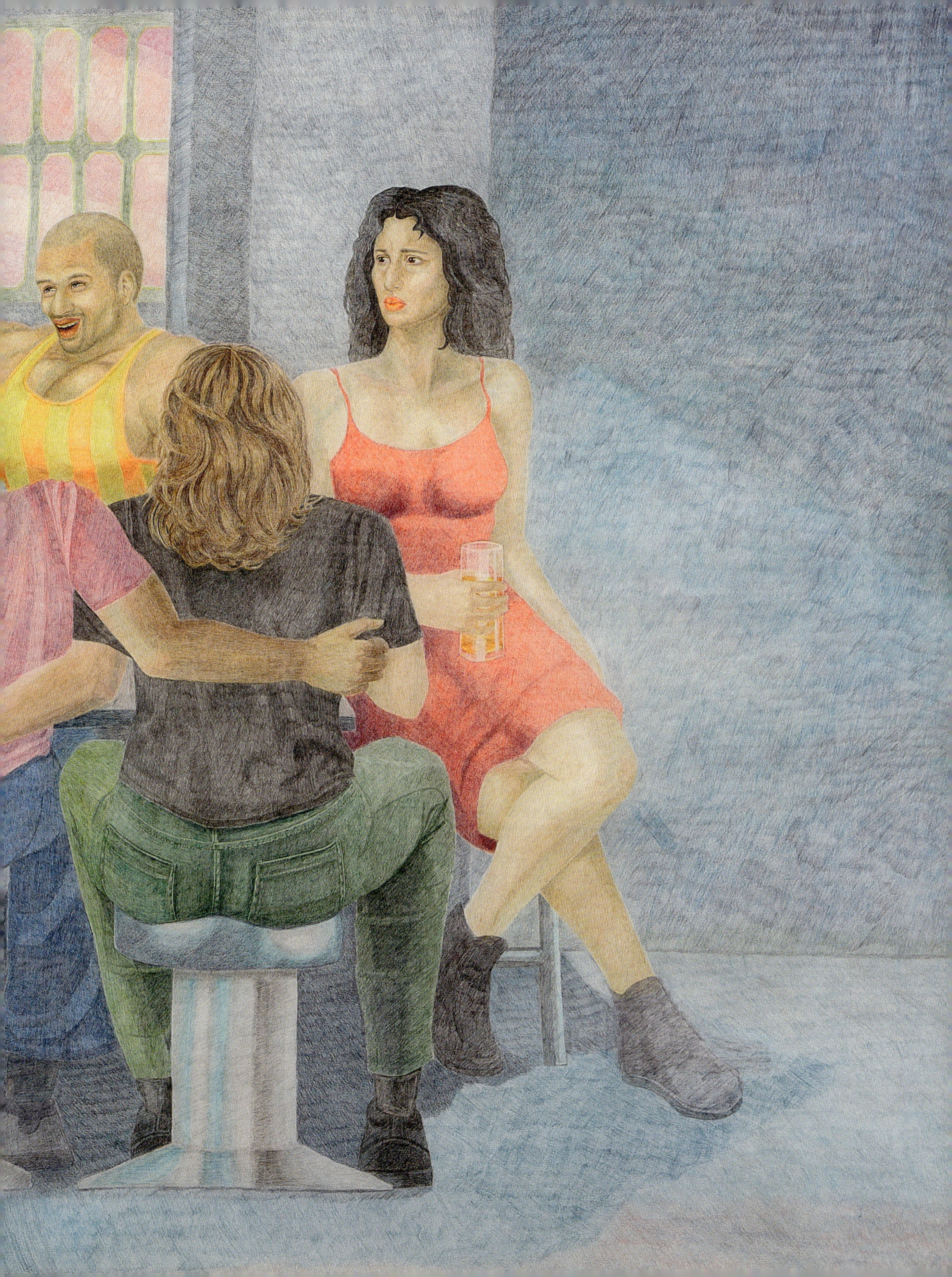

HUNTER REYNOLDS

204 – 07

Athi-Patra Ruga

208 – 09

Tejal Shah

210 – 13

HUNTER REYNOLDS

Patina du Prey's
Drag Pose Series, 1990

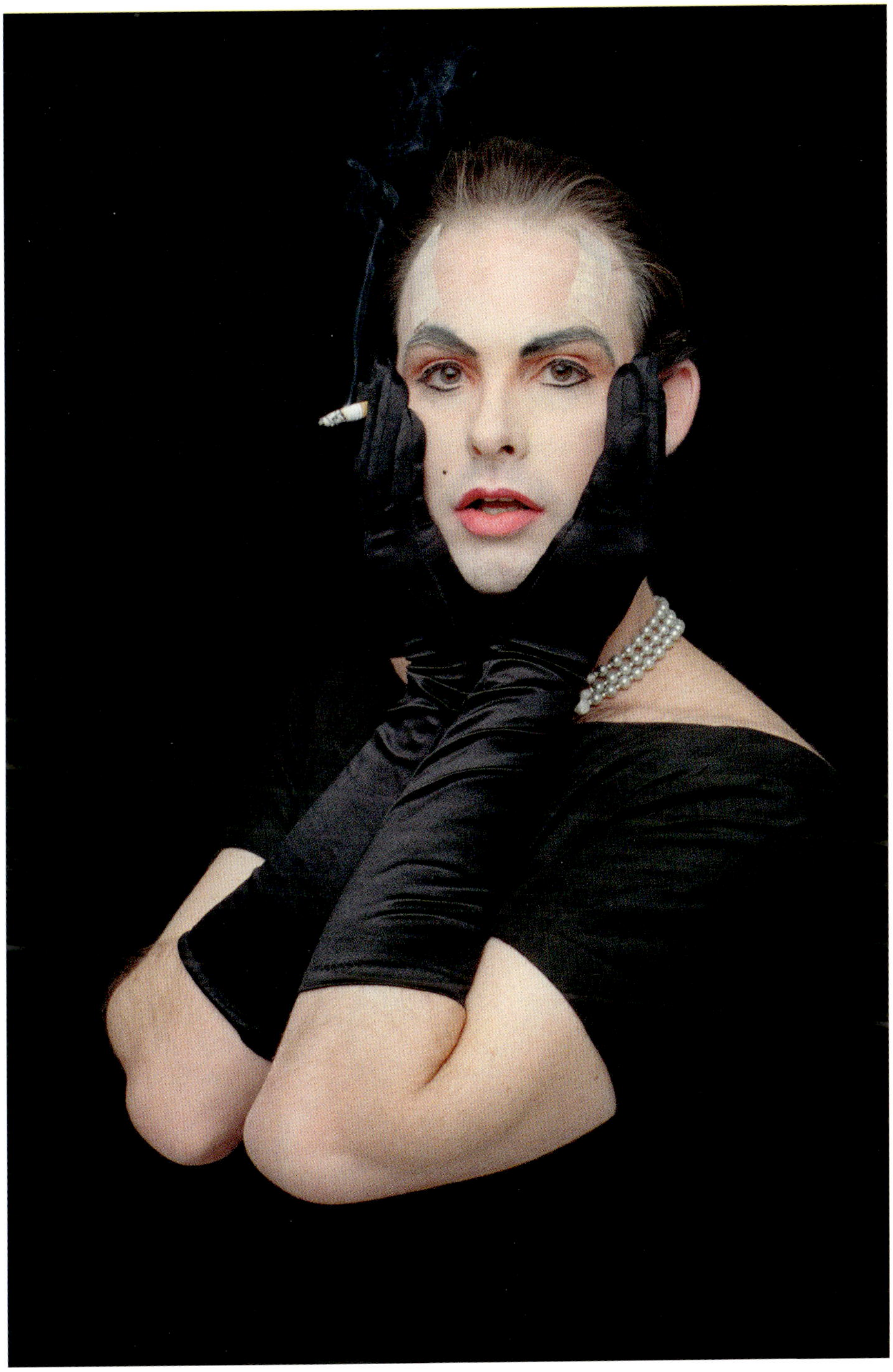

Artist and AIDS activist Hunter Reynolds began performing as his alter ego Patina du Prey in 1989. As Patina, Reynolds discovered that 'sitting on the subway or simply having a coffee at MacDonald's' could be a political action. Reynolds first presented *The Memorial Dress* – a black ball gown printed with the names of 25,000 individuals known to have died of AIDS-related illnesses – at the Institute of Contemporary Art, Boston, in 1993. Standing on a revolving platform before an audience of up to 2,000 people, Reynolds transformed himself into a living memorial, or as he puts it, 'an energetic sacred site of healing'. Throughout the exhibition, Reynolds invited visitors to add the names of people that they had lost to an accompanying memorial book. By 1996, this book held a further 5,000 names. Speaking of his practice as a whole, Reynolds comments that 'making art has been a tool I use to process and deal with my pain as well as transform it'.

HUNTER REYNOLDS

Survival AIDS (ACT Up Chicago with Memorial Dress Photographed by Maxine Henryson), 2015

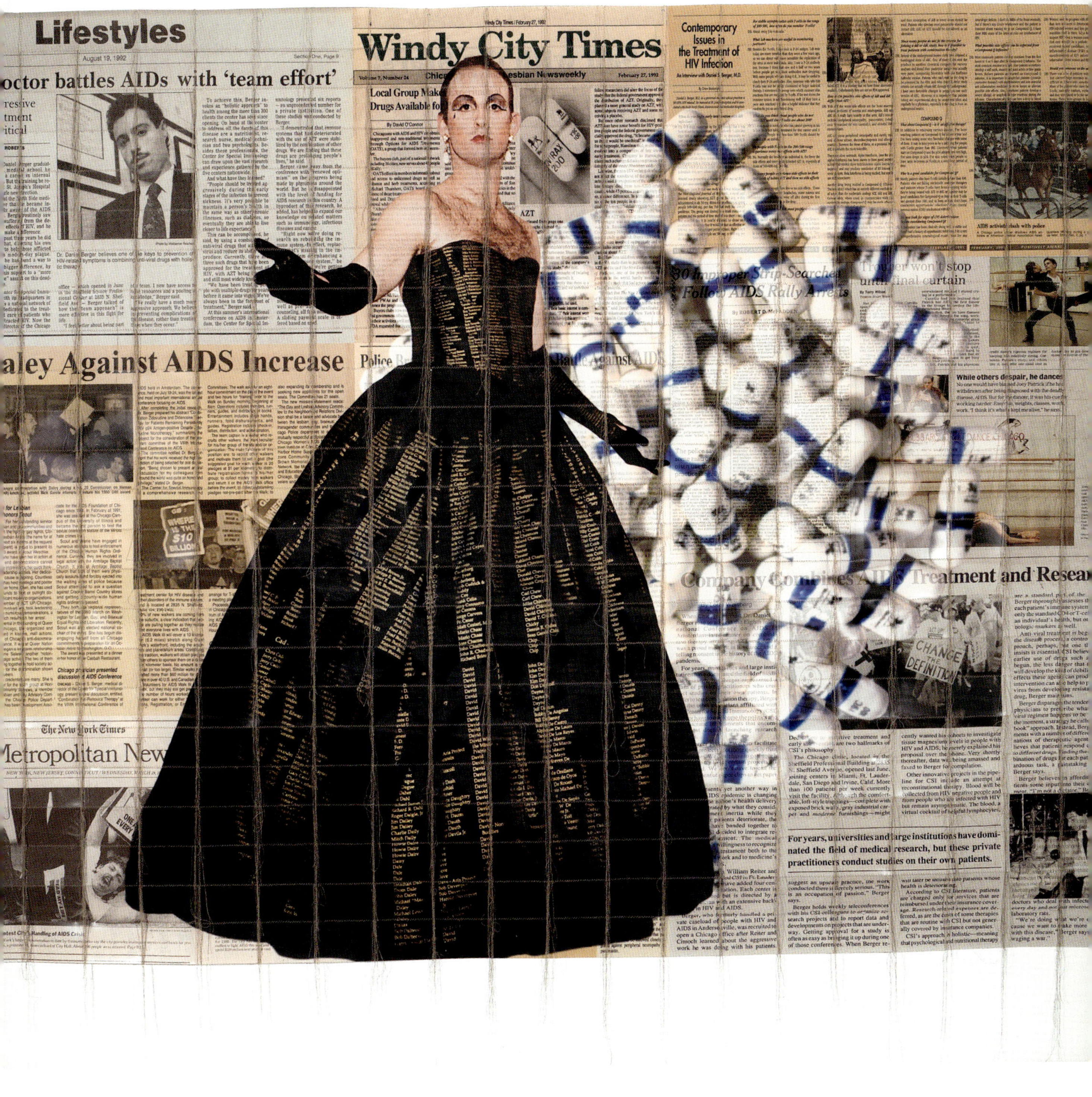
Lifestyles
August 19, 1992
octor battles AIDs with 'team effort'
Windy City Times
Contemporary Issues in the Treatment of HIV Infection
aley Against AIDS Increase
30 Improper Strip-Searches Follow AIDS Rally Arrests
Trouper won't stop until final curtain
While others despair, he dances
The New York Times
Metropolitan New
Company Combines AIDS Treatment and Resea
For years, universities and large institutions have dominated the field of medical research, but these private practitioners conduct studies on their own patients.

ATHI-PATRA RUGA

Azania, 2013

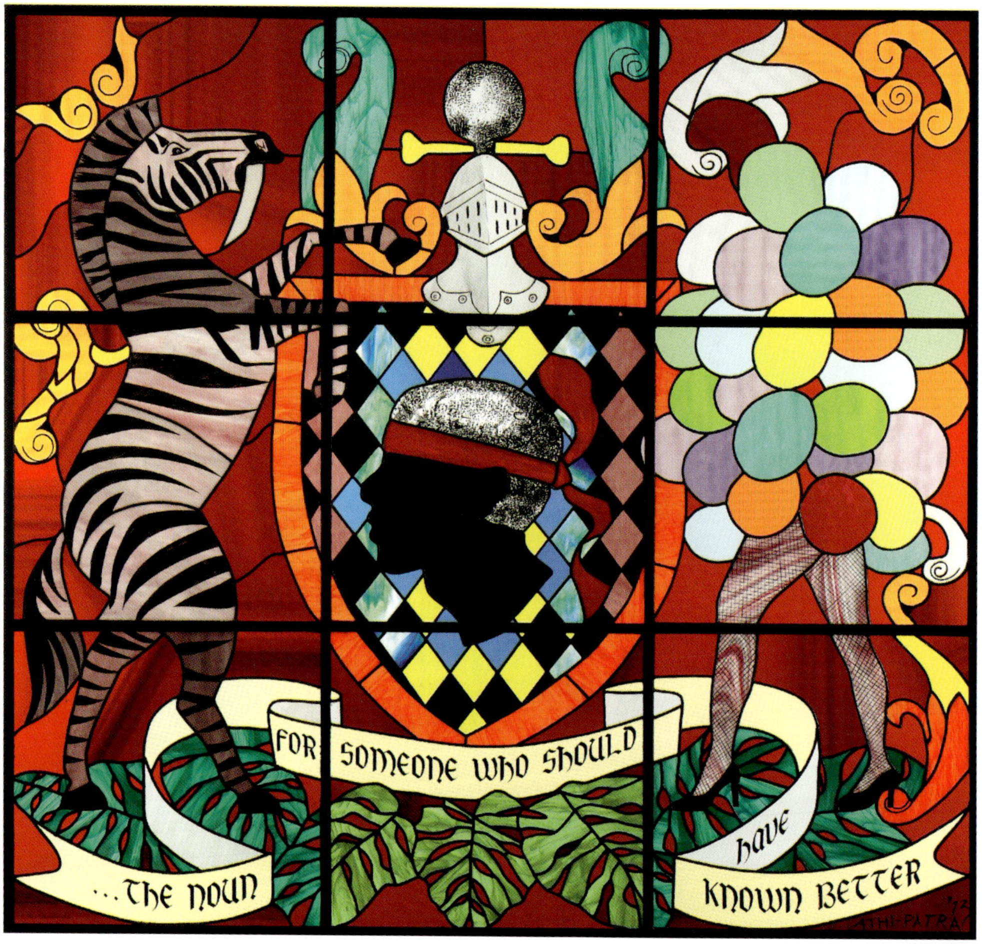

ATHI-PATRA RUGA

The Night of the Long Knives I, 2013

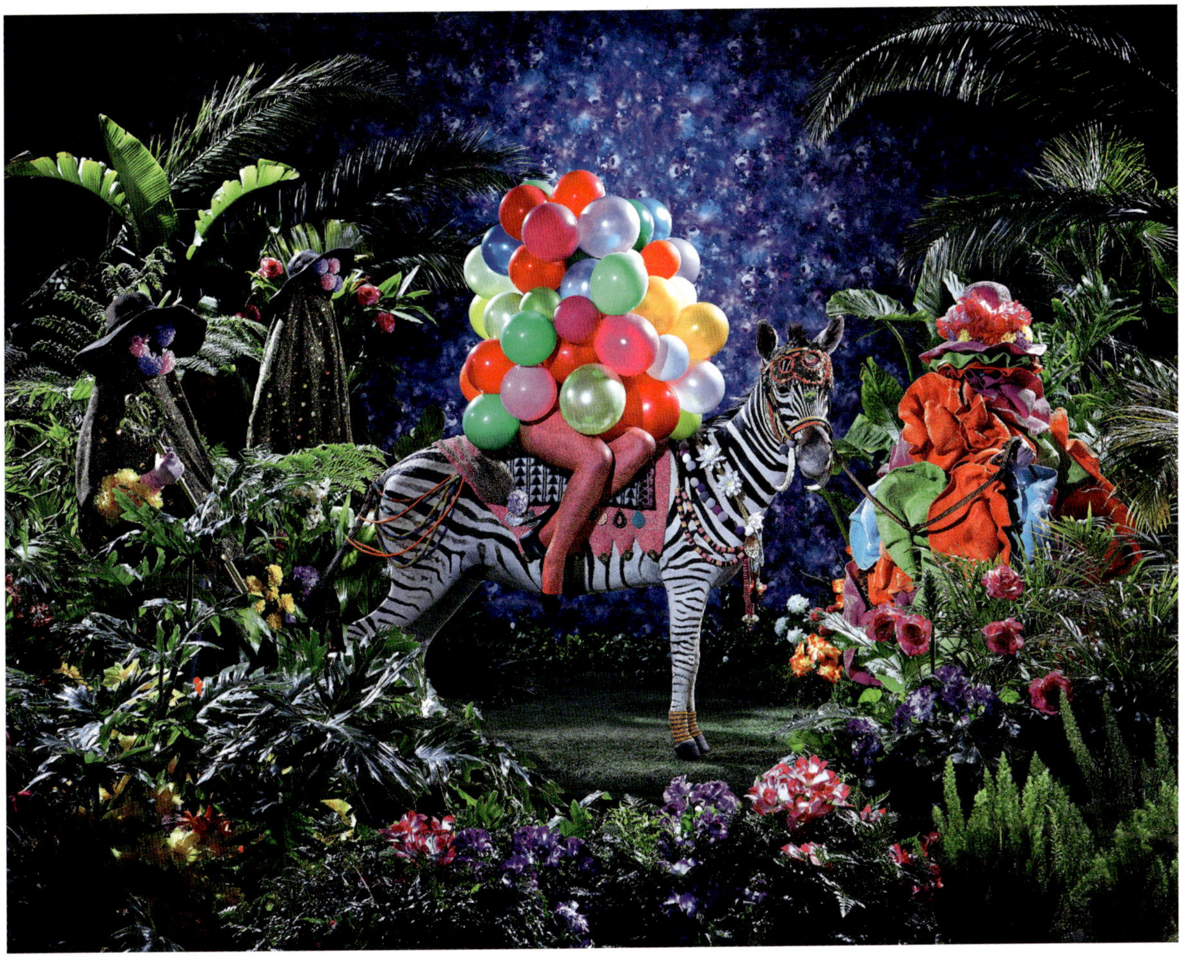

TEJAL SHAH

You too can touch the moon – Yashoda with Krishna, 2006 (*Hijra Fantasy* series)

Tejal Shah is a multidisciplinary artist who works across video, photography, performance, text and installation. 'I am drawn to work at the edges of things,' Shah comments, 'always pushing the boundaries of our assumptions and conventions.' *You too can touch the moon – Yashoda with Krishna* (2006) is part of Shah's *Hijra Fantasy* series. For this series, Shah worked closely with members of the hijra community in Mumbai, inviting them to share their desires and fantasies, or 'what would they be if they could be anything they wished to be.' *You too can touch the moon – Yashoda with Krishna* features Malini, a member of the hijra community, as Yashoda, the mother of the Hindu deity Krishna. The photograph is based on a painting by celebrated nineteenth-century Indian painter Raja Ravi Varma. In Shah's words, the photo-fantasy functions as 'a perverse "queering" of Ravi Varma's mythological pictures, and the colonial history that produced them.'

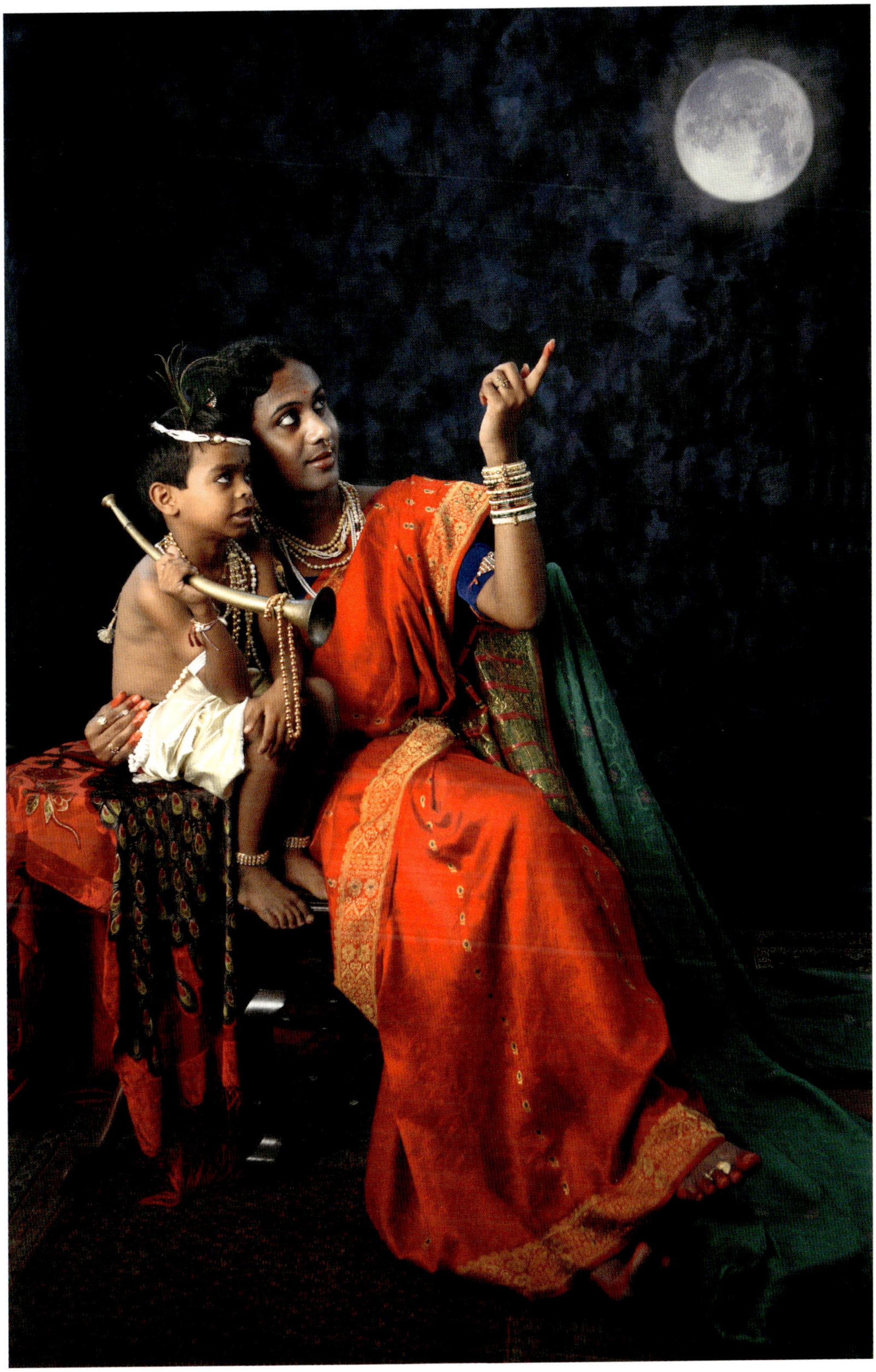

TEJAL SHAH

Hir I, 2013 (*Anonymous Life* series)

Southern Siren – Maheshwari, 2006
(*Hijira Fantasy* series)

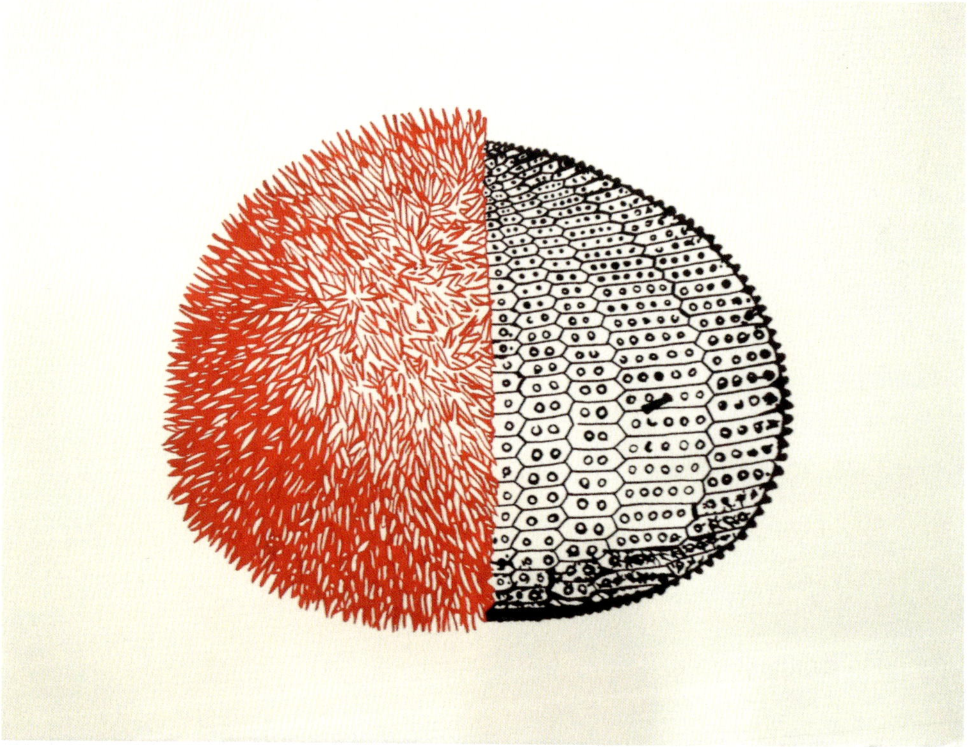

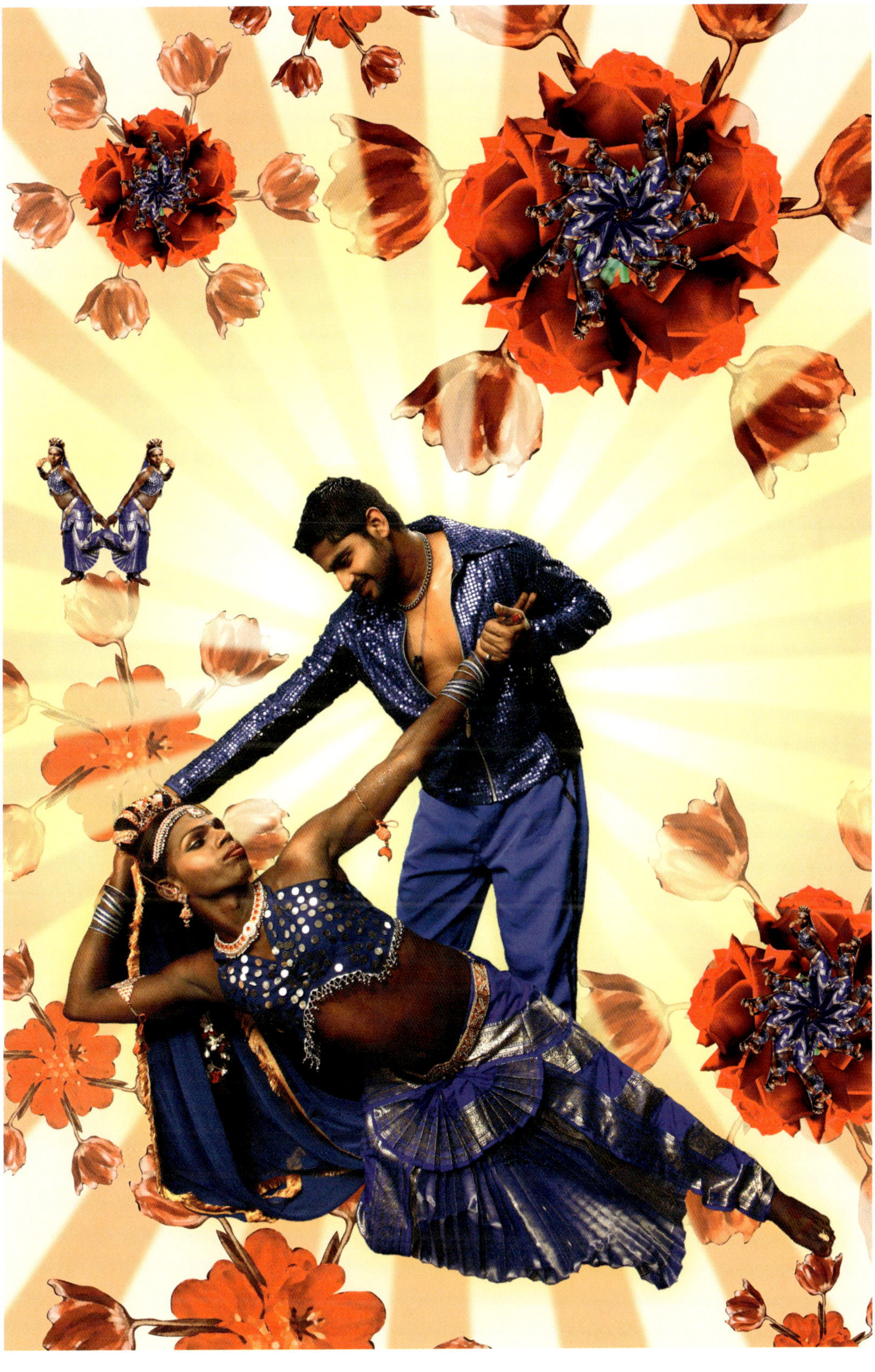

VICTORIA SIN

216–19

Jenkin Van Zyl

220 – 23

Del LaGrace Volcano

224 – 27

VICTORIA SIN

A View from Elsewhere, Act 1,
She Postures in Context, 2018

In this multimedia installation, Victoria Sin uses text, lip-sync, drag, performance and music to craft a speculative narrative that exposes both the transformative potential and dissociative threat of desire. Sin negotiates their diasporic Chinese ethnicity through research-driven performances by engaging diverse source materials that include poems, Cantonese opera, science-fiction novels and queer theory. In their work, Sin uses lip-sync to explore the uncanny embodiment of seemingly 'authentic' origins and universal truths. Fittingly, the texts they lip-sync often describe a sense of physical, linguistic or epistemological dislocation – a fundamental lack. Their words both belong and do not belong to them, under-scoring their enquiry into the porous contours of racialised non-binary subjectivity.

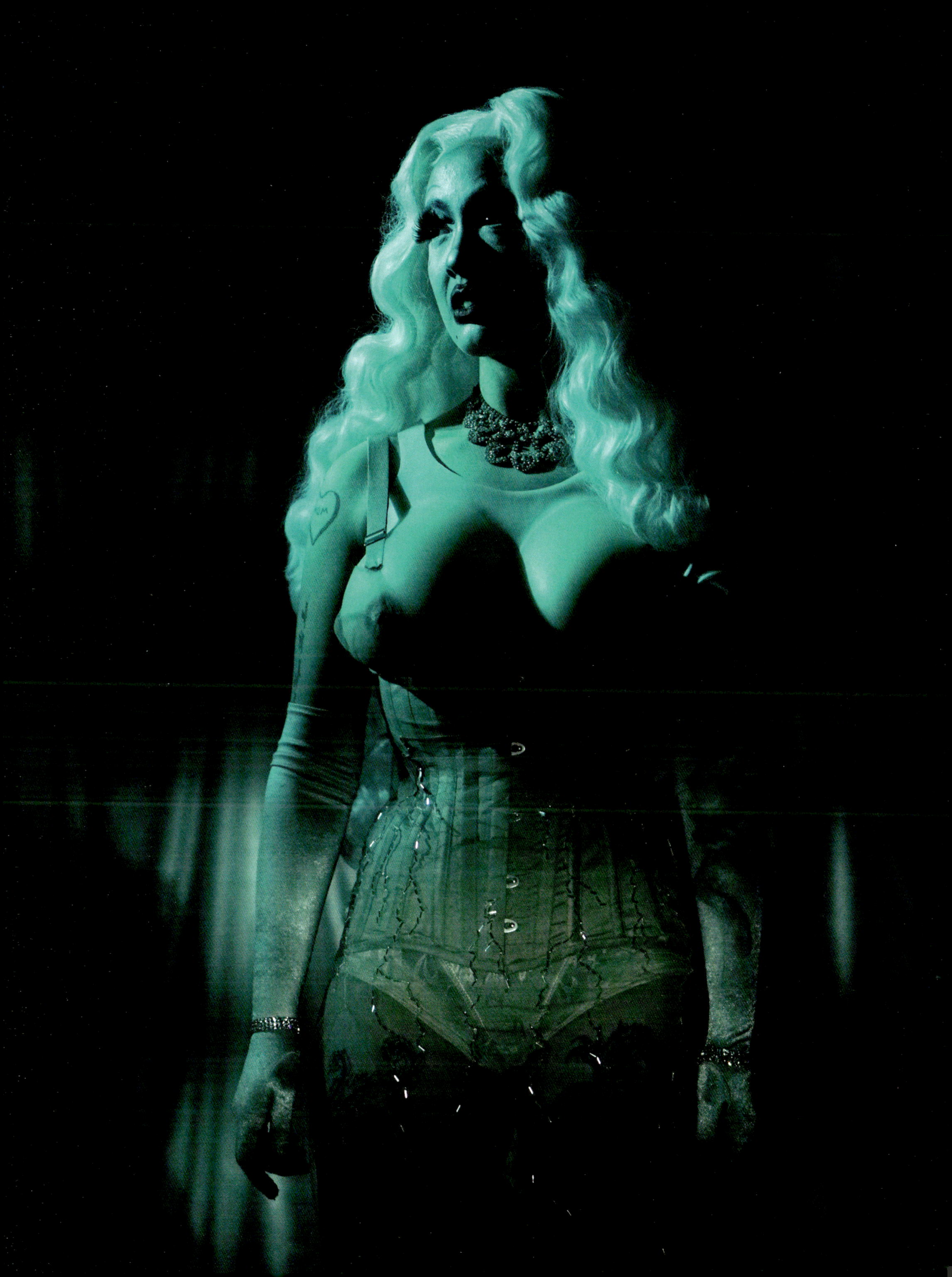

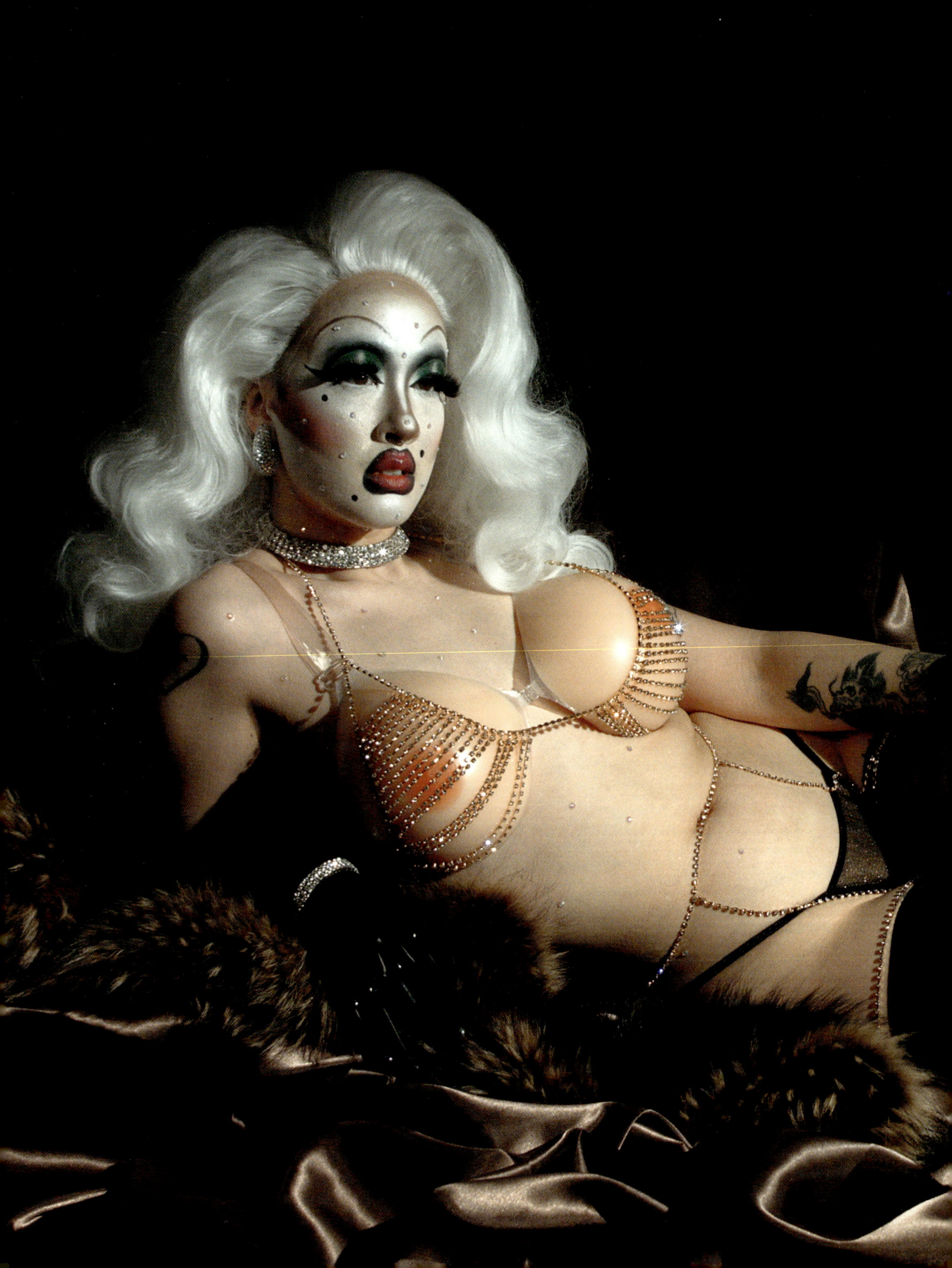

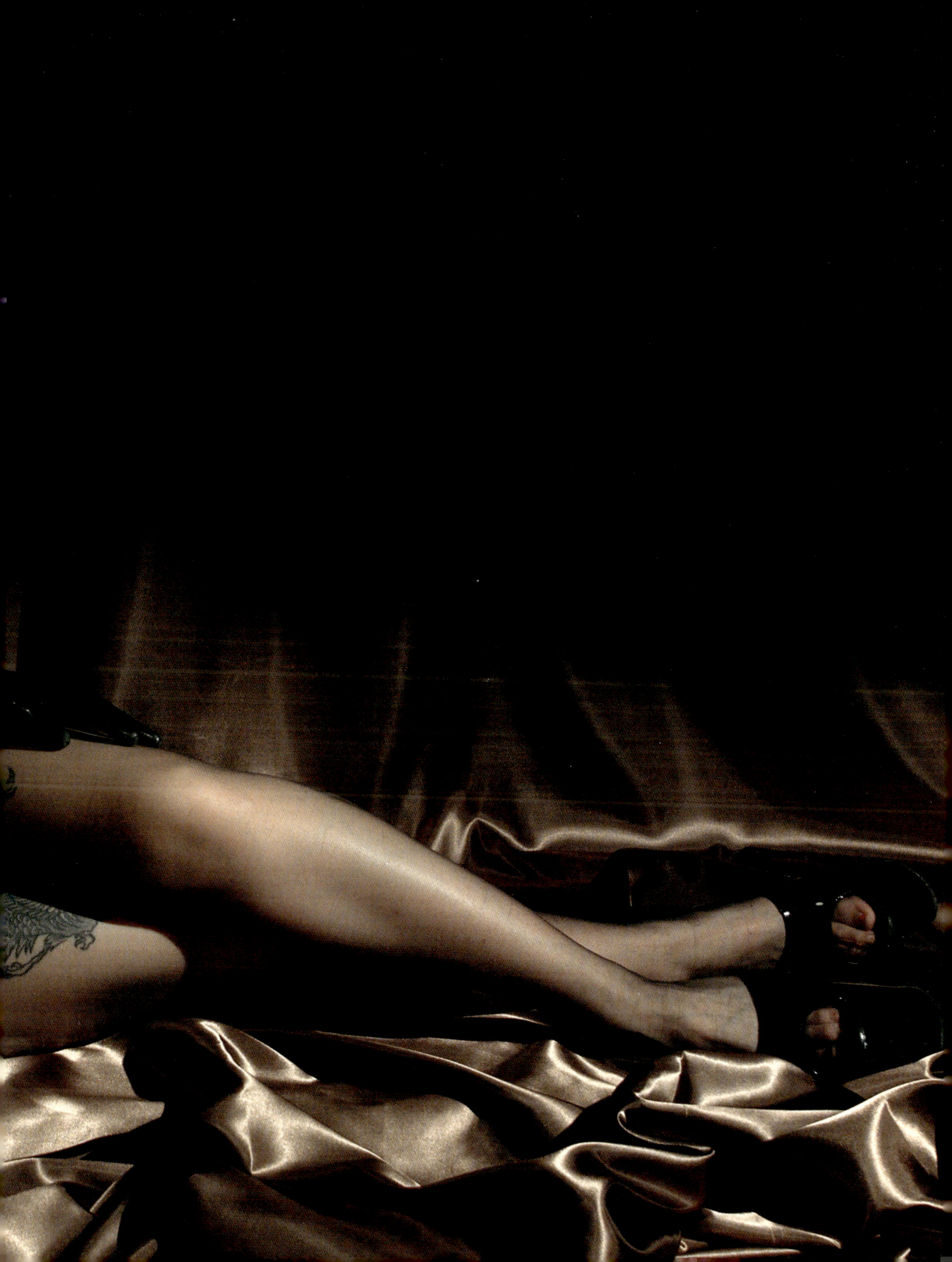

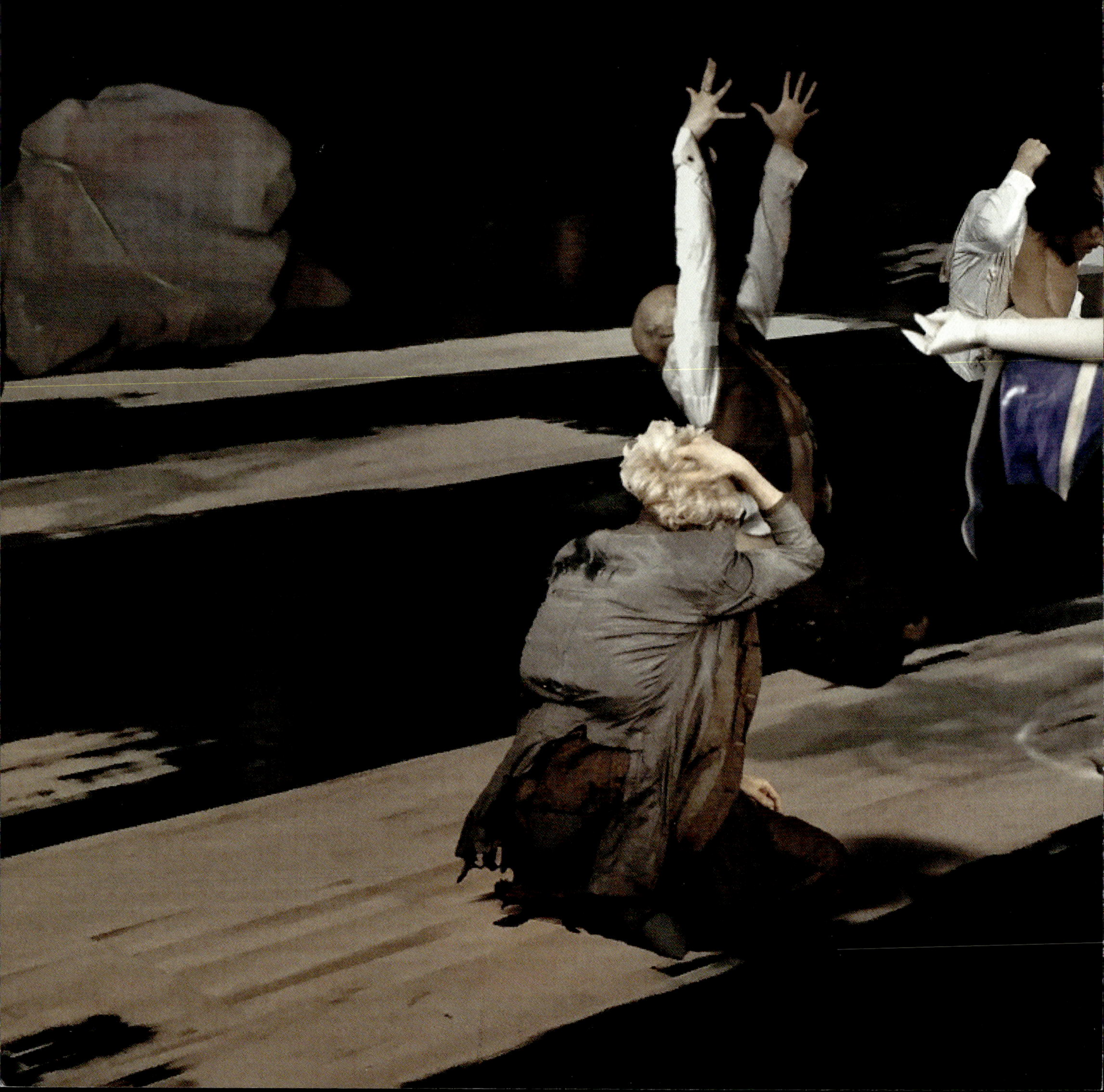

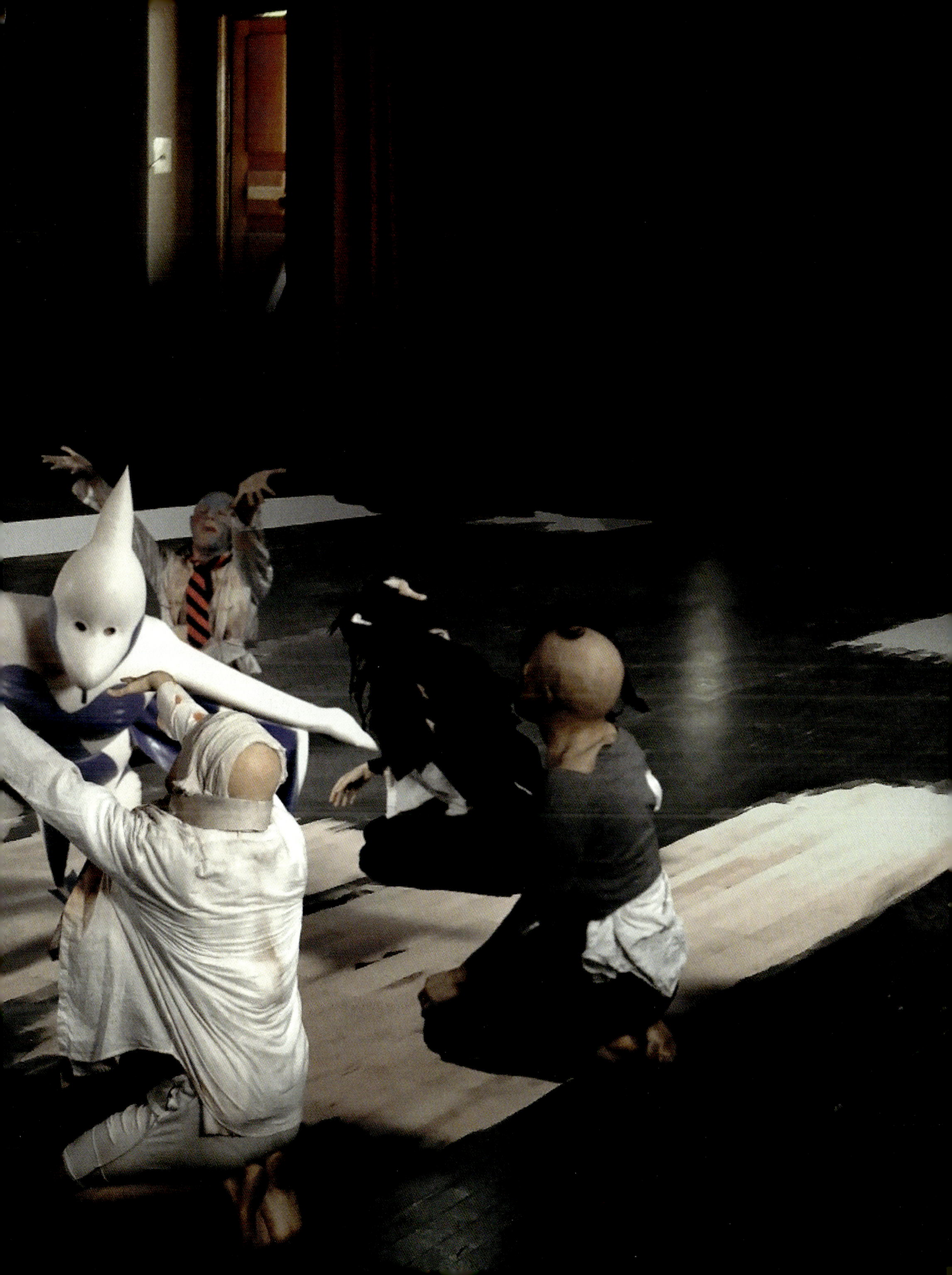

JENKIN VAN ZYL

Looners, 2019

Working across film, installation and sculpture, Jenkin van Zyl dismantles binary classifications – 'real and virtual, front and back stage, male and female, self and other, ruin and repair, time and space, fantasy and rationality' – embracing instead 'multiple selves, instability and deviance'. For *Looners* (2019), Van Zyl creates a series of fantastical worlds in which performers, anonymised by silicone masks, enact scenes of ritualised violence and pleasure in a manner simultaneously ludicrous and grotesque. *Looners* shows us a genderless species somewhere between human and monster, compelled towards abject repetitions by obscure libidinal drives.

Previous, still

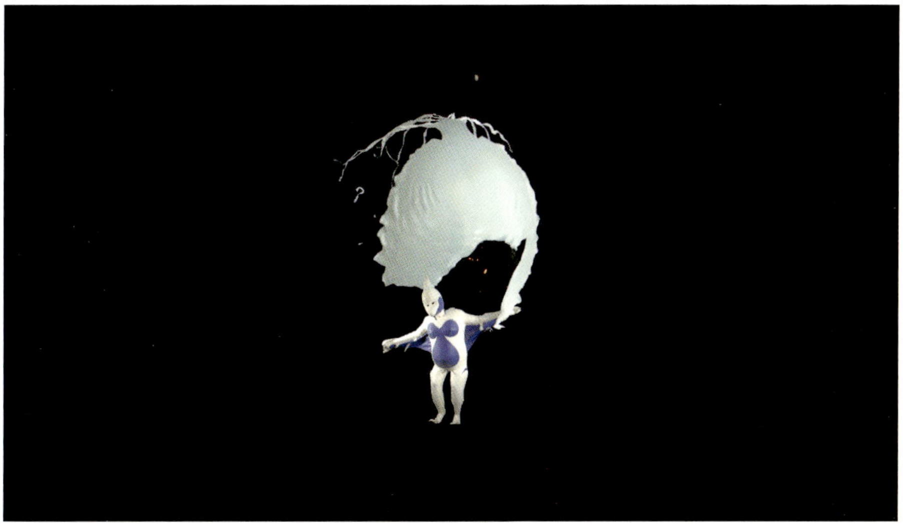

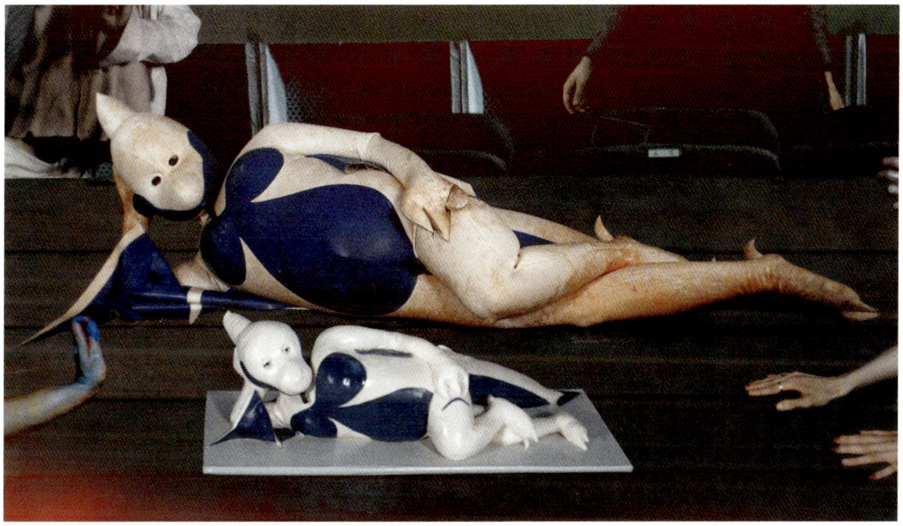

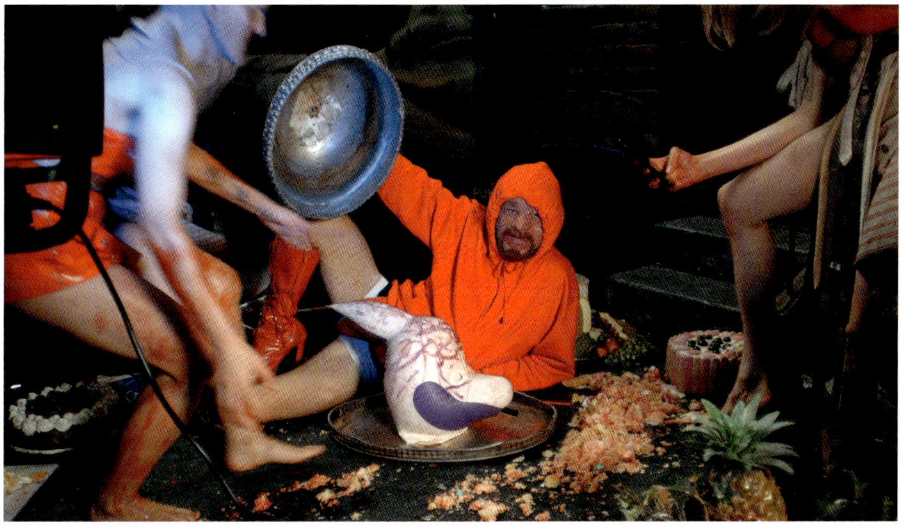

DEL LAGRACE VOLCANO

Robin: Cold Store Romance, London, 1988

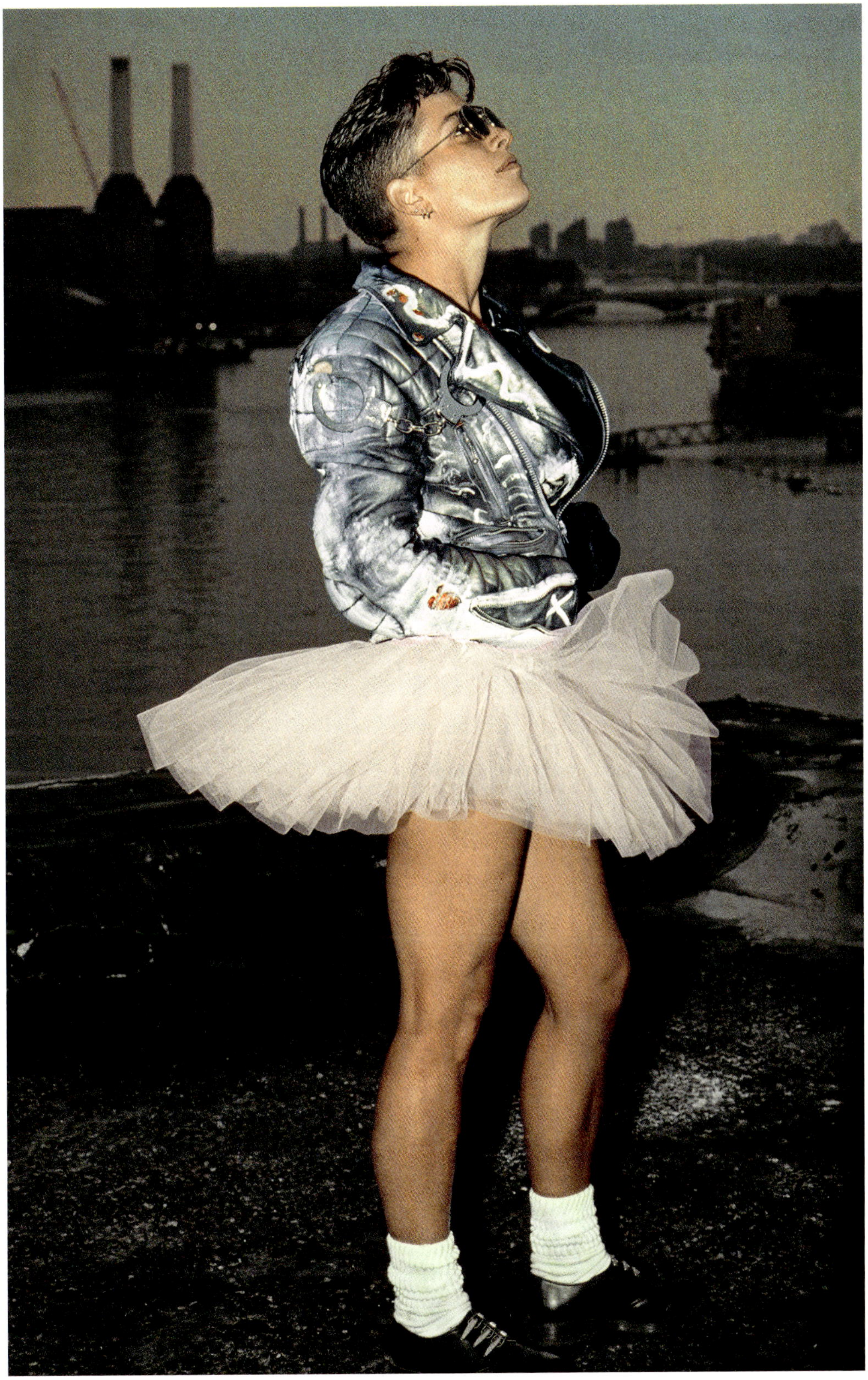

DEL LAGRACE VOLCANO

Marc Angelo Almond, 1992

Jax Back 2, London, 1991

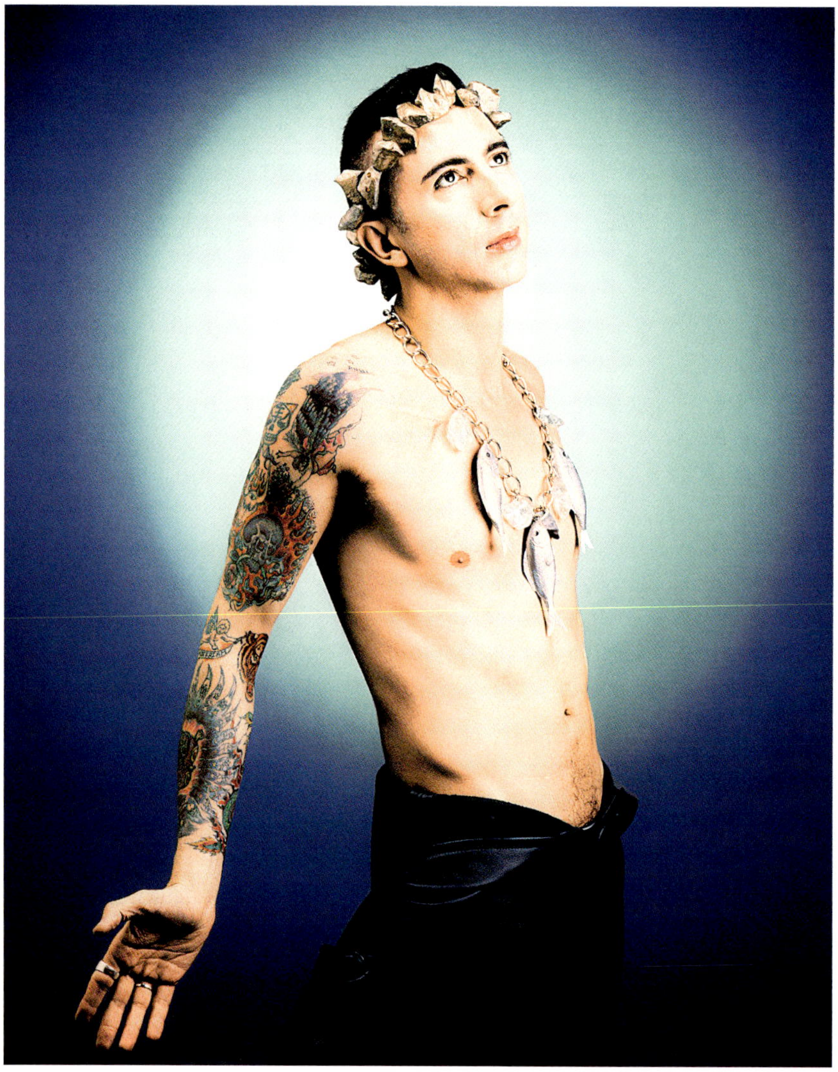

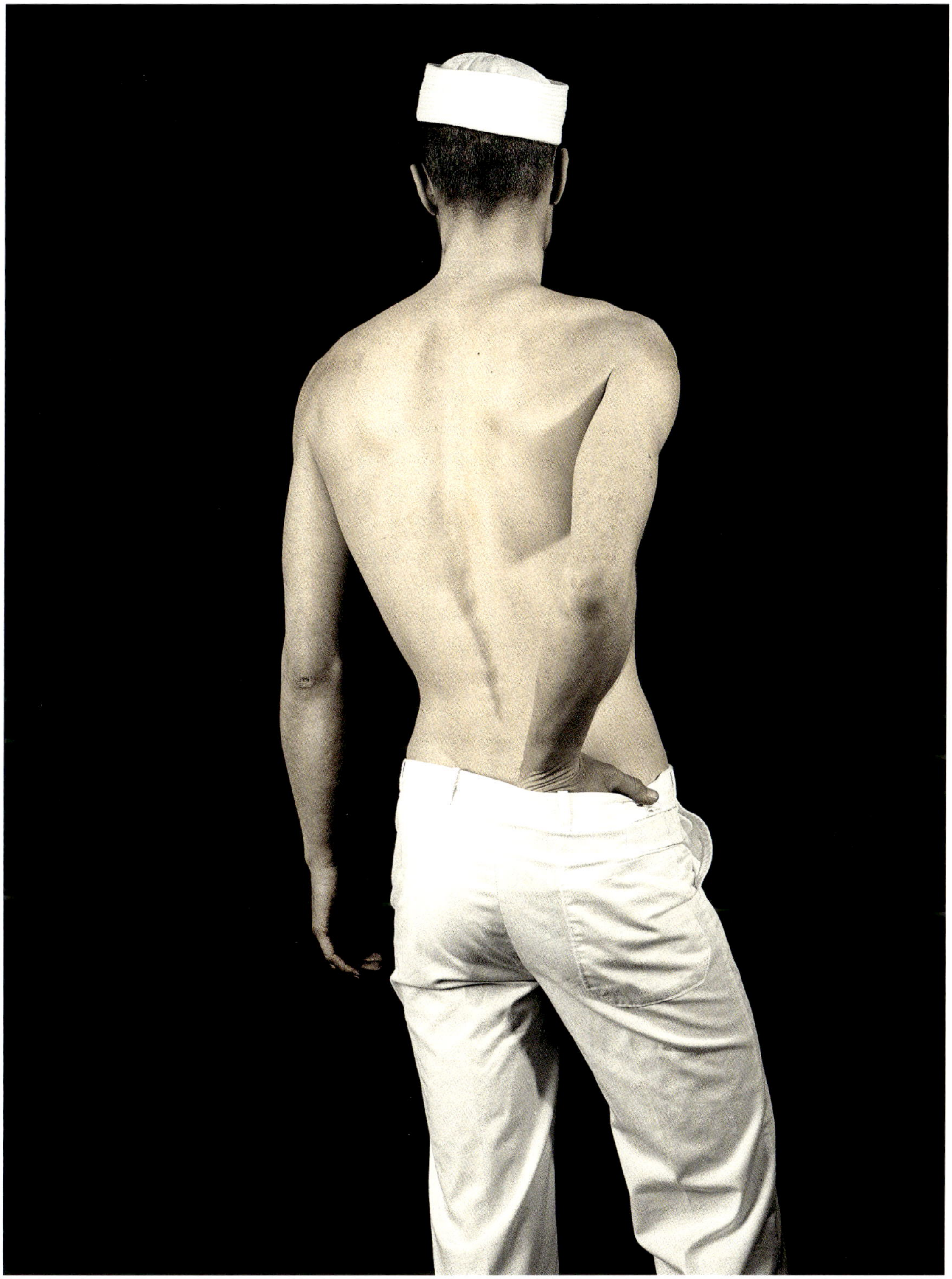

LIST OF WORKS

Measurements are given in centimetres, height x width x depth.
Works given an asterisk are illustrated works only.

Ajamu

Born 1963 in Huddersfield, UK. Lives and works in London, UK.

Body builder in bra, 1990

Photographic print, 55.9 x 66
Courtesy the artist, pp. 82–83

Katchi Kwok, 1990

Photographic print, 33 x 26.7
Courtesy the artist, p. 85

Nickers and garter belt, 1990

Photographic print, 38.1 x 31.7
Courtesy the artist

Cock and glove, 1993

Photographic print, 33 x 26.7
Courtesy the artist, p. 84

Heels, 1993

Photographic print, 33 x 38
Courtesy Dr. Ingrid Pollard, p. 88

Man in gloves, 1993

Photographic print, 72.4 x 55.9
Courtesy the artist, p. 87

Self-portrait with blond wig, 1993

Photographic print, 38.1 x 31.7
Courtesy the artist

Self-portrait, 1998

Photographic print, 72.4 x 55.9
Courtesy the artist

Self-portrait in chaise longue, 1998

Photographic print, 39 x 39
Courtesy the artist

Feet of Duane Cyrus, Dancer, 2015

Photographic print, 43.2 x 33
Collection Professor Lubaina Himid, p. 89

Amrou Al-Kadhi
Holly Falconer

Born 1990 in London, UK, where they live and work.
Born 1984 in Gloucestershire, UK. Lives and works in London, UK.

Glamrou, 2016

Digital c-print on aluminium, 160 x 120
Courtesy Cause & Effect Magazine, p. 91

Lyle Ashton Harris

Born 1965 in New York, NY, USA, where he lives and works.

Billie #1, 2002

Unique polaroid, 61 x 50.8
Courtesy the artist and Baldwin Gallery, Aspen, p. 94

Billie #4, 2002

Unique polaroid, 61 x 50.8
Courtesy the artist and Baldwin Gallery, Aspen, p. 96

Blue Billie, 2002

Unique polaroid, 71.1 x 61
Courtesy the artist and Salon 94, New York, p. 95

Josephine #6, 2002

Unique polaroid, 61 x 50.8
Courtesy the artist and Baldwin Gallery, Aspen, p. 97

Josephine #18, 2002

Unique polaroid, 61 x 50.8
Courtesy the artist and Salon 94, New York

Sadie Benning

Born 1973 in Madison, WI, USA. Lives and works in New York, NY, USA.

Gun Egg, 2017

Wood, aqua resin, casein, acrylic gouache, Euro Lux and photographs, 121.9 x 241.3
Collection of Linda Shirvanian. Courtesy the artist and Vielmetter Los Angeles, pp. 98–99

NAYLAND BLAKE

Born 1960 in New York, NY, USA, where they live and work.

The Big One, 2003

White nylon and fiberfill, 488 x 457 x 15
Courtesy Matthew Marks Gallery, New York, p. 101

PAULINE BOUDRY/ RENATE LORENZ

Born 1972 in Lausanne, Switzerland. Lives and works in Berlin, Germany.
Born 1963 in Berlin, Germany, where she lives and works.

Silent, 2016

HD video installation, 7 min
Courtesy Ellen de Bruijne Projects, Amsterdam and Marcelle Alix, Paris, pp. 104–07

FLO BROOKS

Born 1987 in Devon, UK. Lives and works in London, UK.

new TEENAGER HERE COMES TROUBLE, 2017

Acrylic on wood, 25 x 25
Courtesy the artist and Project Native Informant, London

NOT!, 2017

Acrylic on wood, 21 x 21
Courtesy the artist and Project Native Informant, London

I'm having a mid-teen crisis, 2018

Acrylic on wood, 21 x 21
Courtesy the artist and Project Native Informant, London

I'm just a phase my parents are going through, 2018

Acrylic on wood, 21 x 21
Courtesy the artist and Project Native Informant, London

U Bend but it's still a trap, 2018

Acrylic on wood, 161 x 157 x 4.5
Courtesy the artist and Project Native Informant, London, pp. 112–13

YessSIR! Back off! Tell me who I am again?!, 2018

Acrylic on wood, 197 x 177 x 4.5
Arts Council Collection, Southbank Centre, London, pp. 108–11

LUCIANO CASTELLI

Born 1952 in Lucerne, Switzerland. Lives and works in Zurich, Switzerland.

Lucille Lying on Back, 1973

Watercolour, gold leaf, rose petals and swan feathers on paper, 70 x 100
Collection of Alexandra Castelli

Lucille Self-portrait, 1973

Watercolour and mica on paper, 200 x 140
Courtesy the artist, p. 114

Lucille Self-portrait, 1973

Watercolour, mica, cotton, gold leaf and swan feathers on paper, 100 x 70
Courtesy the artist

Self-portrait with Feather Boa, 1973

[Photo taken with self-timer]
Analogue gelatin silver print, 40 x 30
Courtesy the artist

Golden Record 3, 1974

[Photo taken with self-timer]
Digital c-print, 110 x 75
Courtesy Anjuli Castelli, p. 115

Self-portrait, 1975

[Photo taken with self-timer]
Digital c-print, 70 x 53
Courtesy the artist, pp. 116–17

JIMMY DESANA

Born 1949 in Detroit, MI, USA. Died 1990 in New York, NY, USA.

Sink, 1979

Cibachrome print, 50.8 x 40.6
Courtesy the Jimmy DeSana Trust and Salon 94, New York, p. 123

Submission (Panty Hose), 1979

Black and white gelatin, 25.4 x 20.3
Courtesy the Jimmy DeSana Trust and Salon 94, New York

Marker Cones (No Head), 1982

Vintage cibachrome print, 55.2 x 66
Courtesy the Jimmy DeSana Trust and Salon 94, New York, pp. 120–21

Four Legs with Shoes, undated

Vintage cibachrome print, 66.7 x 55.6
Courtesy the Jimmy DeSana Trust and Salon 94, New York, pp. 124–25

Jes Fan

Born 1990 in Scarborough, Canada. Lives and works in New York, NY, USA.

Testo-Candle, 2017

Beeswax, candle wick and depo-testosterone, 20.3 x 12.7 x 15.2
Courtesy the artist

Systems II, 2018

Silicone, glass, epoxy, melanin, depo-testosterone, estradiol and wood, 132.1 x 63.5 x 50.8
Courtesy the artist, pp. 126–27

Systems III, 2018

Silicone, glass, epoxy, melanin, estradiol and wood, 121.9 x 63.5 x 48.3
Courtesy the artist

Chitra Ganesh

Born 1975 in New York, NY, USA, where she lives and works.

**Rose of My Rose*, 2007

Acrylic and mixed media on panel and wall, dimensions variable, panel 232 x 450
p. 129

**Shimmering Pulse*, 2009

Lightjet print, 167.6 x 121.9
p. 128

At Her Dream's Edge, 2019

Mixed media, dimensions variable
Courtesy the artist

Martine Gutierrez

Born 1989 in Berkeley, CA, USA. Lives and works in New York, NY, USA.

Clubbing, 2012

Colour video with sound, 3 min 6 sec
Collection of The Frances Lehman Loeb Art Center, Vassar College.
Purchase, Advisory Council for Photography 2016.21.2.1

Demons, Chin 'Demon of Lust,' p93 from Indigenous Woman, 2018

C-print mounted on Sintra, hand-painted artist frame, 91.4 x 61
Courtesy the artist and RYAN LEE Gallery, New York, p. 131

Demons, Tlazoteotl 'Eater of Filth,' p92 from Indigenous Woman, 2018

C-print mounted on Sintra, 91.4 x 61
Andrew C. Rose Family Collection, Delaware. Courtesy RYAN LEE Gallery, New York

Demons, Yemaya 'Goddess of the Living Ocean,' p94 from Indigenous Woman, 2018

C-print mounted on Sintra, hand-painted artist frame, 91.4 x 61
Long term loan/Promised gift to the Minnesota Museum of American Art

Masking, 24k Gold Mask, p46 from Indigenous Woman, 2018

C-print mounted on Sintra, 50.8 x 40.6
Courtesy the artist and RYAN LEE Gallery, New York, p. 132

Masking, Cocoa Mask, p50 from Indigenous Woman, 2018

C-print mounted on Sintra, 50.8 x 40.6
Courtesy the artist and RYAN LEE Gallery, New York

Masking, Fish Mask, p48 from Indigenous Woman, 2018

C-print mounted on Sintra, 50.8 x 40.6
Long term loan/Promised gift to the Minnesota Museum of American Art, p. 135

Masking, Garlic Mask, p54 from Indigenous Woman, 2018

C-print mounted on Sintra, 50.8 x 40.6
Courtesy the artist and RYAN LEE Gallery, New York

Masking, Green-Grape Mask, p51 from Indigenous Woman, 2018

C-print mounted on Sintra, 50.8 x 40.6
Courtesy the artist and RYAN LEE Gallery, New York, p. 134

Masking, Red Spath Mask, p49 from Indigenous Woman, 2018

C-print mounted on Sintra, 50.8 x 40.6
Long term loan/Promised gift to the Minneapolis Institute of Art

Masking, Snail Mask, p55 from Indigenous Woman, 2018

C-print mounted on Sintra, 50.8 x 40.6
Courtesy the artist and RYAN LEE Gallery, New York, p. 133

Masking, Watermelon Mask, p57 from Indigenous Woman, 2018

C-print mounted on Sintra, 50.8 x 40.6
Courtesy the artist and RYAN LEE Gallery, New York

Nicholas Hlobo

Born 1975 in Cape Town, South Africa. Lives and works in Johannesburg, South Africa.

Babelana Ngentloko, 2017

Ribbon and leather on linen canvas, 160 x 250
Courtesy Lehmann Maupin, New York, Hong Kong and Seoul, p. 140

Intlantsana, 2017

Ribbon on canvas, 120 x 180
Private Collection, New York. Courtesy Lehmann Maupin, New York, Hong Kong and Seoul

Jong' emva rhamncwa ndini, 2017

Painted leather, wood, ribbon, steel, adjustable papier mâché mannequin, skull and horns, 145 x 65 x 104
Courtesy Lehmann Maupin, New York, Hong Kong and Seoul, p. 139

Unduluko, 2017

Ribbon, leather, plastic, copper and rope, 110 x 310 x 169
Courtesy Lehmann Maupin, New York, Hong Kong and Seoul, p. 141

Peter Hujar

Born 1934 in Trenton, NJ, USA. Died 1987 in New York, NY, USA.

Daniel Ware (Cockette), 1971

Vintage gelatin silver print, 50.8 x 40.6
Courtesy The Peter Hujar Archive LLC, Pace/MacGill Gallery, New York and Fraenkel Gallery, San Francisco

Two Cockettes (Reggie Dunnigan and Goldie Glitters), 1971

Vintage gelatin silver print, 43.2 x 35.6
Courtesy The Peter Hujar Archive LLC, Pace/MacGill Gallery, New York and Fraenkel Gallery, San Francisco, p. 149

Candy Darling on Her Deathbed, 1973/2018

Pigmented ink print, 40.6 x 50.8
Courtesy The Peter Hujar Archive LLC, Pace/MacGill Gallery, New York and Fraenkel Gallery, San Francisco, p. 147

Hudson River, 1975

Vintage gelatin silver print, 37.1 x 37.1
Collection of Alexander Jakowec

Hudson River (IV), 1975

Vintage gelatin silver print, 37.5 x 37.5
Collection of Alexander Jakowec, p. 142

Reclining Nude on Couch, 1978/2019

Pigmented ink print, 40.6 x 50.8
Courtesy The Peter Hujar Archive LLC, Pace/MacGill Gallery, New York and Fraenkel Gallery, San Francisco, p. 150

Ethyl Eichelberger as Nefertiti (II), 1979

Vintage gelatin silver print, 50.8 x 40.6
Courtesy The Peter Hujar Archive LLC, Pace/MacGill Gallery, New York and Fraenkel Gallery, San Francisco

Ethyl Eichelberger as Nefertiti (III), 1979

Vintage gelatin silver print, 50.8 x 40.6
Courtesy The Peter Hujar Archive LLC, Pace/MacGill Gallery, New York and Fraenkel Gallery, San Francisco, p. 151

John Heys in Lana Turner's Gown (I), 1979

Vintage gelatin silver print, 50.8 x 40.6
Courtesy The Peter Hujar Archive LLC, Pace/MacGill Gallery, New York and Fraenkel Gallery, San Francisco, p. 144

John Heys in Lana Turner's Gown (II), 1979

Vintage gelatin silver print, 50.8 x 40.6
Courtesy The Peter Hujar Archive LLC, Pace/MacGill Gallery, New York and Fraenkel Gallery, San Francisco, p. 145

Greer Lankton's Legs, 1983/2019

Pigmented ink print, 50.8 x 40.6
Courtesy The Peter Hujar Archive LLC, Pace/MacGill Gallery, New York and Fraenkel Gallery, San Francisco, p. 143

John Heys with Orange Breasts, 1983

Vintage gelatin silver print, 50.8 x 40.6
Courtesy The Peter Hujar Archive LLC, Pace/MacGill Gallery, New York and Fraenkel Gallery, San Francisco, p. 148

Juliana Huxtable

Born 1987 in Bryan-College Station, TX, USA. Lives and works in New York, NY, USA.

Untitled (Lil' Marvel), 2015

Colour inkjet print, 101.6 x 76.2
Collection of Scott Hoffman. Courtesy Project Native Informant, London, p. 155

Untitled (Psychosocial Stuntin'), 2015

Colour inkjet print, 101.6 x 76.2
Private collection. Courtesy JTT, New York and Project Native Informant, London, p. 154

Untitled in the Rage (Nibiru Cataclysm), 2015

Colour inkjet print, 101.6 x 76.2
Private collection. Courtesy JTT, New York and Project Native Informant, London, p. 153

Transexual Empire, 2017

Inkjet print, vinyl and magnets on metal sheet, 243.8 x 121.9
Courtesy the artist and Reena Spaulings Fine Art, NY/LA

Joan Jett Blakk

Born in Detroit, MI, USA. Lives and works in San Francisco, CA, USA.

Joan Jett Blakk for President, 1992

Wallpaper, dimensions variable
Courtesy the artist, p. 157

Zoe Leonard

Born 1961 in Liberty, NY, USA. Lives and works in New York, NY, USA.

Pin-up #1 (Jennifer Miller does Marilyn Monroe), 1995/1997

C-print, 86.4 x 57.5
Courtesy the artist, Galerie Gisela Capitain, Cologne and Hauser & Wirth, p. 161

Pin-up #3 (starring Jennifer Miller), 1995/1997

C-print, 86.4 x 57.5
Courtesy the artist, Galerie Gisela Capitain, Cologne and Hauser & Wirth

Ad Minoliti

Born 1980 in Buenos Aires, Argentina, where she lives and works.

**The Feminist School of Painting*, 2018

Installation view, KADIST, San Francisco, 2018, pp. 162–63

Playcentre, 2019

Mixed media across site, dimensions variable
Courtesy the artist and Peres Projects, Berlin

Pierre Molinier

Born 1900 in Agen, France. Died 1976 in Bordeaux, France.

Introït, 1967

Vintage gelatin silver print, 12.4 x 17
Courtesy Galerie Christophe Gaillard, Paris, and Galerie 1900-2000, Paris

Grande Mêlée – Photomontage, 1968

Vintage gelatin silver print on soft Agfa paper, 23 x 27
Courtesy Galerie Christophe Gaillard, Paris, and Galerie 1900-2000, Paris, pp. 164–65

Sur le pavois, planche 26 du Chaman (On the Shield, plate 26 of The Shaman), 1968–70

Vintage gelatin silver print, 23.4 x 17.6
Richard Saltoun, London

Le modèle (Jean) (The Model), 1970

Vintage gelatin silver print, 12.5 x 17.5
Richard Saltoun, London

Le Chaman, 1970

Vintage gelatin silver print, 16 x 11
Courtesy kamel mennour, Paris/London, p. 169

Luciano Castelli, 1974

Vintage gelatin silver print, 12.5 x 9
Private collection of Luciano Castelli, p. 167

Luciano Castelli, 1974

Vintage gelatin silver print, 16.5 x 11.4
Private collection of Luciano Castelli

"Pantomine Céleste" (Photo-Montage pour "Le Chaman et ses créatures"), undated

Vintage gelatin silver print, 12 x 17
Courtesy kamel mennour, Paris/London, p. 168

Kent Monkman

Born 1965 in St. Marys, Canada. Lives and works in Toronto, Canada.

Stag Hunting (After Theodor de Bry), 2018

Acrylic on canvas, 182.8 x 274.3
Courtesy the artist, p. 173

The Three Bachelors, 2018

Acrylic on canvas, 213.3 x 335.3
Courtesy the artist, pp. 174–75

Zanele Muholi

Born 1972 in Durban, South Africa. Lives and works in Johannesburg, South Africa.

Isiko I, 2006

Gelatin silver print, 76.5 x 50.5
Courtesy Stevenson, Johannesburg and Cape Town, p. 179

Untitled, 2006

Lambda print, 52.5 x 70
Courtesy Stevenson, Johannesburg and Cape Town

Untitled, 2006

Lambda print, 37.5 x 50
Courtesy Stevenson, Johannesburg and Cape Town, p. 178

Crime Scene #1, 2012

C-print, 33 x 49.5
Courtesy Stevenson, Johannesburg and Cape Town, p. 180

Crime Scene #3, 2012

C-print, 33 x 49.5
Courtesy Stevenson, Johannesburg and Cape Town, p. 181

Crime Scene #4, 2012

C-print, 33 x 49.5
Courtesy Stevenson, Johannesburg and Cape Town

dis-ease, 2012

C-print, 60 x 40
Courtesy Stevenson, Johannesburg and Cape Town

She'll, 2012

C-print, 60 x 40
Courtesy Stevenson, Johannesburg and Cape Town

Souls mo(ve)ments, 2012

HD video installation, 14 min 42 sec
Courtesy Stevenson, Johannesburg and Cape Town

umthombo, 2012

C-print, 60 x 40
Courtesy Stevenson, Johannesburg and Cape Town

Phila I, Parktown, 2016

Wallpaper, dimensions variable
Courtesy Stevenson, Johannesburg and Cape Town, p. 177

Catherine Opie

Born 1961 in Sandusky, OH, USA. Lives and works in Los Angeles, CA, USA.

Jerome Caja, 1993

C-print, 49.2 x 39
Private collection. Courtesy the artist, Thomas Dane Gallery, London, and Regen Projects, Los Angeles

Justin Bond, 1993

C-print, 50.8 x 40.6
Courtesy the artist, Thomas Dane Gallery, London, and Regen Projects, Los Angeles, p. 183

Mike and Sky, 1993

C-print, 50.8 x 40.6
Private collection. Courtesy the artist, Thomas Dane Gallery, London, and Regen Projects, Los Angeles, p. 185

Pig Pen, 1993

C-print, 101.6 x 76.2
Courtesy the artist, Thomas Dane Gallery, London, and Regen Projects, Los Angeles, p. 184

Feet (Ian), 1994

Inkjet print, 20.3 x 20.3
Courtesy the artist, Thomas Dane Gallery, London, and Regen Projects, Los Angeles

Vaginal Davis, 1994

C-print, 152.4 x 76.2
Courtesy the artist, Thomas Dane Gallery, London, and Regen Projects, Los Angeles, p. 186

Amy, 1996

Inkjet print, 20.3 x 20.3
Courtesy the artist, Thomas Dane Gallery, London, and Regen Projects, Los Angeles, p. 187

Hand (Pig Pen), 2009

Inkjet print, 20.3 x 20.3
Courtesy the artist, Thomas Dane Gallery, London, and Regen Projects, Los Angeles

Sunrise 4, 2009

C-print, 127 x 95.3
Courtesy the artist, Thomas Dane Gallery, London, and Regen Projects, Los Angeles, p. 188

Sunset 4, 2009

C-print, 127 x 95.3
Courtesy the artist, Thomas Dane Gallery, London, and Regen Projects, Los Angeles, p. 189

Planningtorock

Born 1972 in Bolton, UK. Lives and works in Berlin, Germany.

Portrait Planningtorock, 2011

C-print, 140 x 93.3
Courtesy Planningtorock, p. 193

Christina Quarles

Born 1985 in Chicago, IL, USA. Lives and works in Los Angeles, CA, USA.

It's Gunna Be All Right, Cause Baby, There Ain't Nuthin' Left, 2016

Mixed media, dimensions variable
Courtesy the artist and Pilar Corrias, pp. 195–97

Hannah Quinlan and Rosie Hastings

Born 1991, Newcastle, UK. Lives and works in London, UK.
Born 1991, London, UK, where they live and work.

The Dudes, 2017

Pencil on paper, 137 x 203
Courtesy Josef Dalle Nogare Collection, pp. 200–01

Something for the Boys, 2018

Video installation, 16 min 34 sec
Courtesy the artists and Arcadia Missa, London, p. 199

Funny Girls, 2019

Graphite on paper, 59 x 115
Courtesy the artists and Arcadia Missa, London

Hunter Reynolds

Born 1959 in Rochester, MI, USA. Lives and works in New York, NY, USA.

Patina du Prey's Drag Pose Series, 1990

Digital c-print, 76.2 x 57.8
Courtesy the artists and PPOW Gallery, New York, p. 205

Patina du Prey's Drag Pose Series, 1990

Digital c-print, 76.2 x 57.8
Courtesy the artists and PPOW Gallery, New York

The Memorial Dress, 1993–2007

Mixed media installation, 240 x 240 x 240
Courtesy the artists and PPOW Gallery, New York

Survival AIDS (ACT Up Chicago with Memorial Dress Photographed by Maxine Henryson), 2015

Archival c-prints and thread, 121.9 x 152.4
Courtesy the artists and PPOW Gallery, New York, p. 207

Athi-Patra Ruga

Born 1984 in Mthatha, South Africa. Lives and works in Cape Town, South Africa.

**Azania*, 2013

Stained glass, lead and powder-coated steel, 184 x 170
p. 208

**The Night of the Long Knives I*, 2013

Archival inkjet print on Photorag Baryta, 190 x 150
p. 209

Site-specific new commission, 2019

Mixed media across site, dimensions variable
Courtesy the artist

Tejal Shah

Born 1979 in Bhilai, India. Lives and works in Goa, India.

Southern Siren – Maheshwari, 2006 (*Hijira Fantasy* series)

Digital photograph on archival paper, 167 x 110
Courtesy the artist, Barbara Gross Galerie, Munich and Project 88, Mumbai, p. 213

You too can touch the moon – Yashoda with Krishna, 2006 (*Hijra Fantasy* series)

Digital photograph on archival paper, 167 x 110
Courtesy the artist, Barbara Gross Galerie, Munich and Project 88, Mumbai, p. 211

Hir I, 2013 (*Anonymous Life* series)

Dry pastel, gouache and ink on paper, 27.9 x 38.1
Courtesy the artist, Barbara Gross Galerie, Munich and Project 88, Mumbai, p. 212

Hir II, 2013 (*Anonymous Life* series)

Dry pastel, gouache and ink on paper, 27.9 x 38.1
Courtesy the artist, Barbara Gross Galerie, Munich and Project 88, Mumbai

Hir IV, 2013 (*Anonymous Life* series)

Dry pastel, gouache and ink on paper, 27.9 x 38.1
Courtesy the artist, Barbara Gross Galerie, Munich and Project 88, Mumbai

Victoria Sin

Born 1991 in Toronto, ON, Canada. Lives and works in London, UK.

A View from Elsewhere, Act 1, She Postures in Context, 2018

Multimedia video installation, 18 min 50 sec
Soundtrack by Shy One (act 1 and 3); videography by Ana de Matos; lighting by Cecilia Gonzalez Barragan (act 2)
Courtesy the artist, pp. 217–19

Jenkin van Zyl

Born 1993 in London, UK, where he lives and works.

Looners, 2019

Multimedia video installation, 30 min
Courtesy the artist, pp. 220–23

Del LaGrace Volcano

Born 1957 in Orange, CA, USA. Lives and works in UK and Sweden.

Robyn: Cold Store Romance, London, 1988

Giclée print, 134 x 91
Courtesy Del LaGrace Volcano, p. 225

Jax Back 2, London, 1991

Giclée print, 91 x 76
Courtesy Del LaGrace Volcano, p. 227

Marc Angelo Almond, 1992

Giclée print, 134 x 111
Courtesy Del LaGrace Volcano, p. 226

Zach's Back, London, 1994

Giclée print, 91 x 76
Courtesy Del LaGrace Volcano

Self-portrait with Blue Beard, 1995

Giclée print, 91 x 76
Courtesy Del LaGrace Volcano

LENDERS

Ajamu

Marcelle Alix, Paris

Arcadia Missa

Arts Council Collection, Southbank Centre, London

Lyle Ashton Harris

Baldwin Gallery

Flo Brooks

Ellen de Bruijne Projects, Amsterdam

Alexandra Castelli

Anjuli Castelli

Luciano Castelli

Thomas Dane Gallery, London

Jimmy DeSana Trust

Holly Falconer

Jes Fan

Galerie Christophe Gaillard

Galerie 1900-2000, Paris

Chitra Ganesh

Hauser & Wirth

Professor Lubaina Himid

The Peter Hujar Archive LLC

Juliana Huxtable

Alexander Jakowec

Joan Jett Blakk

RYAN LEE Gallery

The Frances Lehman Loeb Art Center

Zoe Leonard

Matthew Marks, New York

Lehmann Maupin, New York, Hong Kong and Seoul

Kamel Mennour

Minneapolis Institute of Art

Minnesota Museum of American Art

Ad Minoliti

Kent Monkman

Dr. Ingrid Pollard

PPOW Gallery

Project Native Informant, London

Christina Quarles

Hannah Quinlan and Rosie Hastings

Reena Spaulings Fine Art, NY/LA

Regen Projects, Los Angeles

Hunter Reynolds

Andrew C. Rose Family Collection

Jam Rostron

Athi-Patra Ruga

Salon 94, New York

Richard Saltoun

Tejal Shah

Linda Shirvanian

Victoria Sin

Stevenson Gallery, Johannesburg and Cape Town

Jenkin van Zyl

Del LaGrace Volcano

WHATIFTHEWORLD, Cape Town

And those who wish to remain anonymous.

ACKNOWLEDGEMENTS

This exhibition would not have been possible without
the collaboration of the participating artists, their studios and galleries,
to whom we are greatly indebted.

We are also grateful to the following individuals and organisations
for their collaboration and support:

Isabelle Alfonsi, Marcelle Alix

Marc Barben, Stevenson

Sabrina Blaichman, Hauser & Wirth

Marie Catalano, JTT Gallery

Cause and Effect Magazine

Justine Do Espirito Santo, Arcadia Missa

Rozsa Farkas, Arcadia Missa

Alissa Friedman, Salon 94

Samy Ghiyati, Kamel Mennour

Sree Goswami, Project 88

Trey Hollis, PPOW Gallery

Stephen Koch, The Peter Hujar Archive

Jeffrey Lee, RYAN LEE Gallery

Jane McCarthy, Regen Projects

Katy McKinnon, Regen Projects

Ashleigh McLean, WHATIFTHEWORLD

Clare Morris, Thomas Dane Gallery

Cory Nomura, Matthew Marks Gallery

Wendy Olsoff, PPOW Gallery

Lauren Panzo, Pace/MacGill Gallery

Jeremy Parker, Project Native Informant

Javier Peres, Peres Projects, Berlin

Ariel Lauren Pittman, Susan Vielmetter Los Angeles Projects

Kiki Jai Raj, Baldwin Gallery

Shaun Caley Regen, Regen Projects

Elsa de Rémur, Reena Spaulings

Alexis Rose, Lehmann Maupin

Manuel Segade, Centro de Arte Dos de Mayo, Madrid

Hedi Sorger, The Peter Hujar Archive

Jana Suhani Soin, Pilar Corrias

Stephan Tanbin Sastrawidjaja, Project Native Informant

With special thanks to Thomas Dane Gallery, London and
WHATIFTHEWORLD, Cape Town

EXHIBITION CREDITS

Hayward Gallery

Vincent Honoré, Guest Curator
Eimear Martin, former Associate Curator
Tarini Malik, Assistant Curator
Thomas Sutton, Curatorial Assistant
Eimear O'Raw, Exhibition Organiser
Ana Carolina Roman Rodrigues, Intern
Imogen Winter, Senior Registrar
Alison Maun, Exhibition Bookings and Indemnity Coordinator
Chloe Brooks, Senior Technician
Aoife Leach, General Manager
Juliane Heynert, Installation Manager
Lucy Biddle, Exhibitions Interpretation Manager
Jennifer Hawkins, Administrator
Rachel Ward, Operations Administrator
Marcia Ceppo, Operations and Logistics Manager
Matt Arthurs, Philip Gardner and Kate Parrott, Installation Technicians
Imogen Maxwell, Librarian
Leonie Warner, Senior Visitor Experience Manager
Kate Ford, Duty Manager
Emma Bani-Walker, Duty Manager
Gareth Spencer, Duty Manager

Exhibition Architecture by Diogo Passarinho Studio
Exhibition Graphics Design by Nina Jua Klein
Lighting by Lightwaves Ltd.

Hayward Gallery Publishing

Diana Adell, Project Manager
Alex Glen, Sales Manager
Rebecca Fortey, former Art Publisher

Southbank Centre

Tamsin Ace, Head of Public Programming
Debo Amon, Literature Programmer
Iona Bell, Marketing Officer
Clare Callaghan, Press Officer (Visual Arts)
Kate Chadwick, Exhibitions Coordinator, Site design
Steve Clark, Merchandiser and Book Buyer
Bea Colley, Literature Programmer
Murray Cooper-Melchiors, Head Of Ticketing, Customer Relations and Membership Operations
Paul Denton, Producer, Festival Site Design
Helen Faulkner, Head of Marketing
Julie Flavell, Producer
Edward Gaffney, Philanthropy Executive
Alison Gannage-Stewart, Head of Commercial Events
Chrystal Genesis, Education Manager (Young People)
Matthew Hale, Head of Visitor Experience
Dan Harrington, Website Manager
Roger Hennigan, Technical Manager
Charlotte Hobden, Patrons Manager
Ted Hodgkinson, Head of Literature and Spoken Word
David Holdaway, Head of Legal and Business Affairs
Andrea Ioannou, Philanthropy Manager
Luke Jordan, Senior Health and Safety Advisor
Ben Larpent, Senior Programmer, Classical Music
Ellie Mayes, Corporate Development Manager
Richard McClenaghan, Senior Trusts and Foundations Manager (Maternity)
Lexy Morvaridi, Contemporary Music Programmer
Joanna Newell, Head of Philanthropy
Marie Ortinau, Education Manager (Schools and Courses)
Paul O'Sullivan, Membership Manager
Amanda Pearlman, Head of Retail and Buying
Lucy Peters, Senior Editor
Hilary Philpot, Head of Health and Safety
Justin Pledger, Head of Corporate Development and Partnerships
Clemmie Power, Senior Ticketing and Membership Operations Manager
Jessica Santer, Head of Creative Learning
Joel Stanners, Senior Technician
Trish Thomas, Head of Digital Engagement
Rupert Thomson, Senior Programmer, Performance and Dance
Jordan Tyler, Senior Visitor Experience Manager
Bengi Unsal, Senior Contemporary Music Programmer
Katherine Walsh, Buyer and Merchandise Manager
Lucy Wells, Education Manager (Communities)
Abigail Wilkinson, Marketing Editor
Glen Wilson, Senior Content Editor (Digital)
Clare Wood, Southbank Centre Archivist
Pete Woodhead, Social Media Manager
Madani Younis, Creative Director
Takis Zontiros, Social Media Producer

IMAGE CREDITS

Copyright Credits

Image Credits

All images are courtesy the artist unless otherwise stated:

courtesy Cause & Effect Magazine p. 91 (photo: courtesy Amrou Al-Kadhi and Holly Falconer, originally shot by Holly Falconer, 2016); courtesy the artist and Salon 94, New York pp. 94–95; courtesy the artist, Baldwin Gallery, Aspen pp. 96–97; courtesy the artist and Vielmetter Los Angeles pp. 98–99 (photo: Chris Austin); courtesy Matthew Marks Gallery p. 101 (photo: Jack M. Kucy); courtesy Ellen de Bruijne Projects, Amsterdam and Marcelle Alix, Paris pp. 104–05, 107; Arts Council Collection, Southbank Centre, London pp. 108–09 (detail), 111; courtesy the artist and Project Native Informant London pp. 112, 113 (detail); Jimmy DeSana Trust pp. 120–21, 124–25; courtesy Jimmy DeSana Trust and Salon 94, New York p. 123; courtesy the artist and Gallery Wendi Norris, San Francisco pp. 128–29; courtesy the artist and RYAN LEE Gallery, New York pp. 131–35; courtesy the artist and Lehmann Maupin, New York, Hong Kong, and Seoul pp. 139–41 (photos: Anthea Pokroy); courtesy The Peter Hujar Archive LCC, Pace/MacGill Gallery, New York and Fraenkel Gallery, San Francisco pp. 142–45, 147, 148–51; courtesy the artist and JTT, New York pp. 153–55; courtesy GLBT (Gay Lesbian Bisexual Transgender) Historical Society, San Francisco. Collection CA2M, Mostoles p. 157 (photo: Marc Geller); courtesy the artist, Galerie Gisela Capitain, Cologne and Hauser & Wirth p. 161; courtesy KADIST, San Francisco pp. 162–63 (photos: Jeffmo Warrin); courtesy Galerie Christophe Gaillard and Galerie 1900-2000 pp. 164–65; photo © Centre Pompidou, MNAM-CCI, Dist. RMN-Grand Palais/Philippe Migeat p. 167; courtesy Kamel Mennour, Paris/London p. 168; courtesy Richard Saltoun Gallery, London p. 169; courtesy Stevenson, Cape Town/Johannesburg and Yancey Richardson, New York pp. 177–81; courtesy Regen Projects, Los Angeles and Thomas Dane Gallery, London pp. 183–89; courtesy PLANNINGTOROCK p. 193 (photo: Norman Konrad); courtesy the artist and Pilar Corrias, London pp. 194–97 (photos: Brica Wilcox); courtesy the artists and Arcadia Missa pp. 199, 200–01 (photo: Tim Bowditch); courtesy the artist and P.P.O.W, New York pp. 205, 207 (photo: Stan Narten); courtesy the artist and WHATIFTHEWORLD pp. 208–09; courtesy the artist, Project 88, Mumbai and Barbara Gross Galerie, Munich pp. 211–13; photo: Anne Tetzlaff p. 217.

AUTHOR BIOGRAPHIES

Travis Alabanza is a performer, writer and actor. They have recently starred in the theatre productions *Putting Words in Your Mouth* (2016) and *Jubilee* (2017), as well as their debut theatre show *Burgerz* (2017–18). A resident artist at Tate (2017–18), their work has also appeared in the *Guardian*, BBC, *Huck Magazine* and *Dazed and Confused*, among others. Their poetry book *Before I step Outside (you love me)* was published in 2017.

Jay Bernard is a writer from London. They won the 2018 Ted Hughes Award for *Surge: Side A*, a cross-disciplinary exploration of the New Cross Fire in 1981. Their first collection, *Surge*, will be published by Chatto and Windus in 2019.

Amrou Al-Kadhi is a non-binary British-Iraqi drag performer, writer and filmmaker, whose work focuses on the intersection of queer identity and race. They have three films in development – with Film4, British Film Institute (BFI) and BBC Films – as well as two TV series, with Channel 4 Comedy and BBC Drama. Their memoir *UNICORN* will be published by 4th Estate (HarperCollins) in October 2019.

Paul Clinton is a writer based in London, and a lecturer in curating at Goldsmiths, University of London. Between 2014 and 2018 he was Senior Editor at *frieze* magazine; Clinton continues to write for *frieze* while also regularly contributing to *London Review of Books*, *MOUSSE*, *Art Review*, *Art Monthly* and other publications. His book *Other Hunting* will be published by Ma Bibliotheque in 2019.

Charlie Fox is a writer and artist based in London. His fiction and non-fiction has appeared in *Dazed and Confused*, *Artforum* and the *New York Times*, among other publications. His book *This Young Monster* (2017) is published by Fitzcarraldo Editions. In 2019, he will curate the twin art shows *My Head is a Haunted House* (Sadie Coles, London) and *Dracula's Wedding* (RODEO, London).

Jack Halberstam is Professor of Gender Studies and English at Columbia University. Halberstam is the author of several books including: *Trans* A Quick and Quirky Account of Gender Variability* (University of California, 2018), *Skin Shows: Gothic Horror and the Technology of Monsters* (Duke University Press, 1995), *Female Masculinity* (Duke University Press, 1998), *In a Queer Time and Place: Transgender Bodies, Subcultural Lives* (New York University Press, 2005), *The Queer Art of Failure* (Duke University Press, 2011) and *Gaga Feminism: Sex, Gender, and the End of Normal* (Beacon Press, 2012), and is finishing a book titled *Wild Things: Queerness After Nature*. Halberstam has also been published in numerous journals, magazines and collections.

Vincent Honoré is Director of Exhibitions and Programmes at MoCo, Montpellier Contemporain (France). He was part of the curatorial team opening Palais de Tokyo, Paris (2001–04), and later a curator at Tate Modern, London (2004–07). In 2007, he became founding Director and Chief Curator at the David Roberts Art Foundation (DRAF), London, where he led the exhibitions and education programmes. Honoré was Artistic Director of the Baltic Triennial 13 (2018), which took place across Vilnius, Tallinn, Riga and London. He served as Senior Curator at Hayward Gallery, London (2017–19), where his projects included *DO DISTURB* (2018), a festival of performances co-programmed with Palais de Tokyo; an evening of performances for Art Night 2018; and the group exhibition *DRAG: Self-portraits and Body Politics* (2018).

Tarek Lakhrissi is a visual artist, poet and writer based in Paris. His work has been exhibited in Auto Italia, London; Palais de Tokyo, Paris; Fondation Lafayette Anticipations, Paris; La Galerie, Noisy-Le-Sec, Paris; Artexte, Montreal; Contemporary Art Centre (CAC), Vilnius; and Wendy's Subway, Brooklyn, among others.

Nat Raha is a poet and queer/trans* activist, living in Edinburgh, Scotland. Her poetry includes *of sirens, body & faultlines* (Boiler House Press, 2018), *countersonnets* (Contraband Books, 2013) and *Octet* (Veer Books, 2010). She has been published in numerous magazines and anthologies, and performed her work internationally. In 2018, Raha completed her PhD in queer Marxism and contemporary poetry at the University of Sussex. Raha is co-editor of the *Radical Transfeminism Zine*.

Manuel Segade is director of Centro de Arte Dos de Mayo in Móstoles (Madrid, Spain). He has curated exhibitions at MUSAC, La Casa Encendida, ARCO and TENT, as well as the Spanish Pavillion in the 2017 Venice Biennale. He is the author of the book *Narciso Fin de Siglo* (Melusina, 2008), and in 2018 curated, with Sabel Gavaldón, the exhibition *Elements of Vogue. A Case Study on Radical Performance* (CA2M, 2018).

Susan Stryker is Professor of Gender and Women's Studies at the University of Arizona, where she was director of the Institute for LGBT Studies (2011–16) and established the Transgender Studies Research Cluster. She is the author of *Transgender History: The Roots of Today's Revolution* (Seal Press, 2017) and co-editor of the anthologies *The Transgender Studies Reader* (Routledge, 2006) and *The Transgender Studies Reader 2* (Routledge, 2013). Stryker is also founding co-editor of the Duke University Press journal *TSQ: Transgender Studies Quarterly*.

Published on the occasion of the exhibition

Kiss My Genders

Hayward Gallery, London
12 June – 8 September 2019

Guest Curator: Vincent Honoré
Former Associate Curator: Eimear Martin
Assistant Curator: Tarini Malik
Curatorial Assistant: Thomas Sutton
Exhibition Organiser: Eimear O'Raw

This exhibition has been made possible by the provision of insurance through the Government Indemnity Scheme. Hayward Gallery would like to thank HM Government for providing Government Indemnity and the Department for Culture, Media and Sport and Arts Council England for arranging the indemnity.

Published in 2019 by
Hayward Gallery Publishing
Southbank Centre, Belvedere Road, London SE1 8XX UK
www.southbankcentre.co.uk

Project Manager: Diana Adell
Sales Manager: Alex Glen
Former Art Publisher: Rebecca Fortey
Catalogue designed by Studio Frith
Printed in Belgium by Graphius

Short texts written by Lucy Biddle (pp. 100, 106, 130, 138, 146, 156, 176, 182, 194, 198, 206, 210); Thomas Sutton (pp. 110, 152, 172, 222); Wong Bing Hao (pp. 127, 216)

A catalogue record for this book is available from the British Library.

ISBN 978 1 85332 364 5

Distributed in North America, Central America and South America by
ARTBOOK | D.A.P.
75 Broad Street, Suite 630, New York, NY 10004
tel: +1 212 627 1999
www.artbook.com

Distributed in the UK and Europe by
Cornerhouse Publications
HOME, 2 Tony Wilson Place, Manchester, M15 4FN
tel: +44 (0)161 212 3466
www.cornerhousepublications.org

Front cover: Juliana Huxtable, *Untitled (Lil' Marvel)*, 2015 (detail)

SOUTHBANK CENTRE

LOTTERY FUNDED | Supported using public funding by ARTS COUNCIL ENGLAND